To Z

ROOTS
& Wings

With heartfelt gratitude
for all your help, Zoë,

from

Brendan

17-11-20

First published in 2020
Print edition ISBN 9798691848537

Cover design by Tom Taheny Graphics, Galway

ROOTS

& Wings

MEMORIES AND FICTIONS

Brendan J. Nangle

Author's Note

Sometimes personal memories deserve to be shared. I believe the same may hold for the fruits of one's imagination. I try to do both in this compilation of stories, initially written for my family and for my own enjoyment.

These pages contain some of my childhood memories of Ireland in the 1940s and 1950s, memories that somehow find their way back through the intensifying mists of time. These provide glimpses of my roots. Also included are a few recollections from more recent periods, after I flew the nest. We should not forget the past, trivial as some of our memories may appear. Appreciating the past should, I believe, encourage us to appreciate ourselves and the world bequeathed to us, and to help us look to the future with an enlarged reservoir of hope.

In addition, the book contains some of my short stories, mostly fictional, but some of which span the nebulous interface between fact and fiction. If the mind can be joyously transported away from the many pressures of everyday realities to some distant place and time on the wings of the written word, then surely a story has fulfilled its purpose – be it fact or fiction. It is a way of throwing seeds of thought out into the world, not knowing how they will blossom in other minds and hearts. That's what storytelling, that ancient Irish tradition and artform, is all about, whether written or oral. It's a rich heritage. This is my storytelling.

Four of my poems are also included.

Give the ones you love wings to fly, roots to come back and reasons to stay.

DALAI LAMA

About the Author

Brendan J. Nangle was born in Dublin, Ireland, during the latter years of the Second World War. While his childhood was spent largely in the city's suburbs, his parents frequently exposed him to their respective rural backgrounds, thus cultivating his love for nature – a love that has grown over the years.

Later, with a Ph.D. in chemistry from University College Dublin, Brendan followed a career in chemical industries, both in Ireland and overseas. This involved considerable writing of a scientific nature. Upon his retirement in 2003, he started to explore his other writing skills, initially by composing a series of bedtime stories in rhyme for his many grandchildren. He still enjoys reading these to them.

In addition to preparing a family history, Brendan has drafted a historical novel and has written many short stories. Two of these stories have been published in *Storytellers, New Writing from Ireland*, and three of his brief reflections were published in *The Irish Times*. His collection of childhood memories constitutes a valuable record of life in the Ireland of those bygone days.

Brendan lives in Dalkey, County Dublin, with his wife Suzanne, his most discerning critic. The panoramic view of Dublin Bay from his home, together with his daily walks amid the natural beauty of nearby Dalkey and Killiney Hills, continue to instil in him a wealth of inspiration for his writings.

CONTENTS

MEMORIES   1

The Gun   2

Le Grand Hôtel du Canadel   7

My Mother's Diary   16

Baby William   21

The Locked Room   27

Bell Number Seven   31

My Grandfather's Pocket Watch   34

The Cable   38

My Mother's Cameras   45

My Father's Wireless   50

QWERTY   52

The Wicklow Bus   57

King Conkers   60

Mary Good Luck   63

The Sabre   69

The Candlestick   75

Concrete Mike   79

The Mangle   92

The Shell   95

Where is Home?   98

Our Televisions   105

My Mother's Wish   107

The Royal Hospital Kilmainham   111

The Oil   118

The Quarry   125

The Rare Ould Times 127

He is Here 131

The Whistle 136

FICTIONS 143

The Lighthouse 144

The Castle 152

Robert 158

The Brooch 162

The Lady Mystery 167

The Cottage 173

The Wall 180

Jacinta 189

Red Lady 196

All Souls 205

The Chalet 211

Arabian Fire 221

My Window 230

Charity 234

The Nun 241

The Leprechaun 247

Mr. Talbot 251

POEMS 255

Inspiration 256

I am Dublin 258

Time 260

Roots & Wings 262

ACKNOWLEDGEMENTS 263

MEMORIES

Storytelling is a tool for knowing who we are and what we want.

URSUAL K. LE GUIN

The Gun

I stood in amazement as my father took a revolver from a brown paper package that he had kept hidden on the upper shelf of the large press in his office. I had just turned ten years old at the time. I had seen guns only in pictures and had never known that there actually was such a weapon in our house. He let me hold it for a moment. The cold metal object felt heavy. I learned sometime later that it was his point 38 calibre Webley Revolver. He then took a small cardboard box of bullets from the press and showed me how to open and load the revolver. I gazed, totally intrigued. He told me he had wanted me to see it. He knew I was old enough then to keep a secret – I had to promise I would never tell anyone. Years passed and I kept my promise. It was a special secret between my father and me.

Now as an adult, I'm quietly watching him. The shallow peak of his cloth cap shades his eyes from a glare that doesn't exist. Even when boating, he wears his grey suit and dark coloured tie in keeping with the habits of a man of his age. He had requested that I join him on the lake today and asked me to row. He had told me why. Any further exchange of words between us now seems unnecessary, even inappropriate. I know this is an emotional moment for him. I feel extraneous to the scene. He pulls the gun slowly from the package he had hidden in the inside pocket of his overcoat and holds it in his right hand. He brandishes it, as he must have done so often in the past. Despite its age, its steely grey metal still appears new. I can see from his face that long buried memories are flooding back. I know this is inevitable. I also know that those memories must be of his young days, some fifty years ago, when he regarded that gun as a precious and even vital possession. He was just sixteen years old then. That was during his military training in the

Old Irish Republican Army camp in Ballindoon in County Sligo, not far from where he is now. He raises his gaze and looks across the lake water. Near his abandoned family homestead, he can see Ballindoon Abbey. His family burial plot lies in the shadow of that fourteenth century ruin. The abbey's fragmented walls stand bleak against the backdrop of the Highwood Hills with their scattered collection of white-walled houses. Many young men from that area, some from those very houses, had enlisted in the IRA with him in 1916. It was considered the right thing to do. At that moment in history, the IRA, a paramilitary movement, appeared to present the only viable opportunity to dislodge the British after seven hundred years of occupation. It was in that IRA camp that he was assigned the revolver and was given his first training in the use of firearms. Diligent practice made him an expert marksman. In the turbulent Ireland of the time, he knew his life might depend on it. He had told me that his most vivid memories were of the times spent on active IRA deployments. There were occasions when he fired his revolver in those adrenaline-pumping ambushes against British troop detachments. Those were times he rarely spoke about. But I knew he still held them among his memories, deep rooted and emotional, some undoubtedly rewarding, some understandably painful. His eyes are moist.

His promotion to Camp Adjutant and subsequently to Captain followed rapidly. At the age of twenty-one, he became Officer in Charge of an IRA Company at the Coolany Training Camp in County Sligo, with over one hundred men under his command. His IRA revolver was always with him; it was regarded as part of his uniform. There were satisfying memories when, in 1919, the IRA was recognised by the first Dáil Éireann as the legitimate army of the Irish Republic. He treasured his military service medal, awarded years later, in recognition of his active participation in the IRA during that period. I can see now in his face that touch of pride in remembering that he had fought for what he had believed to be right, he had fought for Ireland. I find myself silently sharing with him that sense of pride. I feel an enhanced admiration for him.

Latterly, there were his many years in An Garda Síochána. Due to his extensive IRA training in firearms, he was one of the few members of the force issued with a Garda service revolver. He progressed rapidly through the ranks. When he eventually retired from the Garda after over forty years' service, he had to surrender that official revolver, which he never kept in his home. But he still retained his old IRA weapon. He had never told me why. Perhaps that most potent and tangible memento of his past was difficult to part with. He never applied for a licence for that weapon. Why should he, he had said. It was never used anymore or even seen as it was stored in that locked press, together with a few rounds of ammunition, for the past fifty odd years. Now it is once again in his hand, its stark appearance looking ominously out of place in the peaceful surroundings of Lough Arrow.

Some moments ago, as he sat in the stern, I had rowed the small boat away from the shore, hearing the swish of the light breeze through the reeds. This is the lake where, as a young boy, he had enjoyed trout fishing. It is the lake for which he had developed a deep love, a love that had never left him. He had returned here almost every year over the past forty years or so for the mayfly fishing, beckoned instinctively when the hawthorn and lilac were in bloom. Normally he would draw in the oars and allow the boat to drift gently to a clump of reeds in Ringbawn Bay, not far from the bank. There he would tie up, watching the mayfly dancing on the wavelets as he prepared his line and bait. That was one of the better places for catching those elusive trout. I had accompanied him on some of those outings when I was younger and I knew his routine. But today, it was not a fishing trip. There was no fishing rod or tackle. This time, he had instructed me to row far away from the shore, out to a place where he knew the water to be deep. There, in response to a motion of his hand, I paused and let the blades of the oars float gracefully in the water. He had already told me what he was planning to do. I know that, for him, this lake is the appropriate location.

He slowly looks around. Beneath an overcast sky, the dark green foliage on two of the lake's several islands breaks the distant horizon. There's a faint scent of bracken in the air. The water laps softly on the hull of the clinker-built boat, with gentle reassuring whispers. The lonesome call of a curlew somewhere inland is interrupted by the splashing of a swan flapping its outstretched wings further along the shore. A dragonfly, conspicuous by its iridescent wings, alights momentarily on my oar, then darts away across the water. We are surrounded by the tranquillity of nature, the soft sounds of solitude. I know he had wanted it to be this way.

There is no one in sight. Intuitively, I know he does not wish me to disturb his thoughts. He holds his revolver nostalgically one last time. He takes a deep breath and slowly edges the gun over the side of the boat. Two small boxes of ammunition follow. He watches them sink into the deep murky waters, as they quickly disappear into a place where they will never be found. As the concentric circles of the perturbance dissipates slowly outwards, only his own distorted reflection becomes visible in the rippling waters. It's the reflection of an old man, behind whose furrowed brow deeply hidden memories have been awakened. In that one small act, he had closed an important chapter of his life. He remains silent. Like many of his generation from that part of the country, his emotions are rarely expressed in words. Like his memories, they are kept locked up deep within. The gun had been a part of him, a tangible part of his past. Perhaps his act was a form of liberation from that tumultuous past. That gun, itself a tiny relic of Irish history, much of it untold, is now gone for all time, resting at the bottom of a County Sligo lake, the lake he so loves. Yet I know his memories still remain and will remain with him forever.

As we slowly head back to the shore, the only sounds are the rhythmic clump of the oars and the swirling of the water around the blades.

Le Grand Hôtel du Canadel

'It's difficult to imagine what those poor soldiers went through.' I made the comment somewhat casually to the elderly gentleman in the wheelchair next to me. The small military commemorative ceremony had come to an end. The speeches were over, the wreaths had been laid and the final martial notes of the Marseillaise, exuding from the small military band, had dissipated into the warm night air. The crowd was beginning to disperse. The small guard of honour had relinquished its position behind the headstones, their banners now neatly furled. The dignitaries in their regalia were being escorted to their vehicles. The roadside cemetery, the smallest of the many French National Cemeteries, was slowly returning to its customary solitude.

'You say it's difficult to imagine, Monsieur?' The frail looking gentleman responded to my comment as he slowly turned his wheelchair to look at me. The shine of several medals pinned to his ill-fitting tunic was just visible in the streetlight.

'It's not difficult to imagine, Monsieur, if you were there,' he continued. I was taken aback. I suddenly realised that I had inadvertently made my comment in English, forgetting that I was in France, and, to my surprise, the gentleman had responded in perfect English, albeit in an accent I didn't recognise.

'You mean you took part in the landings here?' I asked, impressed. He nodded slowly. I knew that members of the *Commandos d'Afrique* had crossed the Mediterranean and come ashore on the small beach just below the cemetery shortly after midnight on the 14th/15th August 1944 in what was called *'Operation Dragoon'*. A small monument marks the spot. Most of the cemetery's thirteen gravestones mark the final resting place of the brave members of that force who had helped liberate France during the Second World War exactly seventy years ago. They were the advance guard for the major landing of Allied Forces on the beaches of Southern France.

'Yes, you should try to imagine.' His small piercing eyes, well set into a sallow and deeply wrinkled face beneath a slanting black beret, were staring at me. He spoke slowly and deliberately in a voice surprisingly strong for his age.

'And you must see the past, see what happened here seventy years ago – you must try to see it clearly, Monsieur.' He momentarily raised a slender finger in the air as if lecturing to me and waited for a moment to let the full significance of those words sink in. I felt compelled to listen as he continued in solemn tones. He tapped the arm of his wheelchair with the bony knuckles of his right hand to emphasise every important syllable.

'You must imagine what those lads felt who silenced the large gun over there on the promontory.' He waved his hand in the direction of Cap Nègre, the rocky headland about two kilometres to the west.

'It was a big gun, you know, a big seventy-seven-millimetre cannon covering the whole coastline. That was a very lethal weapon. It had to be taken before we could land. That was just after midnight when Chief Warrant Officer Texier's lads scaled those cliffs from the sea, almost vertically, up to the gun. That was a very tough assignment, Monsieur. Some very gallant men, including Texier himself, sacrificed their lives. I knew many of them. But they achieved their objective. They silenced the gun.' He paused. His eyes dropped their gaze momentarily, then resumed their steady stare.

'It was around one o'clock in the morning when General Bouvet gave the order and we hit the beach down there, me and my comrades. It was dark – there was no moon, just like tonight. I knew we were in France, in

Provence – I could get the faint scent of the oleanders in the night air.' There was a brief hint of a smile, then he continued calmly and deliberately.

'By then, of course, the element of surprise was lost, with all that shooting at the promontory. They heard us coming. They were ready for us. They started to set off double star flares to light up the whole area. Yes, we knew it wasn't going to be easy, as we scrambled ashore from the LCAs. Each man carried forty pounds of equipment. Can you imagine it, Monsieur?'

'LCAs?' I queried.

'Landing Craft Assault, Monsieur.' He continued. 'We climbed over the tracks and past the small railway station – that was the building just behind me here. The worst was when we moved up the path to the old hotel there. You know, there was a German garrison based there – that was their stronghold for this whole area, Monsieur. We had to take the hotel – that was our first objective.'

There was increased determination in his voice as he continued.

'Yes, we had to take it. The *Résistance* had given us all the information. But we knew it would be difficult. There was a lot of shooting. We probably injured or maybe killed quite a few but I couldn't see exactly what was happening, especially when the flares went out. I know we took several prisoners. There was chaos at first; oh yes, quite a lot of confusion. Then suddenly there was silence – deadly silence.' He paused.

'Is your imagination following me, Monsieur?' I nodded. He continued.

'We encircled the hotel, making our way around through the gardens. The entrance was at the other side, away from the sea.'

His arm gestured in a semi-circular motion.

'We thought we had them all, so we started to enter,

up the steps to the door, very cautiously of course. It was dark. That's when they suddenly opened fire from the hallway inside. One of my comrades, Jacques, fell in the doorway right beside me. He's now lying just there, Monsieur.' With a feeble finger, he pointed towards one of the crosses marking the graves, as he continued.

'He was clutching onto my leg as he took his last breath, poor Jacques. But I couldn't stop, I couldn't even look at him, Monsieur. We immediately sprayed the place with bullets.'

He swung his hand around to illustrate the action.

'They were ricocheting off the walls. Then all went quiet again. I stumbled over some bodies in the entrance hall. Then I turned down into the basement where the maids' rooms were. I guessed their guns and ammunition were stored down there. You see, I had to make sure everything was secure, Monsieur. That's when I met them, face to face – two Germans who were hiding there.' He leaned forward in his wheelchair and reached out with a long shaking hand to pull me closer. His voice developed a soft hoarseness as he continued, his lips beginning to quiver.

'I took them by surprise. They were young lads, very young, probably younger than me. Even in the dim light, I could see the terrible fear in their eyes. I was that close, real close, you see. Their weapons were at the ready but they hesitated. I had to shoot. I thought of Jacques and I fired several rounds.' His stare became even more intense.

'It was either them or me – do you understand? I can still remember their blood spattering onto the floor tiles. Can you imagine, Monsieur? You *must* imagine so that you know what we all really went through that night, each one of us. It was our duty.' He leaned back, straightening his sunken chest, and raised his head erect.

'Grandad, stop talking about that!' A slim girl with long hair, probably in her twenties, emerged from the shadows nearby and approached the wheelchair. 'You know that sort of talk gets you too upset. Anyway, it's time to go now.' She smiled briefly at me as she started to turn the wheelchair towards the road. The old man was straining to continue staring at me.

'They fell on the tiles just a few metres away. You *must* imagine it and remember it, Monsieur.' I stood and watched the wheelchair slowly disappear into the night.

I had read about those landings several times before. I knew it all already and I was glad the old man didn't delay me any longer. I had other thoughts on my mind. We had to leave very early the following morning for an exciting week's skiing in Les Deux Alps, a resort about five hours' drive north. I turned and made my way quickly up the short winding avenue to the apartment block where my family was holidaying for the summer. I had known that the apartment building was erected after the war on the foundations of Le Grand Hôtel du Canadel, the hotel that the old man had referred to. I also knew that the peace of the little village of Le Canadel, its secluded beach and tranquil surroundings was shattered shortly after the occupation of France in the Second World War. The hotel was taken over by the occupying forces, its prominent location providing an ideal vantage point for their garrison. Stories still persisted in the village about atrocities which took place in the hotel, including the torture and murder of members of *La Résistance* in the basement. Shortly after the war, the building was mysteriously burned down, no one seemed to know how and the older villagers didn't want to discuss it. The present apartment block was erected on its foundations shortly afterwards.

The following week, on returning to our Le Canadel apartment, I started to think about the old man in the wheelchair. Later that evening at dusk, something drew me again down to the small cemetery below the apartment. It looked deserted. My thoughts returned to the soldiers lying there. Even though the cemetery was the smallest in France, the whispers I could sense from the graves of those young men were just as loud and persuasive as any of those from the graves in the country's major war cemeteries. In the increasing darkness, those whispers seemed to be telling me of the evil and the indisputable lessons of war. Would that the world would listen! I stood motionless. It was then that I noticed a figure moving slowly towards me from beside one of the crosses. It was the young girl who had been with the old man in the wheelchair. She smiled shyly.

'Are you the man who....?' She hesitated as she looked closely at me. I nodded. 'I was hoping I'd meet you sometime,' she said. 'I wanted to tell you that my grandfather passed away last week.' I was taken aback.

'Oh, I'm so sorry', I said. She continued.

'It was just a few days after the ceremony here. Before he died, he talked about you. He said you were the only person who listened to him. No one else wanted to hear all that sad stuff.' I detected tears beginning to well up in her eyes. Guilt started to clutch at my brain with its cruel claws. I should have listened more sympathetically to the old man's words. I should have told him how I appreciated him telling me about those events and that I was able to imagine it. The girl pulled a folded piece of paper from the back pocket of her jeans and handed it to me.

'He had this with him the night of the landings. He always kept it. We thought he would like you to have it.' Through the tears she forced a brief smile. I looked at the well-worn paper in my hand and drew a breath to thank her, but she was gone.

As night fell, the moon was making her magical presence

felt. I unfolded the piece of paper. It was a faint, rough pencilled sketch of the local coastline showing three locations with times written after each – *Cap Nègre 12.30, Le Canadel 1.00, Cavalaire 1.30*. Along the side a few names were scrawled. One was Jacques followed by a large 'X'. On the top left-hand corner was a date, *14/8/1944*, apparently written sometime later in pen. I stared at the paper. Was I holding a piece of history in my hand? The full impact of the old man's words rapidly enveloped me like a clinging mist. I stood, my mind becoming heavy with emotion. What, I wondered, had drawn me down to the little cemetery that night?

My eyes turned to the line of simple crosses close by. In the moonlight, I could make out the one marked *'Pancrazi, Jacques, C.D.O. Afrique'*. At its base lay a sprig of oleander. Had the young girl left it there on behalf of and in memory of her Grandfather? I began to wonder if, in a few years' time, that young soldier, lying in foreign ground in a land he helped liberate, would be but a meaningless name on a gravestone, remembered by none.

I made my way pensively up the avenue to the apartment block. The rasping sound of the cicadas, which punctuated the daylight hours, had ceased and only the harsh croaks of a couple of toads somewhere in the woods disturbed the silence. The delicate scent of the oleanders imparted a faint sweetness to the air, reminding me of the old man's comments. For the first time, I became conscious of the solitude around me and how it contrasted with the sounds of battle that must have resounded here seventy years earlier. The moonlight, filtering through the overhanging mimosa branches, formed grotesque moving shapes on the tarmac at my feet, each pale moonlit patch fighting with its surrounding shadows, just as good had fought with evil in the chequered history of the place. In my mind, I could still see the piercing eyes of the old man in the wheelchair and hear his words. My thoughts were on him and on his brave young comrades who had struggled up that same avenue on that fateful night in 1944. Despite the passing of those seventy years, I now felt connected to that night. I was walking in the footprints of history.

As I entered the apartment building, I recalled that its basement retained the original maids' rooms of the old hotel, accessed via a narrow passageway still displaying the ornate floor tiles. It was in one of those small basement rooms that we stored our beach equipment, items of fun and freedom in marked contrast to the weapons of war that the old man in the wheelchair told me were once kept there. That fun and freedom we owed in no small measure to that man and his companions, those brave young commandoes, some of whose remains now lay in the tiny cemetery below. That basement had witnessed a lot of traumatic history.

On the following afternoon, I was sitting in the sun on the apartment balcony, gazing at the three islands shimmering peacefully on the horizon, but not seeing them. My mind was still on my encounter with the old man the previous week and subsequently with his granddaughter. The small piece of paper the young girl had given me, that tangible and poignant connection with a tumultuous past, had awakened something within me. My thoughts were interrupted by my eight-year-old granddaughter who had made her way up from our basement storeroom and pulled over a chair to sit beside me.

'It's too scary down there, Grandad.' she said as she opened her story book. 'I felt a very scary feeling as I walked along the tiles in the passageway.' She didn't expect a reply and I didn't venture to offer one. But, somehow, I knew what she meant, I knew what she had felt, and I knew it wasn't her imagination. Those walls, that passageway, those floor tiles, the only existing remnants of Le Grand Hôtel du

Canadel, could never fully expurgate their terrible past.

Later, as night fell, a pale orange moon appeared serenely over the islands, stretching her shimmering walkway of light towards me across the waves, and the faint peaceful scent of oleanders blessed the air.

My Mother's Diary

Carrots
Potatoes
Shoe polish....

I'm looking through the pages of my mother's old diary. It's the Bayer Pharmaceutical Diary for the Fourth Quarter of 1951, distributed by the Pharmaceutical Society of Ireland. Being a pharmacist, or chemist, as a person with that qualification was called at the time, she was a member of that professional society and used their suppliers' diaries as notebooks for her day-to-day affairs. That included her shopping lists. She had several such diaries into which she transcribed her thoughts. Unfortunately, only one, the one I now hold, has survived the years. It's a small diary with a simple brown cardboard cover to which time has not been kind – it's somewhat soiled and it exudes a musty odour from years of storage. Many pages are either lose or missing. But the plain and uninspiring appearance belies the unique treasures that lie scattered within.

I feel nostalgic as I thumb through the pages and see her neat handwriting. Interspersed amid those practical entries I find thought provoking stanzas from some of her poems, many unfinished. I select one, titled 'Autumn Leaves', and I read the first stanza:

A brown leaf trembled on the tree;
The brown leaves quiver'd and were free,
Each seemed on gay adventure bent –
Each leaf, which all its days had spent
Upon a tree, sped joyously,
Arrayed in russet. One could see
The brown leaves quiver and go free,
The brown leaf trembles on the tree.

My mother's diary was where her occasional poetic thoughts first found their way onto paper. She carried it in her handbag where it was always at hand, whenever domestic requirements occurred to her or poetic inspiration came.

A few pages further on, I come across a couple of simple arithmetical problems involving fractions and areas. I suspect that these entries were made while assisting me with my school homework.

Further entries read:

Bacon
Coffee
Oranges
Celery…
Clery's – brown material

That last entry is undoubtedly referring to some garment she planned to make using material she'd purchase at Clery's Department Store in Dublin. The remnants of war time frugality, still prevalent in those times, encouraged *making* rather than *buying* and my mother believed strongly in that principle. She was meticulous in all her work, whether domestic or professional. I recall witnessing the care my white coated mother took in the pharmacy when selecting and weighing tiny samples of various liquids, powders or pastes on her small brass weighing scales. She would mix them with pestle and mortar, carefully following the prescribed formula. In those days, pharmacists prepared most of the medications themselves from the basic ingredients.

My mother was a thoughtful lady of gentle disposition, a lady who loved nature and enjoyed taking walks in the countryside. This is reflected in much of her poetry. She was tall with fine features, slightly sallow in complexion. In the late evenings I can still see her sitting by the fire, always neatly dressed, with her long greying hair tied in a bun and wearing her thin-rimmed reading glasses. She might be reading a newspaper or a book. My father would be upstairs working in his office – he was Garda Duty Officer and his duties involved night work. I would be engaged with my school homework or practicing my piano pieces or constructing something with my Meccano set. But I could still observe my mother. At intervals, she would rake the ashes in the hot grate with the long black poker and perhaps toss a sod or two of turf onto the fire, causing an array of sparks to rise momentarily from the turf dust and scurry up the chimney like a swarm of fireflies. Then she would take her diary and ball point pen from her handbag beside the fender. Placing the diary on her lap, she would quietly start to write, pausing at intervals to gaze thoughtfully into the flickering flames for inspiration.

Interspersed with more domestic requisites from the shops, I come across a further stanza of her poem 'Autumn Leaves':

> *A brown leaf floated to my feet;*
> *The brown leaves scurried down the street*
> *To lie in stillness by the wall,*
> *Or whirl in rustling sudden squall*
> *A-whisp'ring softly to the wind,*
> *Aye! I was truly joyed to find*
> *A brown leaf lying at my feet –*
> *The brown leaves spinning down the street.*

I seldom knew or fully appreciated what her pen, held in those slender fingers, was conveying to the pages of that diary. But I am seeing a small part of it now. The pages contain a miscellany of everything that was of relevance to her on a daily basis. They hold a tiny but precious insight into her life at that time and, to some extent, into the world in which she lived. In looking through this little diary, I'm turning back the pages of history in a very personal way.

The repeated transitions I'm seeing from her notes on day-to-day practicalities to the more profound poetic entries are intriguing, all within a few pages of one small diary. On one page, I am elevated out of reality on the wings of her radiant imagination; on the next, I am jolted back to earth, to the empirical items of ordinary living. Perhaps writing her poetry was her way of lifting her thoughts from the ordinary, of connecting both with herself and with the outside world, of creating and briefly inhabiting another existence. Her mind was essentially scientific, honed by her pharmaceutical training, but it masterfully stretched her tenuous threads of creative thought across disciplines to weave the luminous fabric of her verses. Perhaps she felt some intrinsic relationship between science and poetry. Did she perceive both disciplines as explorers of nature, as expressions of truth?

Even the many corrections and changes which pepper the diary pages, all neatly made as she composed her poems, lend a poignant authenticity to the writings. For me, those alterations also convey a delightfully overt insight into the care she took in composing poems to meet her own exacting standards of satisfaction with regard to language, meter and rhyme.

On a few occasions, my mother won first prize (£2-2s-0d, two guineas) for her poems in the Christmas poetry competition sponsored by *The Garda Review*, the official journal of *An Garda Síochána*. I note that 'Autumn Leaves' was a joint winner in 1951. The diary also contains a couple of addresses but no phone numbers. She rarely needed to phone anyone. Her modes of communication with family and friends were mostly by letter or perhaps by visiting. This was not unusual in those days when not every house had the benefits of a telephone. Her steady hand wrote many letters. And in this diary, I see the same neat handwriting now, its soft well-rounded script free from unnecessary embellishments.

Tragically, while I was still in my young teens, death cruelly snatched her away from me and from this world, like the autumn wind snatches the brown leaves of her poem from the trees. But what cannot be taken away from me are the many inspirational thoughts conveyed in her poetry, together with the memories, so many memories, of her sitting and quietly writing by the fire. I will always have those memories. And thankfully I also have this diary, a small and very personal treasure, a quiet and meaningful messenger from the past, a tangible connection to my dear mother. In her diary, I'm not merely reading her words; in the many entries, especially in the lines of her poems, I'm swimming in a stream of memories, and I'm hearing my mother's voice, wafting softly through the years.

I turn another page and there, fine-tuned after a few alterations, is the final stanza of 'Autumn Leaves'. The poem is a touching reminder of the passage of time, that mysterious and unfeeling continuum that separates our present from our past, that separates my mother from me. While writing these lines, I wonder if perhaps my mother was foreseeing her own passing, less than five short years after she had penned them:

> *The brown leaves hurried down the street —*
> *The brown leaf nestled by my feet*
> *And silent lay. And when at last*
> *Our Autumn comes and life is past,*
> *Released from Earth, with nought to bind,*
> *Life's Great Adventure left behind;*
> *Brown leaves will lie above our feet —*
> *Brown leaves go spinning down the street!*

> *By Eileen Nangle, RIP*

Baby William

'Let's put on your little red socks today,' said Mary Anne as she finished dressing her four-month-old son William. 'We want you looking nice for Fair Day, don't we?'

'But Mammy, people will laugh at him in those bright red socks.' William's older sister chuckled as she helped her mother dress her baby brother.

'Of course not. His Auntie Lily knitted them specially for him and sent them all the way from Wicklow. He'll look just grand.'

Fair Day in Tullow in the 1860s attracted farmers from the surrounding countryside with their cattle, sheep and pigs to sell them in the busy Market Square in the centre of the historic town. Merchants from Carlow Town came to replenish their stocks. Butter and corn were traded in large quantities. Many of the shops on Main Street, together with a few on Bridge Street and Mill Street, displayed their wares on small wooden tables on the pavements. Byrne's General Stores, owned by Baby William's father, had a large variety of goods on display outside. The Byrnes were a well-known and respected family with strong ties to the community. Many years earlier, William Senior's father was leader of a small band of brave men who removed the head of the martyred Father John Murphy, famed from his stance against the English in the battle of Vinegar Hill in County Wexford on 21st June 1798, from the spikes of the Church railings there in Tullow, where Father Murphy had been captured. They reverently interred the head with the body, in defiance of the direct orders of the English Yeomen executioners. A good family pedigree. In addition to managing his store, William was the local auctioneer and hotelier. Today, like all fair days, was a busy time for him.

Crowds made their way between the horse and donkey carts parked on the sides of the busy streets. Any savoury smells from the produce on display were overpowered by the pervasive animal odours. Several horses were tethered to poles and railings outside the blacksmith's forge as they patiently waited their turn to enter the hot smoky interior. Their owners took the opportunity, while in town, to have their shoes replaced. Old Pascal, the town's partially sighted fiddle player, was sitting on his stool at the upper end of the square, playing his usual medley of jigs and reels with his foot tapping in time. His inverted cap was waiting expectantly on the ground beside him. A few local dogs patrolled the streets, barking and snapping at any unwelcome visiting canines.

The weather was kind that particular day, cloudy but warm and dry. The public houses were doing a bustling trade. Many of their eager clients, mostly farmers, consumed their drinks while standing outside the premises, chatting loudly with friends and acquaintances, some of whom they mightn't have met since the last Fair Day. Many strangers from neighbouring townlands were there that day – the menfolk, mostly farm labourers, hoping to get work, the women in their heavy black shawls, seeking domestic employment in the town. Everywhere, of course, noisy bartering was taking place, with voices raised. At times, stout sticks were brandished in the air. Such age-old displays of determination were intended to make the bargaining power as forceful as possible. Getting the best bargain was everyone's challenge.

Mary Anne was used to this busy Fair Day scene as the family hotel in Bridge Street, where they lived, was not far from the town centre. That day, she bundled tiny William into his pram, as she often did, with its black wooden body and large spoked wheels, and wheeled him up into Main Street to purchase some groceries for the family. William's young brothers and sisters were left at home in the care of the one of the maids. The town would be too rough and noisy for them.

'So, you'd be looking for some nice cuts for himself, Mrs. Byrne?' asked Tony, the friendly butcher, as Mary Anne entered his shop. She had parked the pram outside with a couple of other prams nearby. She knew that 'himself', her husband William, after whom their baby was named, expected a good meal when he'd return home hungry that evening after a busy day at the store.

'And how's the new little laddie doing?' The butcher reached for a large side of meat hanging on its hook. He slapped it down on his blood-stained block to set about preparing the required cuts.

'Sure, he's grand, not a bother, thank God.' Mary Anne watched his large knife slicing through the red meat. 'He's just out getting a little fresh air in his pram today.' One of her friends, who had entered, nodded and smiled, commenting, 'A lovely little lad. Isn't he the spit and image of his Dad?'

As Mary Anne emerged from the shop with her purchase of meat in her shopping bag, her heart jumped. For just a moment, she stared at the empty pram in disbelief. Someone had taken William! Her screams attracted the attention of those around. News spread like wildfire: *Mrs. Byrne's baby has been stolen!* The locals were shocked. Stealing a child had never been known in Tullow before. Tony the butcher ran out of his shop. He and a few of the neighbours tried to comfort the distraught Mary Anne, still standing dazed beside the empty pram. They assured her that Baby William couldn't be too far away. He would surely be found quickly. He'd be safe. She shouldn't worry. But Mary Ann couldn't be comforted. She began rushing around the busy town, pushing her way through the crowds, the stalls, the animals and the carts, while shouting to know if anyone had seen her young child. She ran wildly back and forth, not knowing where to look. The town became a blur to her. As she twisted and turned through the crowds, her heart was bursting in her chest. Her brain was confused and throbbing like a pot of boiling water.

William, hearing the commotion, rushed out of his store and joined the crowd outside the butcher's shop. He frantically shouted to several townspeople to help him organise a search party. They spread out in different directions around the square and into the adjoining streets. But there was no trace of Baby William. Nobody in the crowd was seen carrying a baby. People heading for the roads leaving the town were stopped and asked if they had seen anyone with a four-month-old child, but no one had. No sighting was reported. The sun was close to setting as the frantic search continued. It seemed that the jostling mass of people and animals had swallowed the young child.

Séamus, one of the older men in the search party, was looking among the crowds, now thinning out, at the top of the market square. Old Pascal, with fiddle and bow now resting on his lap, called out to him: 'Talk to that group of gypsy women going out the road there. I heard them talking suspiciously as they passed me.' Séamus quickly followed the group of three or four women, who were about to climb onto a donkey cart. He called out to them. They turned and shook their heads. They had seen nothing, they claimed, nothing at all. As Séamus eyed them suspiciously, a flash of bright red wool caught his eye, just visible beneath the hem of one of the younger women's black shawls. He immediately challenged them. 'You stole Mrs. Byrne's baby!' The woman turned away and started to climb onto the cart, helped by one of her companions. As Séamus was about to approach the cart, a burly stranger brandishing a stout stick approached from the direction of the town. He had heard Séamus and immediately shouted to the woman: 'Did you take the baby? Did you take Baby Byrne?' The woman looked at him and hesitated. There was a tiny whimper from beneath the shawl as the red socks moved. 'Give it back right now, you bloody eejit!' the man continued menacingly. 'I've known the Byrnes for over forty years. Shame on you! Hand over that baby immediately or else…' He raised his stick in a threatening manner at the woman who stepped down from the cart, took Baby William from beneath her shawl and, with head bowed, deftly handed the whimpering baby to Séamus. In a moment, all the women had mounted the cart and were gone. Turning to Séamus, the man said: 'Please say sorry to Mr. and Mrs. Byrne. You see, Kathleen lost her own baby a couple of months ago.' He walked away quickly, following the cart. The search was over. Mary Anne wept with joy when she and Baby William were reunited amid a group of jubilant friends who had assembled on hearing the news. William Senior, out of breath, also arrived and hugged his baby son lovingly.

That night, Byrne's Hotel in Bridge Street was alive with festivities as neighbours crowded in. All drinks were on the house. Baby William didn't get much rest with all the noise. He was, after all, the centre of attention. In addition, Mary Anne hung a tiny pair of bright red socks with clothes pegs from the handle of the pram so that everyone could see them. Although Aunt Lily wasn't there, Mary Anne couldn't help whispering to herself: 'Thank God for your colourful knitting, Aunt Lily.'

* * * * *

Note: Sometime in the early 1940s, my late mother wrote an amusing little poem titled *A Pair of Feet* dedicated to her father, William, then in his eighties, when his old feet started to give him trouble. One of the many stanzas read as follows:

One market day – the story goes –
Whilst yet a tiny lad,
A woman stole you from your pram;
Oh, it was very sad!
The hue and cry was raised. 'Tis claimed,
'Tho' fast the woman sped,
In triumph you were carried home
Because your socks were red!

The Locked Room

I slowly pushed open the door. It was obvious that it hadn't been opened for a long time. It was proving difficult, as if it were resisting my somewhat nervous efforts to enter the room. Was it trying to give me a message? The creaking hinges seemed to be shouting at me to stop. The sound was disturbing the silence of the large house. I hesitated, fearing someone would hear. I really didn't want to be found entering a room that was, I sensed, out of bounds. But I knew my mother had gone out shopping, and Granny, who was lolling as usual in her armchair downstairs by the fire, was quite deaf. No one else was around. I persisted.

My bedroom was next to the room I was trying to enter, and more than once during the still of the night, I had heard a faint thudding sound coming from within. It was repeated at intervals and it aroused my curiosity. My mother claimed she didn't hear it and quietly dismissed my query, saying the timber beams and rafters in the three-hundred-year-old building, one of the oldest in Wicklow Town, always creaked at night as the temperature dipped. But I knew the sound I was hearing was certainly not the creaking timbers; my young ears could readily identify those sounds. What I was hearing was different – a soft but definite rhythmic thud, starting and stopping at intervals.

I had known that the room was permanently locked. I didn't know why. I had asked my mother what was in that room. Perhaps I had imprudently chosen the wrong moment to pose the question, while we all sat at table.

'That's Liam's room,' she had whispered, 'but don't talk about it. It might upset Granny.'

I didn't ask again.

Then, one day, I was searching for something in a drawer of an old dresser and found a small metal box, originally for flake tobacco, but now a repository for a miscellany of keys. One of them carried a worn paper label neatly marked *Liam's Room* in faded ink. My inquisitiveness and sense of adventure demanded that I yield to the temptation the key presented.

I stood for a moment at the open door of the room, pulling away a mass of clingy cobwebs that had deposited themselves on my face like dirty lace. The small window opposite was partially obscured by faded curtains, and those windowpanes that still allowed some light to penetrate were covered with layers of dust. Even in daylight, the room was eerily dark. Cobwebs seemed to be everywhere and a musty odour filled my nostrils. In the centre of the room was a bed covered with a once-white sheet. There were no other furnishings. The tops of the floral-patterned wallpaper were peeling away from the damp walls, curling inwards like grotesque wilting flowers. Lower down, against the walls, were many dust-covered boxes of all sizes and two trunks with rust covered locks and hinges. In one corner was an untidy pile of odds and ends, too numerous to identify individually, but I could see that they included many books and a few broken wooden toys. A small wooden rocking horse, which must at one time have brought joy, was standing there with broken reins, abandoned, lonely. Most prominent to my curious eyes was a pair of small wooden crutches, standing upright against one of the trunks. It took me a few moments to absorb the strange scene, a scene devoid of colour, devoid of life, that obviously had lain undisturbed for probably many years. It was as if time had covered it with a dust laden cloak of stillness, a stillness that now enveloped me.

Having gazed all around, my attention was drawn again to the crutches. I had never seen such a small pair before. Were they my size? For a moment, I forgot about my surroundings as I gingerly stepped across the dusty floor and gently lifted the crutches, placing the thickly padded tops under my armpits. Yes, they were obviously for a child of approximately my size – I was seven years old. I couldn't resist taking a few careful paces using the crutches. Handling them took a bit of getting used to, but after I crossed the room once or twice, I had adequately mastered the technique. For me, it was a novel experience, which I was beginning to enjoy.

Then a sudden realisation struck me forcefully – the gentle thuds of the crutches on the bare floorboards was the sound I had been hearing each night from my bedroom. I had no doubt about it. I stopped and stood still. A chill tingled rapidly from the top of my head down the full length of my spine. I became abruptly aware once again of my strange and silent surroundings, as if they were trying to impart some kind of message to me. Something told me that this was not where I should be, that I should leave. It was a very definite and compelling feeling. I carefully returned the crutches to their resting place and left quickly without looking back, pulling the creaking door firmly closed behind me and locking it.

'Come with me while I visit Grandad's grave,' my mother said to me later that day. My grandfather had died just a few weeks earlier, and my mother and I were staying temporarily with Granny, who was showing signs of frailness. We stood in reverence in the damp grass at the foot of the family grave in Rathnew Cemetery, just outside Wicklow Town, while softly reciting a decade of the Rosary together. Several bunches of withered flowers still lay where they had been placed on the grave weeks earlier. A few faded petals lay scattered. The large marble gravestone adorned with a Celtic Cross was inscribed in the Irish language. It stood, sentinel like, displaying a stark record of the passing of loved ones over so many years. My attention was drawn to the inscription bearing the earliest date: *Liam, leanbh sé bliana d'aois, 1906.*

Having completed our prayers, my mother explained that her brother, Liam, had contracted polio as a child and had needed crutches to walk.

'He died when I was just three years old,' she whispered, taking a small embroidered handkerchief from her sleeve to dry away a tear, 'so I have only very faint memories of him. The anniversary of his death was just a few days ago. Poor little boy! And now his dad is with him in heaven.'

I found it difficult to sleep that night. It was very late and the old house was in darkness. Then, in the stillness, I heard that faint sound once again – thud . . . thud . . . thud . . . My heart beat a little faster, but this time I knew who it was. As I lay there, I said a silent prayer for him.

[Original version published in 'Storytellers' (New Writing from Ireland), Edited by Anna Fox, Published in 2017 by Solar Theatre Productions, Co. Dublin, Ireland, paperback ISBN 978 1 78846023 1]

Bell Number Seven

'That's Bell Number Seven.' I could hear my grandfather's voice as we entered the hotel. We had just arrived to visit my grandparents in Wicklow. One of the call bells on the hall bell board was swinging gently on its long elliptical spring as my grandfather's portly frame disappeared up the stairs.

'He'll be down in a minute,' my grandmother assured us. 'He's just gone to see what they want in Number Seven.'

My grandfather was the hotel proprietor and, even though he was succumbing physically to the weight of seventy years or so, he always liked to respond personally to any room service request. In my eyes, as a six-year-old, he was such a talented man. Despite his advancing deafness, he never had to look at the bell board to know which room was requesting service. On that particular visit, his intonation of those words, 'Bell Number Seven', conveyed an air of assertiveness as he made his way up the stairs, like a captain authoritatively defining a course for his ship. For me, his words were also those of an expert in bell tones. Several times I repeated those words to myself, 'Bell Number Seven', like an incantation, trying to pretend I was as important as my grandfather, trying to emulate his mastery of identifying the individual chimes of those bells. There must have been about eight or ten of them hanging on their springs on the wooden board with room numbers on tiny brass plates beneath each one. Those bells, somewhat larger than the typical call bells of the time, were waiting to be activated mechanically by thin cords or 'bell pulls' extending upwards on circuitous paths by walls and ceilings to the individual rooms from where they were controlled by pulling on their tasselled ends. Considering that the hotel, latterly renamed The Bridge Tavern, was over three hundred years old, that mechanically operated bell board, dating from Victorian times, was still regarded as an efficient and practical system of communication.

I watched and waited for another bell to ring, attracted by the almost magical mechanism of their remote activation from rooms hidden somewhere in the vastness of the hotel interior. My delight was enhanced when my grandfather, perceiving my interest, went upstairs and pulled a few of the bell pulls himself, just to demonstrate the clever calling mechanism. It also allowed me to hear the subtle differences between the various bell tones. I was intrigued. To my ears, the bell board was like a miniature carillon. However, I wasn't able to identify an individual bell by sound alone – that talent remained solely within my grandfather's realm of expertise. Nevertheless, of all the bells, Number Seven, the one I first heard my grandfather refer to that day, somehow remained my favourite; it seemed to appeal to my childhood imagination.

Of course, I was also fascinated by the old building itself. Whenever I visited, I liked to explore the small courtyard and stable where, in the early 1800s, the horses for the Bianconi stagecoaches were rested; or the old hotel's many narrow corridors winding through the interior with their uneven floor boards; and the room where the world-famous mariner Captain Robert Halpin, who laid the first functional transatlantic telegraphic cable, was born in 1836 – for me, it was all an adventure. Even as a child, I knew there was a lot of history within those venerable old walls. I could sense it. And I liked to think that those old call bells had also witnessed some of that history. I would always return to the hall and stand by the grandfather clock with its gently swinging pendulum and wait and hope that some of the call bells would ring, especially Bell Number Seven.

Some years later, after my grandfather's passing and before the old hotel was to be sold, my mother had a few of the call bells removed as souvenirs, as reminders of her father and of the hotel itself, her childhood home. I still have one of them, a small solidly cast example of Victorian craftsmanship, with a fragment of its spring still attached. Its appearance is now dulled with the dignity of age, but it still produces a delightfully mellow lingering tone, one of the sounds that must have been so familiar to my mother as a child.

Those bells served my grandfather well as call bells over the course of his almost half a century as hotel proprietor. But I found another use, a very different use, for the one bell I have. When my children were at the age when they would listen for sleigh bells on Christmas Eve, I would creep out into our back garden and gently ring the old Bridge Hotel bell a few times. Returning to the house, I would hear the children exclaiming excitedly that they now knew Santa was on his way – they had definitely heard his sleigh bell so they had to get to bed quickly. Of course, what the children didn't realise was that Santa's *real* sleigh bells would be not be heard until later in the night, closer to midnight, by which time, like all good children, they'd be fast asleep. How my grandfather would have been amused to know how one of his call bells was being used for a function very different to that for which it was originally designed. And how he would have loved to witness the excitement that his bell was bringing to a much younger generation of his family, just as all his bells had enthralled me many years earlier.

The bell is hanging on a wall-mounted bracket in my home. When I hear its soft tone, it evokes fond memories, not just of the joy of Christmases with my children, but also of old The Bridge Hotel in bygone days and, of course, of my mother and my grandfather.

I don't know which one of the hotel's many call bells I have inherited. But somehow, I would like to think that perhaps, just perhaps, it's Bell Number Seven.

My Grandfather's Pocket Watch

Out of curiosity, I give the stem winder three turns. To my amazement, the small second hand starts to rotate, the most visible sign that the old watch is operating. Holding it to my ear, I can hear its tiny heart ticking faintly. This was my grandfather's pocket watch, which has been in the family since the old man passed away in 1948. Sadly, the ravages of time have stripped the venerable timepiece of both its minute hand and the glass that once protected its face. Decorative engravings on the back of its dented casing, including the manufacturer's crest, are worn to almost invisibility. But for me, even in its present imperfect state, it still retains much of its old-world dignity. Seeing that tiny second-hand move is a welcome yet uncanny link to the past. I sit and watch it, and ponder. For a moment, that rotating hand does more than simply record the passing seconds – it transports me back in time.

I clearly remember that watch nestled in my grandfather's waistcoat pocket. Its presence was revealed only by a silver chain with small ornate links stretching in a conspicuous loop from the ring at the top of the watch to one of his buttonholes. It was part of his attire. Even though I was very young at the time, I admired the poise and dignity with which he would slowly withdraw the precious timepiece, cupping it in the palm of his hand, to inspect its dial whenever a time check was required; it was a simple but enthralling ritual. I was always impressed.

Pocket watches, developed in the sixteenth century, became popular for gentlemen of class in the late 1800s. I recall my mother telling me that in her young days in Wicklow, portable timepieces were quite rare. They were even less common in Tullow, in County Carlow, her father's hometown. It was not unusual for my grandfather, apparently perceived to be a man of some status, to be stopped on the street in Tullow with the query 'Do you have the right time, Mister?' This question might come from someone who had forgotten the essential daily task of winding their watch or who doubted its accuracy. More likely, however, the question would be posed by someone lacking the luxury of a personal timepiece. Interestingly, the adjective 'right' was customarily inserted into the question because the *approximate* time, normally adequate for most purposes then, was generally known from the chimes of the church bell or even the position of the sun, if it were visible. Of course, my grandfather was always only too willing to produce his silver-cased treasure, in his usual dignified manner, to proudly enlighten the questioner.

Those small hands, two of which I'm looking at now, while in my grandfather's possession, monitored time throughout the turbulent events in Ireland in the early 1900s. Some months after the Easter Rising of 1916, those hands would have been adjusted by my grandfather to the officially defined Greenwich Mean Time (GMT) as a consequence of the imposition on Ireland of the British time system. This synchronisation of time between Britain and Ireland was deemed necessary due to the development of railway timetables and international telegraphy. GMT was adhered to by the banks, post offices and government departments. However, this change to 'English time' was rejected by many in Ireland, especially in rural areas. The officially discarded Dublin Mean Time (DMT) or 'Old God's Time', as some called it locally, was still tenaciously adhered to. That was the time observed in Ireland before 1916, when mid-day was defined by the moment the sun was directly over Dunsink Observatory, outside Dublin. This was twenty-five minutes and twenty-one seconds behind GMT. One could say that the duality of time systems in those areas gave an additional significance to the phrase 'the *right* time'. My grandfather would, of course, graciously accommodate the nationalistic feelings of those adhering to DMT by ensuring, if asked, that *it* was the time he quoted. And then there were the County Carlow farmers who would claim that their cows didn't know anything about GMT but followed that time defined by the sun for their milking. In a way, it might be said that the cows knew the *right* time.

Wrist watches began to replace pocket watches sometime after the First World War. My grandfather, however, then in his mid-fifties, preferred to retain that gentlemanly dignity still associated with the pocket watch and its decorative chain. He was still using that old timepiece up until the day he passed away.

I look again at that pocket watch with its well-worn silver-plated casing, smooth to the touch. Over the years, its delicate hands must have rotated, second by second, minute by minute, hour by hour, through a lot of history. Each rotation of that second hand that I am now observing once marked a minute of my grandfather's lengthy adult life. It marked a minute of his present, but now, in my hand, it marks a minute of a time he would never witness, a future he would never see. For him, time has stopped, but, for this brief moment in *my* present, the pocket watch is once again obediently marking time. And yet, these life-controlling seconds, minutes and hours are man-made, artificial and irrelevant milestones in the infinite continuum of time. As I look at the faded dial, segmented by its twelve finely inscribed Roman numerals, I wonder if perhaps Einstein was right when he said that time is an illusion.

I gently place the watch, this small marvel of nineteenth-century workmanship, on my study shelf. Its second hand is still rotating. In this modern world of battery-operated quartz-controlled chronometers, which always tell the *right* time, this grand old timepiece, which served my grandfather so reliably over so many years, is now of little practical use. Its second hand will stop recording time shortly as the spring loses its tension, the small quantity of potential energy I had temporarily provided having been depleted. Let it sleep. I wonder who will wind it next at some time in the future, and who will witness that second hand rotate once again to mark just a few more seconds of passing time.

[The original version of this story was published in 'Storytellers' (New Writing from Ireland), Edited by Anna Fox, Published in 2017 by Solar Theatre Productions, Co. Dublin, Ireland, paperback ISBN 978 1 78846023 1]

The Cable

My mother and I sat with my grandfather in the hotel courtyard. I became engrossed as he spoke about his meeting with Anne, mother of the famous Captain Robert Halpin. The meeting was on the occasion of Robert's untimely death some years earlier in 1894. Anne, then probably in her ninetieth year, had been anxious to talk about Robert's life and how he became one of the most famous mariners of his time. Since Grandfather's father-in-law had expressed an interest in buying the hotel for his family, Mrs. Halpin was anxious that the potential new owners were made aware of an important segment of the building's extraordinary history before she passed on. Grandfather vividly recalled Anne's story and related it in great detail exactly as it had been told to him by the old lady. He was a dapper man with a tanned face, greying hair and well-groomed moustache. He was sitting on a small deckchair with arms folded and walking stick propped up beside him. Based on the details he gave my mother and me, this was likely the way in which events unfolded.

It was a day in 1855 and James Halpin, the hotel proprietor, was at the hotel door when he heard the loud voice approaching across the stone bridge from the Murrough. This wasn't the first time he had observed the little Englishman, but always on the other side of the river. This time, he was coming to the hotel's bar, followed by his small admiring entourage. He was conspicuous in his exceptionally tall top hat with his untidy black curls protruding from under its brim. He wore a crumpled three-piece tweed suit with a gold watch on a chain hanging from his waistcoat buttonhole and a large dark coloured cravat. Prominent black sideburns framed a long, tanned face with small beady eyes. A cigar hung precariously from his lips. Despite his small stature, he exuded an imposing presence. 'All that needs to be done now is to complete the station,' he was saying as he swaggered in through the door. 'I've done my bit, now it's up to you Irish to finish the job.'

James, a slim man of middle age, greeted him. 'Welcome, Mr. Brunel, sir. That's great news about the railway line. Well done, sir. Let me take your hat.'

'Thank you. Yes, having a direct line from Dublin to Wicklow will do wonders for the town and also for your hotel business here, my good fellow. Now, the best Irish whiskeys all round, please. And make them large ones. At least the Irish can make good whiskey.'

'Yes. Right away, sir.' James hurriedly retreated behind the bar.

'I'd say you'll get four times the number of customers,' the little man continued as he raised himself onto a wooden barstool, flicking his coat tails out of the way.

'Well, I hope so, sir.'

'Of course, you will. Think big, my dear fellow, think big. That's what I always say. Dargan here will arrange to have those people in Dublin manufacture more rolling stock.' He gestured towards one of his companions. 'They can't be shipped from England because of the different gage, you see. The line will be opening shortly. It will be very popular because of the scenic route I chose along the coast.'

'That's true, sir, very popular, I hope,' James commented, as he poured the requested drinks.

'Anyway,' continued the little man, 'railways take up too much of my time. I want to get back to my ship designing – much more challenging, much more skill required.'

'Yes, I'm sure you do, sir. I heard you designed the *Great Britton*, the largest ship ever built.'

'Yes, my good man, I did indeed. She's a truly

remarkable design, very advanced. But I'll tell you something.' Detecting William's interest, he pulled himself closer to James, took another substantial mouthful of whiskey and lowered his voice. 'I'm designing an even bigger one, much bigger. I've sketched it already. She'll be the largest and most advanced ship ever constructed. She'll have enough coal on board to go to Australia without refuelling.' With his white serviette over his arm, James listened with interest.

'That's very impressive, sir. By the way, our youngest son, Robert, has been crewing many sailing ships on that Australian route.'

'So, your son is a sailor?' He dusted a sprinkling of cigar ashes off his waistcoat.

'Yes, sir, indeed he is. He's been crewing on ships since he was just eleven years old. He tells me that steam is the propulsion of the future.'

'Of course, steam is the future. I foresaw it.' His glass was already half empty. His short legs swung back and forth beneath the stool. 'No more dependence on the vagrancies of the weather. Tell me, my good fellow, what ship is your son on?'

'He's now on the SS *Circassian*, sir.'

'Ah yes, I know that ship. Built by Robert Steele. Good ship, but I would have designed it a little better myself. But tell your son to look out for the *Great Eastern*, that's what I'm going to name my new ship. It will be built within the next three years. It's going to stun the world. Wait and see. My plans never fail.' He swallowed the last mouthful of his drink and turned to his followers. 'Let's finish up, men. I have work to do.' He got up to leave, throwing a gold sovereign on the counter. James ran to open the door for him.

'Thank you, Mr. Brunel. Your hat, sir.' His long coat tails swung jauntily as he strolled out of the doorway, followed by his companions.

'How can you stand that boastful fellow?' James's wife Anne said later. 'I could hear him from the kitchen. He's so full of himself.'

'But, dear, he's a brilliant engineer, very famous. He designs and builds bridges and ships as well as railways.'

'Maybe so, but my mother always said: Don't trust small Englishmen who wear tall top hats to make themselves look taller.'

'That's not the point, dear. He's a genius, a real genius. He's completed many engineering wonders.'

'Well, in my opinion, his huge ambitions will destroy him in the end. People like that eventually wear themselves out. You'll see.'

'Well, be that as it may, I'll advise Robert to look out for this huge new ship he's talking about, the *Great Eastern*. Maybe Robert could become an officer on board someday, or even captain. Imagine what that would do for his career. I'll send him a message…'

James was pleased that the Dublin to Wicklow railway line, which opened just a few months later, *did* bring enhanced business to the Wicklow Bridge House, but not quite in the numbers predicted by Brunel. The newly built Marine Hotel, closer to the railway's Murrough terminal, attracted many of the clients James had hoped for. But the railway also ensured that James and his hotel guests received the English newspapers from Dublin more promptly. Just three years later, the front page of one such paper attracted James's attention. It carried news of the launching on the River Thames of the world's largest and most technically advanced ship, the SS *Great Eastern,* designed by one Isambard Kingdom Brunel. At over 210 metres long, she was fitted out with the most luxurious appointments and could accommodate up to 4,000 passengers. He shared the news with Anne. Brunel's wasn't an idle boast. James excitedly sent a further message to his son Robert, reminding him of the advantages of becoming an officer on such a prestigious ship.

As time would tell, Robert was right to be cautious initially. The great ship failed as a passenger liner due to insufficient numbers of passengers. Two years later, James showed the latest newspaper to Anne: Brunel was dead, exhausted and penniless after his great ship was found to be uneconomical.

'That poor man,' she commented. 'But I told you something like that would happen to him.' The future of the great vessel was uncertain. For a few years, the monster fulfilled various minor roles. Then, about six years after her launch, news came that the huge vessel had been chartered by a business consortium and was converted to a telegraph cable-laying ship. Robert saw his opportunity. To James's and Anne's delight, their son was appointed Chief Officer on board the mighty ship on her first cable laying voyage across the Atlantic. While that endeavour ended in failure when the cable broke in the mid-Atlantic, the same team subsequently laid the first successful trans-Atlantic telegraph cable. Halpin then retrieved and repaired the original cable, and thus laid the second successful cable. For many decades those first durable cables, each 4,000 kilometres long, carried countless historical messages between Valentia Island, County Kerry, and the eastern coast of Newfoundland.

Shortly afterwards, James and Anne were proud to welcome their son on a visit to Wicklow when he presented them with a short section of the historic cable. For them, it was a wonderful memento. Robert went on to lay cables across other oceans and became one of the most important mariners of the nineteenth century. The Halpins followed their son's achievements with pride. In his old age, James sometimes asked himself if history might have taken a different course had Brunel not walked across that stone bridge from his newly completed railway line to drink in the Wicklow Bridge House and, while there, revealed his plans for his new ship, the *Great Eastern*. And then had he, James, not persuaded his son Robert to apply for an officer position on that great ship, how might events have unfolded? James proudly acknowledged that, while Brunel connected cities with railways and bridges, his son connected continents with telegraphic cables.

Ten years after his first and arguably his finest cable laying exploit in the Atlantic, Robert Halpin retired to Rathnew, a few miles from his birthplace in the Wicklow Bridge House in Wicklow town.

A shaft of Autumn sunlight peeped through the branches of the small birch tree in the corner of the courtyard and flickered on my Grandfather's face as he finished speaking and leaned back in his seat.

'I've heard you relate that story previously,' my mother said, 'but I wanted your grandson to hear it from your own lips.'

'Of course,' the old man added, smiling at me. 'And five years after that marvellous encounter with Anne Halpin, your Grandmother's father, Thomas Murphy, purchased the old Bridge House, which he renamed the 'Bridge Hotel', and that's when I became proprietor. As your mother knows, it has been our family home and business ever since.'

Later that evening, to my delight, my Grandfather showed me the remnant of the cable given by Robert Halpin to his parents. What a historic souvenir!

Some years later, after my Grandfather's passing, I accompanied my Uncle Joe as he presented that section of cable to the Wicklow Maritime Museum. By then, that submarine cable had been superseded by several more technically advanced cables and by the advent of international satellite communications.

More recently and perhaps more significantly, a portion of that same obsolete cable, which had lain on the seabed for well over one hundred years, was retrieved off the County Kerry coast by my cousin David. It had snagged the anchor of his small motorboat. Unlike Halpin's sample which, it is thought, was taken from the unused coil on board the *Great Eastern*, the piece given to me by David has undoubtedly served as the actual conduit for those first historical intercontinental messages across the Atlantic. This portion is about ten centimetres long, with a well-insulated copper core of seven interwoven strands.

There's a lot of history buried within the strands of that piece of cable. For me, it is a relic that imparts fond memories of my grandfather and the old Bridge Hotel, as I knew it as a child. But it is also a very personal souvenir of the indirect yet significant part our family's old home played in the history of international telecommunications.

* * * * *

Note: The final section of Brunel's railway line along the Murrough, ending a little distance from the stone bridge at Wicklow Town, was discarded in the 1950s and a new station was built near the upper end of the town.

My Mother's Cameras

My young grandson Rory was thumbing through one of my mother's old photo albums taken from a cardboard box of miscellaneous memorabilia that I had just brought down from the attic.

'Look at those tiny pictures, Grandad. Where did they come from?' The small photos he referred to were part of a large collection of black and white prints meticulously pasted onto the brown album pages by my mother many years previously. Their small size, just 2¼ x 2¼ inches, revealed their origin: they were taken with my mother's old box camera, one of the very basic 'Brownies' of the early 1900s. It was the first of a long running series of simple and inexpensive cameras. Regrettably that old box camera is long gone, presumably discarded in the face of advancing camera design. However, its irreplaceable legacy of tiny photos, or 'snapshots' as they were called, still remains.

I can vaguely remember that camera – a small black box with a tiny glass lens on one side and a knurled wheel near one corner, used to wind the roll of film onwards after each snapshot. A short black leather carrying strap on the top was just large enough for a few fingers to hold. I showed Rory a picture of a similar camera on the Internet. 'That's a camera?' he exclaimed. His mind was trying vainly to liken it to his father's complex looking digital camera with large telephoto lens or even to the tiny cameras incorporated into his older brothers' smart phones. Such associations were understandably difficult.

The old Brownie box camera had belonged to my mother long before she was married. She used it liberally. Light reflected from many scenes had penetrated that tiny lens to form images on the roll of light sensitive film stretched against the internal back plate of the small box. My mother's photos captured scenes from London, Bristol, Madrid, Lisbon, Rome and Milan, as well as various parts of Ireland, her homeland. Events feature in much of her collection – various Wicklow Regattas and Saint Patrick's Day parades and the Eucharistic Congress in Dublin in 1932. In the absence of a telephoto lens, some of the principal subjects in those scenes appear tiny in the photos. But they are still discernible.

Memorable family events from my mother's young days also adorn the album pages, each captured by a click of her camera. My mother's neat handwriting identifies the subject matter in most of the photos but there are some without any inscription, whose subjects will unfortunately never be identified. Many faces peer out of the snapshots, faces frozen in time, faces of long departed relatives, friends and others, many of whom sadly I will never know. These are the faces of people who once inhabited a fleeting moment, an unrepeatable fragment of existence in the infinitude of time. In addition, many of those photos depict other items of interest from days gone by. Each is a tiny window through which one can get a unique glimpse into the distant past, a little piece of family history unearthed. This was a past so remote from Rory's comprehension that he simply gazed in quiet wonderment as the photos attempted to bridge that elusive gap of several generations.

But Rory spotted another object of interest in that box from the attic – an object about the size of a narrow book, with soft black leatherette covering and a small carrying handle. This curiosity was obviously a strange sight for a modern seven-year-old, especially when I told Rory it was another camera. 'Another camera?' was his incredulous response. Yes, this was a Kodak Six20 Folding Brownie, a popular type of camera introduced in 1937. There was a sense of expectation as I carefully opened it for Rory. It was as if we were awakening an old family pet from its hibernation, as the black bellows slowly unfolded. The bellows had lost some of its flexibility as its many age-related holes were patched with orange coloured sticking plaster – a practical if rather inelegant solution to protecting the sensitive film from unwanted light. I showed Rory the tiny lens and activated the shutter release to let him hear that reassuring 'click', a sound I remember well from my childhood. My nostalgia was heightened by the faint once-familiar odour of old roll films that used to occupy the camera's dark interior.

This was my mother's more recent camera, a more portable successor to her original box. It produced photos of a slightly larger size, 2¼ x 3¼ inches, many of which are still displayed on the pages of her later albums. This folding Brownie eventually became our family camera. Its photos provide permanent reminders of some key events in my own young life – my baby photos, my first timid steps, my first tricycle, my First Communion, my Confirmation, my first bicycle. 'Is that really you, Grandad?' Rory exclaimed on seeing me sitting in my old-fashioned pram with its ornate body, curved handle and large spoked wheels. My own young face had joined those other lifeless faces peering out of the past.

Each photo evokes memories – sunny summer holidays with my parents, picnics up the Dublin Mountains, boating on the lakes up the Murrough in Wicklow, fishing from a rowing boat on Lough Arrow in Sligo, sea bathing in Portmarnock and Enniscrone, fun with cousins and friends and with family pets – the memories from each album page are almost endless. I pointed to a photo of myself sitting on a donkey with a wickerwork creel of turf strapped on either side, a snapshot taken somewhere in County Sligo in the 1940s. I explained to Rory:

'My Dad asked the donkey's owner to let me sit on the animal for the photo.'

'Lucky you,' he exclaimed, somewhat to my surprise. He had never seen a donkey carrying turf, never mind one also carrying his grandad. Rory also peered closely at images of his great grandparents whom he had never known.

On more than one occasion, I remember my father attaching a length of fine thread to the shutter release so that he could take a family photo, himself included – those were the days before shutter timers became commonplace on such simple cameras. Rory was incredulous at such primitive ingenuity. That Brownie's small meniscus lens had lovingly followed my childhood, step by step, year by year, like a friendly eye watching over me, recording the more memorable moments. As the years go by, I appreciate it having performed that task all the more.

I was given my own camera at the age of fifteen, a 35mm Ilford Sportsman. Colour had arrived for the first time in our family photo albums. The old folding Brownie was relegated to the attic where it now remains, a mere curiosity, its days of contributing to our family life, and indeed to our family history, having come to an end. But many of its valuable contributions, and especially those of its predecessor, the old Brownie box camera, still remain to give younger generations a small and very personal window into bygone days. Those were the days when family photography was still in its infancy and photos were not as common or numerous as they are today. As I explained to Rory, there was excitement and expectation while awaiting the developed film and its associated photos to be produced by the chemist's shop and then handed across the counter in that sand coloured Kodak paper wallet. That event was eagerly greeted by the inevitable question 'How did they come out?', as we jostled to see the results.

Those cameras must have brought such pleasure to my mother. At that time, they were *new*. Ironically, those same cameras and their photos bring me immeasurable pleasure because they are *old*. What precious memories my mother's old cameras have captured and preserved. And it is those memories, while somewhat dimmed with the mists of time, that still have the unique power to restore the colour, the sound and even the movement to those tiny grainy black and white images, to bring the past back to life.

Rory watched as I carefully folded the camera and returned it together with the photo albums to the box in the attic. Perhaps one day he'll show those small photos and that strange looking camera to his own children when he may, I think, expect the same incredulous reaction: 'A camera?' Meanwhile, those photos will rest in that box, just as the many memories they provoke, rest in a crevice of my mind.

My Father's Wireless

'Shhhhhh!' I could always detect the urgency in my father's demand for silence. He would lean towards his Pye radio set (or 'wireless' as it was called) in its polished wooden casing. With his large hands, he would carefully manipulate the knobs as he strove to obtain the clearest signal while watching the tiny illuminated dial near the top. My mother would sit and wait, her arm around me. As a three-to-four-year-old, I found it difficult to understand how those strange hissing and crackling noises could demand such undivided attention. But it wasn't those sounds that my parents were straining to hear, it was a voice, sometimes barely audible amid the noise. Had I been a little older, I might have noted some telling words such as bombing … aircraft … troops … Allies … Germans … casualties….

Standing about two-foot-high, the wireless held a commanding position on the sitting room side table. My father would put his ear close to the large speaker to hear those sounds better. While it was called a 'wireless', it did have wires. One wire stretched from the back of the apparatus to the top of the window from where it hung outside. This, my father explained, was to catch the radio waves which travelled all the way from London. A second wire, called the earth, wound its way to somewhere under the table. The reason the radio set was called a 'wireless', he explained when I was a little older, was because those sounds from far off London did not come through wires, like on a telephone. Those mysterious invisible talking waves could fly through the air. That wireless was a thing of wonder. And I marvelled that my father knew how to turn the knobs in order to capture those magical waves on his wireless.

The second world war was raging the year I was born. How my parents must have worried about the future of the child they had brought into the world. While Ireland was nominally neutral, a 500 lb German bomb had fallen on the North Strand area of Dublin within days of my birth, resulting in many casualties. This followed two earlier bombings on other areas of the city. Could more bombs be expected? What if the Allies lost the war? So much uncertainty, so much anxiety.

While my memories are extremely faint, I can recall sensing my parents' keen interest in those crackly BBC news bulletins delivered with emotionless English accents. Ireland's only official radio station, Radio Éireann (originally termed '2RN') broadcasting from the General Post Office in Dublin, did not provide detailed information on the war's progress due to questionable government censorship. Hence, my parents relied more on BBC news, broadcast at certain times each day. When my father uttered his customary 'Shhhhhh', it was for a very good reason.

Time passed, and I remember my parents telling me of the celebrations after the ceasefire was declared at one minute past midnight on Tuesday the eighth of May 1945 on what was known as 'Victory in Europe Day' or simply 'V.E. Day'. While hostilities continued in the Pacific region, the war in Europe was over. The need to listen with such anxiety to my father's Pye radio set had now abated. That wonderful wireless, which had served us so well during the war, became the bearer of happier news for many years during my young life before being discarded with the advent of newer radio receivers. But I would like to think that perhaps it still sits somewhere, a proud relic of the early days of the wireless.

[A shorter version of this story was published in The Irish Times, Friday, May 3, 2019.]

QWERTY

'What do the letters Q W E R T Y spell, Daddy?' As a five-year-old, I didn't understand why the keyboard of that complicated looking machine began with a word which didn't seem to make any sense. The only word I could recognise was 'AS' at the start of the second line of keys. Yet I marvelled at how my father could make his typewriter generate so many different words with those same keys.

I was studying my father's Remington, a heavy and formidable looking machine occupying a prominent place on his office desk. As Garda Duty Officer, his office was in our house, an official residence in Garda Headquarters based at that time in the Royal Hospital Kilmainham, in the western outskirts of Dublin City. His hours of duty were for the periods outside normal office hours. This occasionally allowed me to observe him at work, usually before I went to bed. Of course, I knew that I should not disturb his concentration. As I'd peep through the office door, he'd sometimes say "Come on in, Brendan Boy." That bit of encouragement was all I needed.

My father was a big man of heavy build, not unusual for those who were recruited for the police force in its infancy in the early 1920s. I can still see him in the night hours, sitting in that sparsely furnished office. It was a large room, with two windows. The grey painted walls displayed only a large calendar hung from a nail to the left of his desk. Facing the door was a fireplace with black fender and a metal turf box beside it. The room was lit by a solitary light bulb suspended from the ceiling by a twisted electric cable. I would peer over the top of his wooden desk. Close to the inkwell and blotter was his large black telephone with its brown wires curling like snakes to a little black box on the wall. There would be phone calls, sometimes lots of them, and the scribbling of notes with his purposefully pared pencils. I would sit on a stool near the metal wastepaper box, captivated by the importance of what I was witnessing.

Then, when he was ready, it would start. I would watch in expectation as he pulled the big black Remington towards him with an air of determination, clearing his throat as he did so, as if preparing for an important assignment. He would insert several sheets of typing paper, separated by flimsy sheets of black carbon paper to make copies, and wind them into place around the hard rubber roller of this complex mechanical wonder. Leaning forward over the keyboard with his thick rimmed spectacles and his large hands at the ready, he would assume the look of one asserting his authority over the machine. Then the thick middle finger of each hand would start pounding the keys, jumping from side to side, up and down, as he quickly selected each letter with stern concentration. Words emerged in rapid succession onto the paper and remained captured there. I would watch the type ribbon, impregnated with continuous strips of black and red inks, jerkily uncoiling from one spool and winding its way through the type carriage onto the other. It was a noisy performance, the hammering of the keystrokes enhanced by what was undoubtedly my father's excessive force on the keys. The persistent stream of sharp noisy clicks conveyed a sense of importance to the whole procedure. And it seemed that the more force my father used on those rows of keys, the more certitude was pounded into the finished document.

My father never learned to touch-type. Why should he? he would say; he was getting along just as well with his two fingers. And after many years of typing his Garda reports, he was quite adept at handling the machine. He would glance only occasionally at the wad of pages gradually moving upwards in tiny jerks from the roller. Once he got started, the only brief respites from the pounding were at those intervals when he would inspect his pencilled notes, while keeping his hands poised over the keys. Frequent sharp pings would indicate that he had reached the end of a line of type and he would snap over the carriage return lever to start a new line. He would hold down the SHIFT key at intervals to type an upper-case character. Any errors would be corrected with an ink erasing rubber and the correct character then carefully typed over the exact spot. I'd watch until he'd pull the completed wad of pages, together with the carbon papers, from the roller. This he would do with a satisfied swing of his arm, a gesture perhaps exaggerated somewhat for my benefit. That was the spectacular climax of an important accomplishment. To me, that Remington, under my father's expert control, was an amazing machine. There would be my bedtime hug before I left the room.

My father's Garda reports varied in length and complexity depending on the number and nature of the reportable incidents that occurred during his hours of duty. It was his Remington that typed the initial Garda reports on many occurrences that made headlines during the 1930s, '40s and '50s. One such occurrence was the IRA's daring raid on the Irish Army's Magazine Fort in the Phoenix Park on 23rd December 1939, when a large quantity of guns and ammunition was taken. A more horrific example was the dropping of four bombs by German aircraft on Dublin on 31st May 1941, when twenty-eight people were killed and many injured; that was at the height of the second World War and ten days after my birth. There were, of course, many other notable events that came initially through those snakelike telephone wires and that black telephone to my father's desk and were then diligently recorded by his typewriter. A lot of history passed through those well-pounded Remington keys.

When my father had nothing major to report, the Remington would have an easy time resting patiently on his desk. On such occasions, he would justify his relative inactivity by quoting the last line of John Milton's poem *'When I Consider'*: *"They also serve who only stand and waite."* If his faithful old Remington could speak, it might well have said the same.

As I grew a little older, I would gingerly try typing on the Remington myself, at times when my father was not on duty. While I could never achieve my father's typing speeds, my feeble attempts, usually with a single finger, gradually familiarised me with the location of the letters on the QWERTY keyboard, an experience from which I undoubtedly benefitted in later life. I feel I owe something to that old Remington. Indeed, as I sit at my modern computer keyboard, I am reminded that little has changed. The QWERTY layout and the SHIFT key, now in ubiquitous use, are the undying legacies of Remington machines dating from the 1870s. The keyboard was designed to separate frequently used keys in order to reduce the risk of adjacent type bars on the original Remington machines jamming when used in quick succession.

When my father retired from the Garda in 1965, he had to leave his old Remington behind. Undoubtedly that obsolete machine is now long discarded, probably consigned unceremoniously to some scrap heap, its days of loyal service under my father's two pounding fingers well over. I think he missed it. He bought himself a small portable Olivetti typewriter, a more silent and demure-looking machine, but one which didn't have the same imposing stature as his old Remington.

I don't recall my father ever trying to answer my childhood question about what QWERTY meant. But he didn't need to. I quickly came to realise that the typewriter keys were not laid out in a sequence in which the letters necessarily spelt words. Nevertheless, when I open my laptop and look at the keyboard, I sometimes like to think of QWERTY as a word, a special word that brings back fond memories of watching my father pounding away on his faithful old Remington.

The Wicklow Bus

I have faint recollections of threading carefully across the uneven planks of the original Parnell Footbridge in Wicklow Town in the very early 1940s. It was always a little adventure as I peered through the cracks between the timbers at the fast-flowing river below me. That was the wooden footbridge built in 1860. It provided a convenient means for those from the upper part of the town to cross the river to the Murrough, that large wetland area bordering the coast.

We usually travelled to Wicklow in my father's black Hillman Minx to visit my grandparents there. But I especially remember my first trip by bus. As we waited on Dublin's Eden Quay, I felt proud, as a five-year-old, knowing we had to board a green Córas Iompair Éireann (CIE) single decker, not a blue and yellow Great Northern Railway (GNR) bus bound for Belfast.

I watched the driver, a Wicklow man named Gus whom my mother knew, wind the fabric destination scroll using the exterior winder until it displayed 'Wicklow'. Seeing that name appear brought a tinge of excitement. Meanwhile, the conductor, climbing the ladder at the rear, loaded the passengers' bags, cases and bicycles onto the large luggage area on the roof displaying a billboard on either side. My mother and I sat in the front seat on the left-hand side from where I could see the road ahead. That was much better than looking through the side windows or at the backs of my parents' heads from the rear seat of the Hillman during that long drive.

With Gus at the wheel, the noisy engine in the front started, the inspector on the kerbside gave us a wave and we set off. Once we passed Donnybrook, we were in the countryside. As we rumbled along the winding roads, my mother named some of the quiet villages along the way –

Stillorgan, Cornelscourt, Cabinteely, Shankill. Then in her early forties, she was very familiar with the route as she had traversed it so often while travelling between her parents' Wicklow home and her own family home in Dublin. I was impressed at all she could tell me, sometimes including a little bit of local history. This was her way of making the long journey more interesting for me.

In Bray, some passengers alighted while a few others boarded. My mother and I got off briefly. In a grocery shop close to the bus stop, she bought me a special treat – a curved yellow fruit. It was the first time I had seen a banana. World War II, not long over, had restricted the importation of such niceties from far afield. Back on board the bus, my mother showed me how to peel it. As I was enjoying that tasty novelty, she happened to comment that, during times of particular hardship in the past, some people used banana skins to polish their shoes. I was intrigued by the dual function of this amazing fruit – it could satisfy one's taste buds and also beautify one's shoes. To test its shining ability, I started to rub the skin on my shoes, only to be stopped by my mother – she had already polished them with good quality *Nugget* polish for our visit to my grandad and granny, and she didn't want her efforts spoiled.

Having wound its way through the wooded Wicklow hills, the bus arrived at its destination. While most passengers got off in Main Street, Gus stopped the bus in Bridge Street to let my mother and me disembark close to my grandparents' home. We thanked Gus and his friendly conductor. I insisted on waiting to see the bus reversing into its shed on South Quay, a building now renovated and used as storage for one of the town's retail outlets. At my grandparents' house, my mother promptly discarded the banana skin. *What a waste of a good shoe polisher,* I thought.

The next day, my mother and I took the short walk by the river to the Parnell Footbridge. I was dismayed to see that the old wooden structure that I loved had been replaced by a modern concrete bridge. That reconstruction had taken place in 1946 under the supervision of my Uncle Joe, who was County Engineer. For me, however, Uncle Joe had taken away that little sense of adventure I had experienced on crossing the original fragile wooden bridge.

I always associate the Wicklow bus with that Parnell footbridge … and my first banana.

[A shortened version of this piece was published in The Irish Times, Friday, February 1, 2019.]

King Conkers

With my foot, I slowly sift through some withered leaves to find a few chestnuts, fallen from the branches of the old horse chestnut tree. Time slows down as I stand in my father's old secluded garden. I remember enjoying the same sensation as a young boy. Memories flood back as I pick up one of the nuts.

There was excitement in waiting for those little green treasures to free themselves from their spindly stalks and fall to the ground. I would try to hasten those events by throwing stones at the branches in the hope of dislodging some of the chestnuts. I was always impressed at nature providing such fleshy coverings, each with its soft interior, like little cradles for the fresh chestnuts born into the world. If those shells didn't split open by themselves, I would try to prise them open to reveal the precious nuts, shiny and brown, smooth to the touch, each with its whitish circular cap. I would gather as many chestnuts as I could, choosing the largest I could find, and carry them home. I had a mission – to prepare for the game of conkers with my classmates in the school yard.

Careful preparation was necessary, of course. With my mother's help, I would drive a hole through the centre of each nut using a skewer, then roast them in the oven for a short while to harden them – they had a tough job ahead. Then I would thread a piece of string, perhaps about eighteen inches long, through the hole in each nut. When the string emerged from the other side, I would tie a large knot, thereby securing it in place. The conkers were ready.

The half dozen or so conkers in my bulging pocket would lighten my step to school the next morning. I had something to look forward to – challenges in the school yard to determine whose conker could withstand being repeatedly struck by its rivals, which one was to claim the title 'King Conker.' We would take turns, swinging the conkers on their strings with determination and hitting the suspended rival conkers as hard as possible. The rules, strictly enforced, allowed for just three attempts. If my conker succeeded in breaking another, it became a '*one-er*'; if it smashed two rivals, it was a '*two-er*', and so on as it climbed the ladder of success. There was disappointment, of course, if my conker was the first to break in these duels. But I always had a few more in my pocket, similarly prepared, to initiate further challenges. My only problem was that school breaks were not long enough.

I regarded the horse chestnut tree as my friend, the provider of those special items of fun. *My* tree, I convinced myself, produced the best conkers, the ones destined to become those coveted 'King Conkers'. It mattered little that the tree itself hadn't intended its carefully grown nuts to be used in this pursuit; it hadn't occurred to me that, hidden within each of those nuts, was the potential beginnings of another giant chestnut tree – one of the miracles of nature. To me, the nuts were donated for my pleasure, gifts from those friendly leafy branches. Eventually, however, the day came when I started to attend a new school, a school for bigger boys. The days of conkers were over. And when we moved house, my tree was no longer part of my life.

Now, revisiting the garden, I marvel at how well the tree has withstood the passage of time. It is still producing its annual supply of shiny nuts. But now those nuts just lie there on the ground, unwanted by the children of today who are absorbed in far more sophisticated games than mine. Times have changed. The simple pleasures derived from duelling conkers seem to be largely forgotten, dissolved into the shadows of the past.

I fondle the chestnut in my hand, a large one already released from its spikey cradle. I run my fingers over its smooth surface and instinctively place it in my pocket. I don't know why. I suppose just having it is a reminder of the simple joys of my boyhood, of my old chestnut tree and, of course, of the many 'King Conkers' that tree provided for me to enjoy. I take a last look at my old arboreal friend with its roots deep in mother earth and its leafy branches stretching to the heavens, its hand-like clusters of leaflets waving placidly to the light Autumn breeze. I turn and leave, fingering the chestnut in my pocket.

I keep that little memento on my desk.

Mary Good Luck

'Where did Grandad get this boat, Auntie Kitty?' I asked. The water was lapping gently against the bow like tiny castanets of varying pitches as we raised our oars and let the boat drift for a few moments. I watched the drips from our long-bladed sea oars make tiny ever-expanding concentric circles, dissipating slowly into the lake's own tiny wavelets. As a seven-year-old, I looked forward to these small interludes. They provided a break from rowing, a chance to relax and absorb the stillness of the lake and the beauty of the wooded Wicklow shoreline. I leaned on my oar. Roy, my aunt's black and white collie, sat erect at the bow like a sentry, scanning the shore for any wildlife.

'Well, it's a strange story,' my aunt replied, as she partially turned towards me from the aft seat. 'Many, many years ago, a local lifeboat man named Ned was out sea-fishing when he found this boat adrift several miles off the coast. She was obviously very old and he felt she might have been a ship's lifeboat. There was no name on her. Perhaps her mother ship had sunk. There had been many storms in those years and several ships had foundered. Many shipwrecks lie off the Wicklow coast, you know. Anyway, Ned brought the old boat into the harbour. Nobody ever claimed her and eventually Ned asked your grandfather, who was a young man then, if he would take her. Grandfather re-painted her caringly and named her *Mary Good Luck* and our whole family have enjoyed her ever since. Isn't she a nice boat?'

I nodded. There was a great deal to take in. We sat in silence for a while. Eventually I asked:

'Auntie Kitty, why do you always say *she* for the boat and not *it*? The boat isn't a girl.'

'Well, that's true', she replied. 'Many people say *it* for

small boats like this, while a ship is usually referred to as *she* – that's been a tradition among sailors for a few centuries now. But I prefer to think of our lovely boat as a lady, as if she were our small ship. That's why I like to say *she*.'

A dog barked somewhere on the distant shore and Roy, with his front paws on the gunwale, growled softly in response. A flock of noisy birds circled around the far-off trees, asserting ownership of their arboreal territory. Auntie Kitty and I slipped into silence again, allowing nature to speak to us, telling us of the beauty of her stillness. The faint salty smell of the sea wafted in across the Murrough. It was not just our surroundings that were peaceful – the boat herself seemed to be part of that peace, a tranquil lady at one with nature. Temporarily free from the thrust of our oars, she was almost stationary on the placid water of Broad Lough. Clinker built, she was about six metres in length, with a hull painted light grey and a gunwale in faded green. She had three seats or thwarts for rowers. Reflecting on my aunt's words, I began to look on our small craft as a lady, a gentle lady of unknown origins but nevertheless a lady of some character. A small quantity of bilge water gurgled occasionally, hidden from view beneath the floorboards. I swayed slightly from side to side, the sounds becoming more continuous with the gentle rocking motion. I liked to imagine those gurgling noises were *Lady Good Luck* talking softly to me, her watery voice telling me stories perhaps about her mysterious past. Where did she come from? Did she have magical adventures in seas far away? Was she telling me sea-faring secrets, perhaps even tales about pirates and buried treasures?

My aunt interrupted my thoughts. 'Let's start rowing home before the tide changes.' I could see small eddies on the surface indicating that the direction of the current was altering near the outflow from the lake. I knew we had to get back before the ebb tide brought the water level too low to allow us to berth at our small jetty just beyond the stone bridge. This mixture of fresh and brackish water had been pushed by the incoming tide upriver, now it was the river's turn to push it back out to sea, like a giant slowly awakening from his slumbers and asserting his authority. I turned the boat slowly with my oar and we again started to row. As usual, being on the centre thwart, I synchronised my stroke with my aunt's. With the rhythmic creaking of our oars in the rowlocks and the soft swish of the water with each stroke, we exited the lake and headed down the short Leitrim River with the Murrough, that coastal wetland area, on our port side. Choosing a course in the centre of the river, I watched the many black-headed gulls on one bank and the occasional grey heron and cormorant in the shallows beside the reeds on the other. Roy, our ever-vigilant look-out, was eyeing a pair of elegant swans as they crossed nonchalantly, heads held proudly, some distance in front of our bow. After a few moments, we could hear the distant happy chatter of children at Jack Barlow's Cosy Corner ice cream parlour on the Murrough.

'Don't forget to feather your oar after each stroke,' Auntie Kitty advised, as a small breeze hit us. 'It makes the rowing easier.' We passed smoothly under Parnell Bridge, the small footbridge, and approached the large seven-arch stone bridge as its notoriously fast flowing current was gathering momentum. The water, having rested placidly in the lake up to a short time previously, was now once again coming to life, the awakening river giant showing us his strength, challenging our boating skills. 'Now, choose your arch,' Auntie Kitty instructed, 'point her straight, take two hard pulls with me, then ship your oar as we go through with the flow.'

A few minutes later, as Auntie Kitty secured the boat to the jetty, a further question occurred to me.

'Auntie Kitty, why did Grandad name her *Mary Good*

Luck?'

'Well, that's another interesting story,' Aunt Kitty replied as Roy jumped out and we removed our belongings from the boat. 'Let me tell you at teatime.'

Over tea that evening, my aunt provided the answer. She began by reminding me of a story my mother had told me previously, the mysterious tale of the *Mary Celeste.* That was a two-mast merchant sailing ship, which departed from New York in November 1872, bound for Genoa. The captain, his wife and young daughter and a seven-man crew were on board. Some weeks later, she was found abandoned and adrift in the Atlantic, far from anywhere, with sails still hoisted. The fate of the crew remained a mystery. A court of enquiry could find no reasonable explanation. Subsequent owners experienced incessant bad luck with the *Mary Celeste* and she was wrecked by her last owner on a reef off Haiti in order to make a false insurance claim, a sad end to the mysterious ship.

My aunt explained: 'So, when our rowing boat was discovered abandoned in the Irish Sea with no sign of life on board and no name, lifeboat man Ned called her *Mary Celeste II.* But the real *Mary Celeste* was thought to be a haunted ship, a ship which brought bad luck. So, because of that, your grandfather didn't like that name. Instead, he called the boat *Mary Good Luck,* and we've had nothing but good luck with her ever since.'

'I think that's a nice name,' I said.

That first trip in *Mary Good Luck* upriver to the lakes was followed by many others. In addition, we would sometimes take our lovely boat down-stream, through Wicklow Harbour, past the red and white lighthouse on the East Pier, and out to sea. She felt at home confidently riding the sea waves, just as she did in the calm waters of the lake. We learned to trust her – it was just her and us alone, gently rising and falling with the smooth waves in the great expanse of sea. I used to imagine that she was enjoying those little voyages as much as we were. We were all on an adventure together. We never wore life jackets; in those days, such life-saving apparel was considered appropriate only for lifeboat men going to sea in dangerous conditions. We would troll a line with a few feather-covered hooks as we rowed parallel to the Murrough shoreline with the Sugar Loaf as its backdrop, pushing its distinctive rounded peak into the distant sky. Roy and I would watch excitedly as the silvery wriggling mackerel were pulled aboard. We rarely came home without at least a few fresh fish for tea. As always, we had to time such sea voyages to ensure we were not caught out by the tides; rowing up-river against the strong current could be almost impossible and on a few occasions we had to moor *Mary Good Luck* in the harbour until the next favourable tide allowed us to bring her home. But that was all part of the adventure. *Mary Good Luck* seemed to know how to turn every trip into a memorable adventure.

Many years later, when I returned to Wicklow with my own children, *Mary Good Luck* was no longer there. I was told that the old boat had needed too much maintenance – her timbers were rotting and she was leaking badly. She had been given to one of the local fishermen. He had her tied in the river while waiting to start some repair work on her. Then one night there was a severe storm with a strongly flowing river and next morning she was gone – she had broken her moorings. Someone said they saw her disappearing out to sea. Sometime later, an oar was found washed up on the rocks near Arklow, but whether this was from our *Mary Good Luck* was never determined.

The story left me feeling a little nostalgic. What had happened to our lovely *Mary Good Luck*? Was she found adrift by someone and taken to another harbour? Did she drift on the currents over to the Welsh coast? Or did she eventually sink and re-join her mother ship, if indeed she ever had one, on the bed of the Irish Sea, beneath those same waves on which she had taken us on so many fun-filled fishing trips? One of my children suggested that perhaps our *Mary Good Luck* had felt that she had given all she could to our family and had departed, Mary Poppins-like, to give joy to another young family elsewhere. I rather liked that thought. Was that oar her final farewell gift to us, her way of saying goodbye? Having given such pleasure to three generations of our family, our *Mary Good Luck*, that lovely lady, had disappeared from our lives just as mysteriously as she had arrived.

The Sabre

'How much bigger can they make them?' Ray, one of the local fishermen, downed the last sip of his stout and placed the froth-lined glass on the wooden table. 'The *Oceanic* is now the largest ship in the world, they say.'

'Yes, and apparently she's been very well fitted out,' commented Bill. 'Now those who can afford it can sail cross the Atlantic in style during the 1900s.' Through the smoky atmosphere of the snug, there filtered conversations on many topics with both local and visiting mariners participating. There were stories of storms, of shipwrecks and the challenges of the sea. Stories of various unusual cargos and ports of commerce, of distant lands and customs. Stories of life on board the many ships, both sail and steam, that had arrived and lay tied up in Wicklow's small but busy trading harbour. Experiences were shared. Each night, as the frothy stout flowed, voices would become louder and more boisterous and the sawdust covered stone floor became the depository for the occasional spillages as well as discarded empty cigarette packages. That snug was the place for sailors to gather, to mingle with fellow sailors and with friendly locals, to partake in an atmosphere of conviviality while enjoying a good pint, the best in town, some would say. The snug, part of the Bridge Hotel bar, was closest to the harbour, a natural choice of venue for thirsty mariners who might arrive after many days at sea and were anxious to feel *terra firma* beneath their feet, yearning to relax with some of the local brew. The latest maritime news was always a topic of conversation.

'Should be an amazing liner, the *Oceanic*,' said another. 'She's even longer than the old *Great Eastern*, they say.'

'Yes, that's true, and I heard she's designed to do 21 knots. Just imagine: over 17,000 tonnes bearing down on you at 21 knots. You'd be wise to get out of her way fast.' There were some chuckles. The conversation continued to flow back and forth between sips, like waves on a confused sea.

'You're damn right! I'll tell you: not even pirates would dare stop *her* on the high seas.' There were nods of agreement.

'Well, anyway, I don't think you'd see many pirates around nowadays.'

'I hope you're right, but there was talk of pirates coming around here some years ago, up the Irish Sea.'

'Oh yes, there was talk of mermaids coming up the Irish Sea too. Don't believe those stories. Remember, the Barbary Pirates were defeated by the British and the Dutch back in 1816 and driven out of the Mediterranean. And the Sallee pirates too. All defeated, they were.'

'Yes, but where did those villains go? That's the question. They weren't all killed in 1816. I've heard it said that some of their ships escaped the British and Dutch attack. They didn't disappear into thin air, you know.'

'Those are all sea faring tales, sailors' imagination. All rubbish, if you ask me.'

'Well, let me tell you all something.' One of the locals, a brawny man named Jeff, spoke up from the corner as he slowly tipped the ashes from his cigarette. 'My grandfather told me that pirates raided this very place, the Bridge Hotel bar, one night sometime around 1830 or so, I think.' Everyone looked in his direction. 'Of course, William, that was long before your time here.' He directed his gaze towards the bar. William, who had become proprietor of the hotel just one year earlier, was serving the drinks as usual. He was a slim man of medium height in his early thirties, with light brown hair and a neatly trimmed moustache. A dapper man, he always wore his tweed waistcoat while at the bar. Jeff continued. 'I heard they made off with a substantial quantity of liquor from the bar – that's what they were really looking for. They also took whatever money was in the till and all the victuals from the larder.' The drinkers listened as Jeff went on to explain that the pirates had entered from the river, having failed to break into the more secure hotel entrances on the street.

'Well, I think that's rubbish,' said Ray, blowing more cigarette smoke into the air. 'They were probably just local robbers. If that raid *did* happen, how did your grandfather know they were real pirates?'

'They *were* real pirates!' said Jeff emphatically, and he went on to claim that his grandfather, who had been friendly with the previous hotel owners, told him that the hotel staff had been threatened by dark skinned men in strange clothes, speaking a strange language, each brandishing a sabre. 'That type of sabre,' Jeff claimed, 'was the hallmark of those North African pirates in the early 1800s.'

'How did they know they were sabres, not swords?' Ray asked. 'I'm sure there are still plenty of old swords around the country if you went to the trouble of looking for them.'

'There's a big difference,' Jeff asserted. 'Swords have straight blades; sabres, sometime called scimitars, have curved blades. You stab with a sword, you slash with a sabre. Those North African pirates always used sabres.' He demonstrated with several wild swings of his arm as if he were wielding a sabre, almost toppling his neighbour's glass off the table.

'Will you stop that talk? We didn't come here to hear all that gruesome stuff,' commented one of the elderly drinkers stooped contently over his glass. 'Anyway, I'm sure it's all rubbish.'

'Well, it may be gruesome, but it's true,' claimed Jeff, and he continued: 'Those men were carrying sabres. The hotel staff were sure of that. As they made their getaway, they were seen rowing down the river in the moonlight in two small skiffs. Their boats were then hauled aboard a small twin-masted schooner in the bay. That schooner was never seen again.' The bar went silent for a few moments as those present digested Jeff's dramatic story.

William had listened with more than casual interest. The hotel building was thought to be secure at the front but could possibly be broken into from the river at the rear. The hotel had its own jetty close to the stone bridge and this could be reached by small boats at high tide. From the jetty, the premises were accessible through an archway with a wooden door leading into the stable. There was nothing of value in the stable. A horse carriage, or trap as it was called, was the only major item stored there. It had been there when his family had acquired the hotel. It would be of little use to pirates who would have proceeded from the stable through the courtyard and then broken into the hotel building, probably through the windows in the scullery or kitchen. While Jeff's story sounded plausible, William was sceptical. Jeff was known to be quite a storyteller, but William began to suspect that his tales were not always blessed with the attribute of authenticity. Furthermore, the previous hotel owners had never mentioned the incident. But, of course, he suspected they would not have wanted to cause any concern about the vulnerability of the building prior to its sale to William's family.

As the premises was closing that night, Michael, one of the older customers, leaned across the bar to where William was tidying up.

'That story about the pirates, William – to be honest, I heard stories myself about pirates raiding this place from the river many years ago, so there could be some truth there. But, even if they were true, those pirates wouldn't have come all the way from North Africa. Jeff's story about them brandishing sabres – I wouldn't believe that, if I were you.

You have to get to know old Jeff – he means well, but you just can't believe every word that comes out of his mouth.'

Many years went by and William, now in his mid-forties, continued to serve in the bar himself. He always looked forward to participating in the local gossip and hearing interesting stories from the many foreign sailors who frequented the place. As time passed, his popularity with both locals and visiting mariners increased. The bar walls were festooned with postcards, most from distant lands, all praising his hospitality. Some were even stuck onto the *'Players Please'* and *'Sweet Afton'* advertisements. 'You'll have to start pinning them on the ceiling soon,' one of his regulars joked. He had also accrued a sizeable collection of foreign stamps and coins. William had become a member of the Wicklow Harbour Board and worked diligently for the improvement of the port facilities including moorings for the many visiting ships. Business was thriving.

One evening, an elderly dark-skinned man, over six-foot-tall, entered the busy bar. He was conspicuous because, despite the unusually warm October night air, he was wearing a bulky black overcoat and black knitted cap. His bearded weather-beaten face harboured dark brown eyes under heavy black brows. He stood at the door and slowly surveyed the scene, then he took his seat on a stool at the back of the snug, ordered a drink and took out a cigarette. He was a man of few words. Despite the many conversations taking place around him, including discussions on the newly launched RMS *Olympic*, another monster vessel, the dark-skinned man was mostly silent.

Closing time came and the many happy drinkers slowly swallowed their last few sips and gradually dispersed into the night, their loud talk still stoked with the stimulus of the alcohol. The dark-skinned man was hesitating. William called time again and the man, now the last one in the snug, stubbed his cigarette butt on an ashtray and slowly raised himself to his feet. He approached the bar.

'Is this the hotel with a stable at the back by the river?' he asked in an accent William couldn't identify.

'Yes, it is,' William replied, puzzled.

'And is there a cart for a horse in it?'

'Yes, indeed there is. Here we call it a trap. Tell me, sir, how did you know that?' The man hesitated for a moment and took another look around the bar.

'My grandfather told me,' he whispered. Through the neck of his bulky overcoat, he fumbled in an inside pocket and drew out a one-hundred-pound note, which he laid on the counter with an air of solemnity. William stared at it for a moment.

'Well, we don't see many of those around here. Do you have nothing smaller?' The man shook his head slowly while his dark eyes were focussed in a friendly gaze on William, who handed the note back. 'Keep it. Your drink tonight is on the house. Come visit me again sometime.' A faint smile crossed the man's dark face.

'Thank you, but if you could get the change, I'd really appreciate it,' he said, returning the note to the counter with a large callus-encrusted hand.

'Well, I don't have change for that here in the bar. But if you wait a moment, I'll see if I have change in the back room.' Something about the quiet stranger told William he could trust leaving him alone in the bar for a moment. When he returned, the man had gone, disappeared into the night. The one hundred pound note still lay on the counter. On top of it rested a long steely grey sabre.

* * * * *

Note. That sabre passed from William, my grandfather, to his son, my Uncle Joe, and on to me. However, there remains a slight doubt as to its actual origin.

The Candlestick

It was magic! The bird with outstretched wings moving gracefully, the squirrel with one eye blinking as his front paws waved at me, the fish with his tail swishing gently, a sailing ship with hoisted sails, slowly rocking on the waves. I watched, enthralled, as the shadows moved. My grandfather was displaying his skills at casting images on the bedroom wall with his carefully entwined hands held upright between the wall and the lighten candle.

I was spending a night in his house and he was giving me the same bedtime treat he used to give my mother many years previously. Dressed in his customary tweed jacket, his dapper appearance was enhanced by his neatly trimmed moustache. I had seen him create those images using a flashlight, but they seemed even more magical, perhaps more mysterious, when formed by candlelight.

The candle was always mounted in my grandfather's brass candlestick, his constant companion during the nights before electricity had brought its own style of magic to his home. Indeed, even after the advent of the electric light, my grandfather still preferred the natural gentleness of candlelight. It seemed to match his own genteel nature. The candlestick was less than half a foot tall and had a ring-like handle on one side of the circular base, allowing my grandfather to carry it around the house with ease. The solid base was padded on its underside with soft green felt. As a six-year-old, I was impressed at how heavy the small object was.

On that night at my grandfather's house, he allowed me to stay up late. When he asked me in his customary quiet tones, I counted nine chimes coming from the old grandfather clock in the hall. 'That means it's time for bed,' he said. I watched him carefully clean the old wax from his candlestick with his penknife and insert a tall new candle. Then he tore a strip from an old newspaper, folded it into a taper and, with a slim hand trembling slightly with age, inserted one end carefully into the smouldering embers of the turf-fuelled fire. A small flame appeared at the taper's end and he transferred this to the candle's exposed wick. It was a magical procedure. As he carefully carried the candlestick with its lighted candle up the stairs, the flame tilted backwards with each step. He seemed to enjoy the ritual. Perhaps for him, it was a way of reliving times past, almost as if he were emulating some Charles Dickens character. I followed his tall slim frame, watching the shadows of the banister uprights move in the opposite direction on the far wall, like soldiers marching silently in a row.

Entering the dark bedroom, he placed his candlestick on the bedside table. The tiny flame, reflecting off the candlestick's broad base, gave a magic feeling of warmth, a sense of homeliness. The burning candle exuded a soft faint odour. As my grandfather positioned his chair, I watched as little beads of melted beeswax slowly dripped in rivulets down the sides of the translucent candle, solidifying into lumpy ridges as they flowed further from the flame, sometimes even reaching the lip of the candlestick. The once smooth cylindrical candle slowly began to adopt a more gaunt and irregular shape. That small living flame flickered with even the slightest draught in the room. Watching it had an almost hypnotic effect. Once I was under the blanket, the show began. His fingers, slightly twisted by the onset of arthritis, worked their magic, aided by some purposefully folded pieces of paper. Even when he held his hands still, the images moved gracefully, slightly changing shape, like ripples on the sea, as the candle flame flickered. And the captivating images were accompanied by stories. There were stories about a magic puppy who flew up into the sky and landed in another land where he met a friendly dragon, stories about a pirate ship that sailed to an island far away where the crew buried their treasure, now waiting there for me to find it. It was that candle flame, he told me, that poured out the inspiration for his stories. It would also give me pleasant dreams, he assured me. And it probably did.

During the second World War, despite the fact that Ireland was officially neutral, it was considered advisable to switch off or obscure all lights which might act as navigational aids to German bombers. This was especially important on Ireland's east coast, a favoured route for the aircraft. Rather than screen all windows in the large building, my grandfather would switch off the lights. The family would listen together in silence to the heavy drone of German aircraft as they flew over their Wicklow home on their way to drop their dreaded loads on Belfast or Liverpool. My mother told me that the eerie shadows stalking every corner of the house seemed to symbolise the terrifying darkness of the war. Her father would light a candle in his special candlestick and would carry it around, that pinpoint of light bravely challenging the darkness. He would tell her that his tiny flame, in contrast to the deadly flames created by those bombers, was a symbol of hope, of trust in the future, and of peace to come. Even when the candle flame was extinguished, he maintained, those aspirations would still burn in her heart. And so, she claimed, they did.

Of course, there came a time when those magic shadows were no more. I don't know what eventually happened to that old candlestick. It had always stood by my grandfather's bedside and it was there, I was told, when he passed away. It was probably discarded as useless when the old house was sold years later. I thought of it and of his stories as I watched the flames of the six candles in their highly ornate candlesticks imparting an air of solemnity to his funeral Mass. There were no more pictured stories of flying puppies or pirate ships. My grandfather's flame of life, like that of his candles, had been quenched, but that flame of hope, trust and peace he engendered in his family still lives on.

Concrete Mike

'Hello. I'm your next-door neighbour and I want to tell you your boat is too wide for this berth.' I was taken aback. I stood and looked at the gentleman, who had quietly stepped off the boat moored next to ours and delivered that somewhat confrontational remark. He was a thin wiry individual, probably in his early seventies, with scant sandy hair and a prominent nose, dressed in well-worn red plaid t-shirt and shabby blue shorts. There was a look of determination on his thin weather-beaten face, a look of assertiveness, the expression in his sunken eyes telling me he didn't want to be challenged.

My wife and I had just reversed our brand-new motor cruiser into the berth we had purchased some time previously in the marina, a berth selected specifically with the dimensions of our boat in mind, a requirement of the *Capitainerie.*

'Sorry, but I think you're mistaken,' I said. But before I could continue, he snapped:

'I've checked the measurements of your boat.' I was incredulous. I started to prepare myself mentally for a major confrontation, but somehow it didn't seem appropriate to begin a relationship in such a way with the person whose strange looking boat was moored next to ours. I hesitated. Before I could decide how to voice my feelings, he stepped closer and his countenance changed dramatically. A wry smile appeared on his sallow face and his head tilted slightly:

'Well, I'll tell you – *my* boat is also too wide, so if *you* don't say anything, *I* won't say anything.'

Thus began a curious friendship with this unusual quayside neighbour. That was eight years ago. As I sit here on board my boat now, I can't help thinking of him. The Winter sun is starting its decent behind the marina apartments and I look across the water to see St. Tropez in the distance taking on its customary red glow. I close a few of the cabin windows and prepare for the coolness of the approaching night. January nights are always chilly here. I've completed all I came to do during the past week in order to keep the boat in good condition during the lengthy periods of non-use. I sit and relax for a while before bed. And I think.

His name was Mike. He was English, as was obvious from his rather upper-class English accent but, judging by his clothing, he appeared to be a man of little means. Slow to make friends, he rarely showed himself eager to initiate a conversation. He seldom accepted our invitations to join us on board our boat for a beer, but on the few occasions he did, he seemed unwilling to speak about himself. Once he said to us:

'You don't know anything about me,' with a smug smile, a remark that obviously whetted our curiosity. But he quickly changed the conversation as if he wanted to enjoy the little tease and keep his secrets to himself. And indeed, I was happy not to probe him further – whatever mysteries lay in his past were perhaps better left unexplored. A little bit of undisturbed mystery can do no harm.

Over the ensuing months, however, encouraged by the occasional offer of a beer, his veneer of aloofness softened somewhat and he gradually showed less reluctance to converse with us. Small pieces of his past filtered through. Many years previously, while in the United Kingdom, he had built a small sailing boat using ferro cement, a somewhat unusual marine building material, which is basically a form of concrete. He explained to me that it is a material composed of a sand and cement plaster applied over interwoven layers of metal mesh. Patented by a Frenchman in 1855, it was, Mike claimed, the most practical material for amateur boat builders.

Accompanied only by his cat, Mike sailed in this small boat from the south coast of England to the Mediterranean, a rather ambitious voyage for such a craft. Some years later, encouraged by his experiences, he returned to the UK and designed and built a much larger boat, once again using ferro cement. This heavy boat was about fifteen metres in length and resembled a barge with five tiny circular portholes along each side of the hull. An open cockpit at the stern was equipped with a large tiller and basic engine controls. Mike fitted his boat with two stout wooden masts with radio antennae strung between them, large canvas sails and a relatively small diesel engine. Apart from the engine, most equipment on board was constructed by Mike himself. He then motor-sailed his unusual craft to the south coast of France. He acquired a berth in the marina where we met him, and settled there, living permanently on board his boat. Somewhat surprisingly, he claimed he would never visit the UK again, but never gave a reason. His boat, with a blue and white hull and white deck, was conspicuous in that it was the only concrete boat in the large marina. Mike referred disparagingly to the other GRP-hulled boats, including ours, as 'plastic tubs'.

'Concrete Mike', as we secretly called him, almost rarely spoke to any of his other quayside neighbours, although he was somewhat friendly with an English couple who lived in another part of the marina. Little was known about him in the marina. But despite his aloofness, he was a man with an active curiosity. One day, having seen me talking with a fellow boater on the quayside, he made a point of waiting until my acquaintance had left before emerging through his forward hatch and, as he fiddled with something trivial on deck, asked:

'Is he French?' There were many nationalities on our quayside.

'No,' I replied, 'He's German.' After a pause, he

muttered:

'Don't like the Germans!' and disappeared below deck. Some days later, I noticed him peering from his hatch again as I spoke to another boating friend.

'Is he German?' he asked shortly afterwards, as he tidied a lose rope on his aft deck.

'No', I replied, 'he's French.'

'Don't like the French!' was his comment as he retreated beneath the cover of his deck. It was becoming apparent that he didn't have a great liking for people in general.

Unlike ourselves and most other pleasure boaters, Mike never took his strange craft out to sea for pleasure trips but lived a quiet life on board with his cat. While there, he rarely appeared above deck except to perform some maintenance work or to sit for a while on his aft deck in the Mediterranean sunshine. His old bicycle was always parked against the electricity box next to his boat. At ten o'clock each morning, he rode his bicycle to the supermarket for his day's meagre provisions, which he carried in a home-made wooden box fitted to the carrier. He was always back before midday. His punctuality was remarkable. And every Sunday morning at eight o'clock, he would wash his few well-worn clothes in a small basin by the quayside tap, all the while assiduously avoiding any conversation with other boaters. The ritual never changed.

Then, in May, several months after our arrival, we observed Mike bringing sizeable quantities of canned foods, including cat food, on board his boat. One morning, we saw the covers come off his sails and heard his engine start for the first time. He took his bicycle on board and called out to us that he was leaving for Corsica that evening. Detecting my surprise, he informed us that he spent all of his summers in a secluded anchorage far down the west coast of Corsica, 'to get away from people', as he put it. It was the time when the summer crowds were already invading the St. Tropez area. To reach his anchorage, he would motor-sail his concrete boat south at about six to eight knots, the trip taking him over thirty-six hours. He informed us of his summertime location just north of the Senetosa Lighthouse on Corsica's west coast and, somewhat to our surprise, invited us to visit him if we were in the area. For a man seeking total seclusion, we felt uniquely privileged to be issued with such an invitation.

In the evening sunlight, his unwieldy looking craft moved slowly out of its berth with Mike smiling somewhat smugly from the aft cockpit. As I threw his mooring lines aboard, he shouted:

'See you in September – or maybe before, if you care to visit me.' I quickly walked to the harbour wall and watched his heavy boat plod solidly away between the zigzag wakes of the many modern high-speed pleasure craft in the busy Golfe de St. Tropez. In the red glow of the setting sun, the boat eventually disappeared into the uncertainties beyond the horizon. I marvelled at Mike undertaking such a lengthy voyage on his own into the notoriously temperamental Mediterranean in a concrete craft which was many years old and, I felt, of questionable seaworthiness. It was an adventure into the relative unknown by a man himself virtually unknowable.

Later that summer, we undertook our first voyage to Tunisia on our motor cruiser, a memorable and exciting trip. On our way back, with Mike's coordinates programmed into on our GPS, we located his boat anchored in a remote cove surrounded by Corsica's deserted rocky hills. There were no other boats in the vicinity. He had told us that he left his heavy mooring chains permanently anchored there in readiness for his annual visits and dived to the bottom each year to retrieve them. His well secured boat resembled a spider in the centre of its web with lines stretching out in all directions. A marker boldly displaying the name of his boat, floating some metres from his bow, subtly implied exclusivity of the small anchorage. As we drew close, we were a little concerned when we saw no sign of life on board. We sounded our horn, then after a few moments a completely naked Mike climbed out of a deck hatch to greet us. During a meal on board our boat, for which he obligingly donned his well-worn shirt and torn shorts, he told us he never wore clothes while in his anchorage – it saved him the trouble of washing them. He was surprisingly chatty. Once a week, when weather permitted, he would travel northwards along the rocky coast in his two-metre wooden dinghy to purchase fresh provisions, the round trip taking him about two hours. Apart from that, he had no contact with people, preferring total solitude with his cat. Before we said goodbye, we offered him the contents of our 'fridge and he gladly helped himself to some fresh fruit and vegetables.

Some months later, the cement craft quietly arrived back into her moorings next to us in the St. Tropez marina. The summer crowds had largely gone and Mike prepared for the quieter winter months. He once again placed his old bicycle in its usual spot by the electricity connection box on the quayside. He would become angry if any visitors happened to leave their bikes in what he regarded as 'his place'. He was outwardly distrustful of people. One afternoon an obviously distressed Mike called out to us:

'They destroyed my bike!' He described how he had left his bike temporarily by the roadside to check on his electricity metre and the marina rubbish truck had reversed over it.

'They did it on purpose – they just want to get rid of me.' he claimed. We doubted the reason he gave for the incident but nevertheless felt sorry for him.

'I just threw the bike into the rubbish,' he said

defiantly. 'It's totally destroyed!' He had complained to the *Capitainerie* but, he claimed, they just laughed at him. We wondered what he would do without his beloved bicycle. However, the next day the enterprising Mike had second thoughts. He retrieved his damaged old bicycle from the rubbish bin and was able to bring it back to life. At every opportunity thereafter, he would repeat that he felt the port authorities wanted to get him out of the marina. His old concrete boat, in the midst of so many modern streamlined craft, was probably not in keeping with the character of the place.

Mike liked to paint his boat every second year. When his cat walked on his newly painted white deck and then, jumping on board our boat, deposited paint paw prints liberally on our canvas windshield cover, Mike just laughed. He didn't want to be involved with any problems. He was also surprisingly agile for a man of his age. By that time, he was probably in his mid-seventies, although somehow I felt it inappropriate to ask. Occasionally we would see his wiry frame climb to the top of his foremast to fix or adjust one of his antennae. With his torn shorts and no underwear, there was a lot visible during such climbs to any observer below. We bought him a new pair of shorts and, while he appeared grateful, he continued to wear the old pair. We also bought him a stain remover for his few much-stained clothes, but he returned it saying it might be too harsh on his hands. The stains remained, permanent souvenirs of many years of work on his boat.

The following summer during one of our cruises, we visited Concrete Mike once again in his anchorage in Corsica. He seemed pleased to see us, possibly because he knew we would not be intruding on his solitude for long. He told us he had been very upset when another boat dared to anchor near his in the inlet and remained for several days. He obviously felt he had exclusive right to the solitude that the place afforded. During a meal on board our boat, we ventured to ask him about his array of antennae on his two mastheads. He told us he used them for his amateur radio contacts. He had, for a while, communicated regularly by radio with a few friends in Britain. But he complained that he didn't use the equipment much now as most of his friends were dead. Instead, he spent his time watching old movies, for which he had a sizeable supply of video cassettes on board. Then, in a surprising moment of talkativeness, he chuckled as he told us that, some years previously, members of the *Gendarmerie Maritime*, seeing his elaborate antennae, had boarded him there, suspecting he might be involved in some covert spying operation by radio. It was the time of the Gulf War. When they saw how old his equipment was, however, they knew it could not have been used for any meaningful espionage.

Later, back in the marina, we invited him on board our boat for a meal to celebrate his birthday in October, before we departed for home in Dublin. He listed precisely what the meal should consist of – he was very particular about what he ate and how it should be prepared. At table, he chastised me for not knowing my body weight and for not even having a weighing scales on board. He had two scales on his boat and checked his weight on each every day, he told us, in order to monitor his health. The birthday meal became an annual event, as did his Christmas dinner with the English couple in the marina.

As the years passed, we became used to having Concrete Mike as our quiet and reliable neighbour who disappeared each year for some months in Corsica. He gradually became more friendly and was helpful in many small practical ways. When we were having difficulty in accessing local televisions stations, he took pleasure in telling us that our modern TracVision system, designed to lock onto Sky satellites while the boat was in motion, was ridiculously sophisticated. On the following day, displaying a coy smile, he presented us with a small aerial he had fabricated from a length of cable and two small pieces of wood. While the contraption did the job required, the need to stand on deck and hold it aloft while orientating it carefully made it impractical to use. But we were grateful for his effort.

On another occasion, he called out to me from his deck: 'Do you not have a bicycle?' It was during a brief December visit that I made to our boat when I didn't have the use of a car and he had observed me walking for groceries. On telling him that I had no bicycle, he retreated below deck and I was taken aback when he reappeared with an old bicycle which he presented to me with a proud smile. 'I never use this one,' he said, 'so you can keep it.' I thanked him. It was an old and very basic Russian-made machine with copious amounts of rust unashamedly displaying its age and its very poor state of repair. '*Pour la poubelle*?', one of the neighbours later asked in jest, suggesting the dump was the appropriate place for it. But it served me adequately for the occasional short ride. Once, when I left the decrepit looking bike on the quayside for a moment to fetch something from the boat, the observant Mike immediately chastised me for not locking it. 'It could have been stolen. Wouldn't it make a really beautiful Christmas present for someone?' I paid greater attention to the security of the old bike when parking it close to Mike.

To minimise the effort of setting up his large TV dish each time he returned from Corsica, Mike created a cone-like structure on the quayside to support the dish. And, not surprisingly, he made it from concrete, the material with which he was very adept. He seemed unconcerned that this solid and permanent structure, about half a metre high, might pose an obstruction to those walking on the quayside. However, it worked well for him and that was all that mattered.

Mike was always ready to offer advice if requested. He liked discussing things maritime, although he was usually critical of the contents of any boat-related books or articles that I might give him. He was unshakable in his opinions and had a wry sense of humour. We came to accept his habits and little eccentricities, too many to recall. Apart from the English couple, we appeared to be the only boaters he ever spoke to.

One September, on returning from his Corsican trip, he complained of toothache and also of great weakness in his legs. We attributed the latter to his not having walked or cycled for the months he had spent on his boat at anchor in Corsica. We thought it a little strange, however, that he had never complained of a similar problem after any of his previous Corsican trips. He didn't believe in consulting any doctors, he told us adamantly – they were far too expensive and they knew very little anyway. But after some persuasion, he agreed to see a dentist. When it rains in the South of France, it generally rains heavily. The following day was one of those days. I have memories of Concrete Mike departing on his old bicycle early that morning in a downpour, presumably to see the dentist. We became a little perturbed when the usually very punctual Mike did not return by mid-day. Our concern increased when one o'clock came, then two o'clock, with still no sign of Mike.

The subsequent traumatic events are somewhat of a blur in my mind. The Harbour Master's assistant came to our boat that afternoon to tell us Mike was in hospital and had asked us to feed his cat. Later, when we arrived at the hospital, we had to explain repeatedly that we were not his next of kin and that we did not know any relatives. Shortly thereafter, we were totally shocked when we were abruptly informed that he had passed away. We were taken to see him lying there and were handed his wallet and the watch directly off his limp wrist. There was nobody else to give them to. Later, still feeling the shock, I retrieved his old bicycle from where he had fallen off it on the roadside and returned it to the deck of his boat. Next day we had the eerie experience of entering his boat with an officer from the *Gendarmarie Nationale* to find his passport, which was required by the authorities. Finally, with the help of the English couple, arrangements were made for his cremation. There were few attendees. Each of us placed a red rose on his coffin.

It was a traumatic and very distressful sequence of events lasting several days immediately prior to our prearranged departure for Dublin. We were told he had died of a heart attack. I gave the English couple his watch and wallet. Mike's cat was adopted by a local family with children who would look after it. Later that winter, the English couple quietly sprinkled his ashes far from shore in the Mediterranean Sea, that vast body of water over which he had made his annual solitude-seeking voyages to Corsica. He probably would have wanted it that way.

During the subsequent months, the English couple were gradually able to unearth further information in the United Kingdom about Mike's mysterious past. He was born to a well-to-do family in Jersey in the Channel Islands and was flown each day by private plane to and from school on the British mainland. He had hoped to become a Royal Air Force pilot but was turned down as his eyesight was deemed to be inadequate. Instead, he trained as an RAF radio officer but abandoned that career, selecting instead the freedom of a life at sea. Strangely, he chose to have no further contact with his family. There was a girlfriend in his life. She, it was said, had given him an ultimatum – it was either her or his boat; as we all knew, he had chosen the latter. It was also discovered that he had a very sizeable sum of money in his bank account – despite appearances, he was by no means a pauper. And finally, it was established he was a titled gentleman – he was *Sir* Michael! I sometimes wonder if he would really have wanted us to know that, or would he have preferred to have his secret past remain forever a secret…

As I sit here now on board my boat with Winter darkness engulfing the marina, all of these reflections circle through my mind. At this time of year, there are few other boaters around. The quayside is still. The marina water laps gently on the hull and the breeze whistles softly through the rigging of the sailing boats close by. That solitude that Mike so craved surrounds me. This was his world. For him, solitude was his sanctuary, his escape from the realities of the world, with which he seemed never to engage fully. Yet, he strived to portray the impression that he had lived a full and worldly life and had done everything he wanted to. I continue to think of him. I think of his heavy anchor chains which will forever wait for him on the seabed in that small Corsican cove, a place which harboured the solitude he desired.

It is now two years since he departed this world. He told us he didn't believe in an afterlife. His concrete boat, a product of his versatile hands, is still moored next to mine. Our gunwales are almost touching – he was correct when he secretly admitted that his boat was too wide. His old bicycle with its homemade wooden box on the carrier, is still on the deck leaning against the mast where I left it many months ago. Its tyres must now be flat. No one has been on board since. Tomorrow his boat is to be towed away and broken up. I can't help taking a last look at his unusual craft through one of my cabin windows. One of his tiny portholes is directly opposite, less than a half a metre away. I can just make out the dark interior. His many video cassettes are lined up on the shelf. His old radio equipment is still there on his table, just as he left it, a maze of black boxes with knobs and dials, tangled wires, headphones and a microphone. Were it not for the small TV screen and computer, I could be looking into one of the Churchill War Rooms in London, constructed during the Second World War. In my imagination I can see him sitting there now, a man who had diligently extricated himself from his past, who chose to walk alone through life, a life now sadly at an end. The image is too real. I turn away.

Tomorrow, when his concrete boat and its contents are destroyed, the only tangible relic of Sir Michael will be his solid dish-supporting cone still standing there on the quayside like a little memorial, a small concrete reminder of Concrete Mike.

The Mangle

I entered the small back yard and there it was – the old mangle. It had been over sixty years since I had last seen it or even been in the old house. The present occupants had kindly shown me around, but the house interior had changed too much to bring back many of the childhood memories I had hoped to relive. The recent renovations presented a very different world to the one living in my memory. The mangle, however, lit a spark in my mind. It was still intact, standing in the corner of the yard, almost as if it were awaiting my visit, like a long-lost friend. I stood and gazed, being magically transported back through the mists of years into my distant childhood. It had occupied a prominent position in the scullery, that small room next to the kitchen where my mother had done the weekly wash. But sometime over the intervening years, with the installation of a modern washing machine incorporating a spin cycle, there was no longer any need for the mangle to wring excess water from the clothes before they were hung on the line to dry. So that marvellous machine had become redundant and had been relegated to a corner of the yard, where it now stands unused and, I thought, looking sad.

I doubt that my adult children, and certainly my grandchildren, have ever seen a mangle or clothes wringer, as it is sometimes called. That time saving machine was thought to have been invented around the middle of the nineteenth century when it first appeared in the United States as a small device attached to the top of washing machines. The first geared wringer mangle in the UK is thought to date from around 1850. Over time, the machine played an integral part in the weekly family washing routine in many households. Our upright version of the mangle probably dated from the early twentieth century.

As I stood there, memories came flooding back. On Mondays, my mother would collect the wet clothes in the large enamelled basin, all well-scrubbed on the wooden ribbed scrubbing board and rinsed several times in the scullery's stone sink. The unmistakable smell of the liberally applied *'Sunshine'* soap would still linger in the room as the grey suds-laden water swirled around and down the drain. Then it was time for the exciting part of the procedure.

"Mammy, can I turn the handle?" I would ask expectantly. It made me feel important to be participating in that critical weekly ritual. As a young boy, I was fascinated by the mangle's mechanism. The large crank handle operated the cogwheels, which rotated the wide wooden rollers. It was between those rollers that the wet clothes were wrung. For me, it was a mechanical marvel, a huge gaunt looking monster, but a friendly monster, steadily sucking our clothes in between its gigantic wooden lips, as if digesting our intimate family secrets. But turning that handle also gave me a sense of power – I was controlling this great invention, like the driver of a powerful threshing machine or a train driver operating his mighty steam locomotive. I was in command. It was an invigorating feeling.

Handkerchiefs were always the easiest to wring, moving between the rollers with little effort and depositing their rather small allotment of water into the bucket carefully positioned on the stone floor below. Underclothes and socks were also processed smoothly, but sometimes with a little more effort applied to the handle. Tablecloths, bed linen and other large items had to be folded to an appropriate size and carefully positioned to be drawn in by the machine. Woollen items were a little more difficult to wring because of their greater bulk. But the towels – they were the worst. Even after adjusting the large compression spring over the upper roller, my mother would sometimes have to help me turn the handle to get such thick items introduced between the rollers and adequately squeezed. I felt the hungry monster must have enjoyed digesting such succulent items.

While my mother would be feeding the machine and attending to the flattened clothes exiting from the other side of the rollers, I was more interested in observing the small stream of water falling into the bucket. The greater the volume of collected water, the greater was my sense of achievement. Somehow, I felt it was my job to keep that trickle flowing constantly, a tiny waterfall of success. And one could never have imagined how much water those bulkier items could have retained – the bucket might even be full before we were finished.

The mangle had served us well over the years. I'm sure my mother could never have imagined wash days without it. After its many years of loyal service, it now stands motionless there in the yard, discarded, exposed to the elements, its large cog wheels, coated with rust, no longer turning the rollers. Its solid yet ornate cast iron frame is now almost bare of paint. Did it still retain our family secrets within its solid wooden rollers? Was it perhaps waiting for me to turn the handle once again and bring it to life, to bring back the past? It has been left there, abandoned, because it serves no purpose now, I was told. But for me that day, it *did* serve a purpose, a very valuable purpose – it provided me with a wealth of treasured memories.

The Shell

'Grandad, I have something for you.' It was Róisín, just five years old, her bright brown eyes looking up at me with eager expectation of my reaction.

'Really?' I said. 'I can't wait to see it. I wonder what it is.'

Róisín had been walking on the beach with her mother and older sister and had rushed in through the door with something cupped between her hands. She waited for a moment, looking at me as the smile on her faced broadened. She had mastered a certain expertise of letting the excitement build up. When she sensed that the moment was right, she opened her hands while continuing to gaze at me, and there was my present – a small white seashell.

'Wow!' I exclaimed. 'That's really nice, Róisín.' She waited and watched while I fingered the delicate looking shell with its beautifully intricate network of rough fanlike ribs on its convex side and the smooth white surface on its concave surface.

'I found it on the beach and brought it back for you, Grandad.' By recounting the incident, she wanted to derive full benefit from the experience of giving me a present she had selected especially for me. I smiled and gave her a thank-you hug. Then she listened as I started to explain that the type of shell was probably, at one time, joined to another identical shell by a flexible hinge at the tip. A scallop called a bivalve would probably have lived between the two shells.

'And, Grandad, that scallop living there would have got little bits of food from the sea water it sucked in.' Róisín was proud to let me know that she knew it all already. I smiled and nodded approvingly.

Róisín's thoughtful action immediately brought back brief memories of my own childhood holidays on the beach.

Exploring the beach after the waters had receded evoked a sense of anticipation. There I would find flotsam and jetsam of all sorts, thrown up by the generous waves, it would seem, for the benefit of my young inquisitive mind. Of my various finds however, the seashells were the most fascinating. I was told that the shells still magically retained the sounds of the sea. Having listened carefully, my imagination was such that I almost convinced myself it was true.

Róisín's small gift was also a reminder of the excitement of finding a sufficient number of similar shells that I could use as decorative borders for imaginary roadways for my toy cars and trucks on the kitchen table – one of the simple joys of childhood. I could have used pebbles for the same purpose, of course, but somehow a collection of seashells seemed more unique, more exciting. They were small magical gifts created somewhere in the vast waters of the ocean.

Róisín ran off happily to play with her sister, her special little mission completed, her moment of joy now dissipated by the excitement of their games. But I allowed that brief moment of intimacy to linger in my mind as I looked again at the seashell in my hand, with a few grains of sand still adhering to its surface. It's just a common seashell, one of many different types formed by such an enormous variety of creatures living in the deep. Their once protective calcareous home to a scallop or similar marine mollusc was both ornate and functional, a tiny yet wondrous creation formed far from our eyes in the mysterious realm of the sea. Its small inhabitant was just a single representative of the great diversity and complexity of life in that watery world. I wondered if it is some part of our primordial instinct that draws us to the sea, thought to be the origin of all life, and hence to creations from its depths.

Róisín had given me more than a shell – she had provided me with a brief moment of contemplation, a nostalgic look into the past, a small reminder of my own childhood joys and, more importantly, of the unfathomable wonders of nature. There are probably many thousands of shells washed up each day on the sandy beach, perhaps millions. Yet *this* small shell means something special to me – it was presented to me by Róisín, a gesture touching in its simplicity, a gesture of love for her grandad. I keep it on my desk.

Where is Home?

Presenting her blue Trinidad passport to the immigration officer always gave her that sense of belonging. This was her country. This was where she was born. This was where she spent her formative years. As she exited into the Arrivals Hall at Piarco Airport, the sweet notes of a small steel band playing one of the latest calypsos greeted her ears, a nice gesture to welcome passengers arriving from overseas. The melodious tones instantly released memories, which had lain dormant for so long – memories of sitting on the back-gallery doorstep of her family's old home in nearby Port of Spain and being captivated by those magical sounds emanating from the local steel band. Despite the long and tiring flights required to get here from Dublin, Suzanne's energy was instantly revived, and she couldn't resist chipping along to the intoxicating rhythm as she pushed her luggage cart – it came naturally to her. It was Carnival Time in Trinidad. And she was here!

This annual display of unrestrained exuberance, soca and calypso, wild colourful costumes, bacchanal and general frivolity takes place on the Monday and Tuesday before Ash Wednesday. With eager anticipation, Suzanne found herself quickly immersed in the busy preparations for it, reliving memories of her young days in the happy land she called home before she emigrated to Ireland many years previously. The atmosphere, the heat, the relaxed Trinidadian way of life – it all meant so much to her. Now, amid the clamour of Trinidadian voices, with their vibrancy and musicality, she slipped effortlessly back into that environment, the unrivalled display of orchestrated turmoil, of uniquely organised chaos. She relished the local foods, the savoury rotis with polouri, the doubles, or bake and shark, with their tantalizing aromas exuding from the stalls at every street corner. Each odour re-awakened happy memories of her childhood. And she delighted in complementing these gastronomic experiences by sipping sorrel or cold coconut water from the nuts freshly chopped open by the vendors in their jitneys around the Savannah, that large grassy area in the heart of Port of Spain.

Within days of her arrival, she had carefully selected a frivolously outrageous and colourful costume for Carnival, as she had always done, designed around the theme chosen by her favourite band. Then came the dancing at the many nightly fêtes in the Caiso Tents and laughing with her friends at the parodying lyrics of the talented calypsonians. She enjoyed the excitement of cheering on the steel bands, some comprising up to one hundred pannists. She enthusiastically supported them initially in their 'panyards' and finally in the big and noisy Panorama competition on the Savannah stage, with its kaleidoscope of vivid colours. She waited expectantly for the judging of this year's calypsos at Dimanche Gras and the glamorous crowning of the Calypso King and Queen.

For Suzanne, the most exciting event however was joining her fellow revellers at three o'clock on Carnival Monday morning to 'chip' along with the steel bands on the cool streets of Port of Spain for that ever-so-wild J'Ouvert. That's when any old rags replaced normal clothing and any semblance of reality was buried in joyous exuberance. And then after sunrise and a quick shower, she chipped and jumped up tirelessly through the hot city with her favourite band or DJ until dusk on Monday, oblivious to her aching feet. With that tireless energy derived from the captivating beat of the calypso music, she couldn't wait to repeat that wild masquerading in the scorching sun all day on Carnival Tuesday, the climax of the event. That is Carnival in Trinidad, a recognition of the innate desire to temporarily forget the real world, to immerse oneself in an alternative reality, to shed inhibitions, to re-energise, to play. Throughout the years, Suzanne's annual participation in that unique event has helped to keep her young at heart.

To recover from the joyful excesses of Carnival, she spent time on Ash Wednesday and the following few days on the magnificent white coconut tree lined beaches of Maracus or Blanchisseuse and also on those on the small neighbouring island of Tobago, known as *Robin Crusoe's Island*. Of course, she spent time with relatives and some old school friends, not seen for what seemed such a long time. She had waited a whole year since the previous Carnival to relive all these unique and very personal experiences, but at last she was here in her homeland – she had come home. Yes, this felt like home, her home. Or was it perhaps just the excitement of the Carnival with its many highly emotional memories that gave her that feeling of being at home...?

Suzanne's memories of Trinidad, the land of the hummingbird, were those of a peaceful tropical paradise during the time when it was under British rule, part of the British Empire. She had grown up in idyllic surroundings – lush vegetation in which to roam carefree, with the unique song of the yellow-breasted kiskadees, the squawks of the multi-coloured parrots and the shrill chirps of the tiny green parakeets entertaining her from the blossom bearing branches above. There were exotic fruits like mango julie and pomme cité that she'd pick liberally from the trees in her back yard, and those broad sandy beaches caressed by warm enticing waves on which she'd body surf with her many cousins. She'd roller skate on the sparsely trafficked streets with the neighbouring children. In the latter part of each year, she'd walk to school through the Savannah on a carpet of pink and yellow poui tree blossoms, enjoying the fresh fragrances. The Savannah meant a lot to her. But above all, there was the hot all-enveloping sunshine day after day. The intense heat didn't bother her – she had grown up in it and had accepted it as the norm. And each Carnival Time, the captivating rhythms of the steel pan, that melodious instrument invented in Trinidad, would entice her to jump up Trinidadian style and happily 'chip' along with the bands on the streets. That was her childhood, a happy and carefree childhood. Trinidad was in her blood. She was proud to call herself a Trinidadian.

But now, as Carnival came to an end each year, the realities of life as it is on that now independent Caribbean island would begin to take hold. Of course, she knew this would happen – it happened to her at the end of every visit. Despite the number of white Trinidadians still living in that multi-ethnic society, it irritated her now to be mistaken for a foreigner. To anyone who asked her where she was from, she'd retort indignantly:

'I'm a local – this is my country.' sliding purposely into a more accentuated version of her natural Trinidad accent, which she had never lost. Trinidad had changed over the years. She had expected this. It was inevitable. She reminded herself that it happens in every country throughout the world, and Trinidad is certainly no exception. While the country still retained its abundant natural beauty, it was the small changes she found difficult to accept. Many of the exotic fruits she enjoyed as a child were now difficult to find. Some of her favourite poui trees, homes to the noisy parrots and parakeets, were gone, their sad stumps and twisted roots protruding at intervals from the coarse Savannah grass. Their faint sweet aroma was largely replaced by nauseating traffic fumes as myriads of cars raced around the 3.5-kilometre perimeter of what is said to be the world's largest roundabout. It upset her to see that the artistically designed and much-admired colonial houses, which had imparted a unique character to the streets bordering the Savannah, were being demolished one by one and replaced by modern rectangular office blocks. *Is destroying such unique parts of our heritage really necessary?* she'd ask herself. Approaching Carnival time, all such buildings were now boarded up for fear of intrusion by over exuberant revellers. And on a very personal level, she was saddened to see that the ornate church where her grandmother was both baptised and married had been demolished and the site now covered by a car park.

Even Carnival itself, the main purpose of her visit, was not the same. Many of the melodious steel bands, which for her had always been the focus of the event, had been replaced by speaker-blaring DJ trucks forcing her into the discomfort of earplugs. The calypsos, the primary music of Carnival, were not based on melodies as tuneful or on lyrics as imaginative as those of long ago. Now volume seemed to take precedent over quality. The many imaginatively artistic themes portrayed by the bands in the past have few cleverly designed equivalents. Carnival costumes in many cases were becoming distasteful in their scantiness. The wholesome atmosphere of Carnival past was disappearing. But Suzanne still made the most of it and had to admit to herself that she enjoyed it thoroughly.

More significantly, however, Suzanne knew she could not roam as freely as she used to, especially as the rapid tropical sunsets approached and the friendly daylight receded. The relatively high crime rate, notably in her native Port of Spain, was a perpetual worry. Now the need for continuous caution for fear of being robbed, or worse, would start to become more of a burden the longer she stayed. It distressed her to realise that many of the places where she had spent such a carefree childhood were now entered with apprehension or, in many cases, had become no-go areas. As the days went by, the invasive unease started to weigh heavily on her. Were her feelings accentuated by the dramatic contrast with such pleasant childhood memories? Even if so, she found the changes difficult to accept or relate to.

'This place isn't what it used to be,' she would say to herself repeatedly as the days went by and the joys of another Carnival subsided into blissful memories. 'I couldn't live here. This is not my Trinidad.'

On board her departing overnight trans-Atlantic flight, a mixture of emotions surged relentlessly within her. She gazed through the small window at the lights of Port of Spain, the city of her birth, slowly fading, like her memories, into the darkness. She tried to relax as she turned her eyes skywards to the almost pitch-black firmament. She stared at that infinite and mysterious repository of thoughts and dreams, lonely and unfeeling, speckled with myriads of aloof stars, icy bright dots in countless constellations. Her mind floated freely through that impartial cosmos like an unfettered spirit. She found herself yearning for a place that no longer existed, a place she had left many years ago, a place now living only in her memory. Perhaps more significantly, she realised that her lasting association with that nebulous place made it difficult for her to fully associate with any other place. An internal clamour of identities was flooding her mind. To where did she really belong? Where or what is home? Is it something within her, or is it nowhere? She drifted through that star filled universe, with its cold and vast inter-stellar spaces, as sleep slowly descended.

Some hours later, the light of a new day gradually awoke her. She thought once again of the country she had left behind some hours previously. It was so far away now. While it was no longer her home, somehow she still felt drawn to it. She had happy memories, not only of times long ago but also, she realised, of the Carnival just passed. Still a Trinidadian at heart, she felt compelled to return next year to experience the joys of another Carnival with her beloved steel bands and all the related excitement. After all, for her that was something very special. And the country itself, changed as it was, was still a place like no other, a place to be proud of – it was Trinidad.

Upon exiting from the Aer Lingus flight onto the misty tarmac at Dublin Airport, the cold March breeze enveloped her, causing her to wince sharply as it instantly stung her exposed sallow skin like a host of little needles.

'How can I feel at home here – this place is far too cold for me,' she thought, wrapping her woollen scarf more tightly around her neck. *'I just wasn't made for this.'* Then, as she walked from the Customs Area into the Arrivals Hall, three of her young grandchildren ran shouting to greet her with warm affectionate hugs.

'Hi Granny! WELCOME HOME!'

Our Televisions

I entered the room with a sense of expectation. It was 1950 and Uncle Joe had acquired his first television set. We had driven to his home in Wicklow to see this modern phenomenon. The set, in its polished wooden case, sat on a small table in the corner of his heavily furnished sitting room with its flowered wallpaper and thick curtains. He had a large aerial installed on his roof to capture those illusive signals from across the Irish Sea.

With an aura of ceremony, he switched on the set. As a nine-year-old, I was intrigued to see him patiently and masterfully tuning the device, converting that flickering snowy screen into shadowy moving images transmitted live from the BBC. I watched those grainy, black and white pictures with awe and I think Uncle Joe was proud to demonstrate that wonderful technology to me.

Uncle Joe would not have known then that he himself would play a small but significant part in a little piece of related history – the setting up of Ireland's first television transmitting mast. In 1959, as County Engineer for Wicklow, he collaborated with the Board of Works (now renamed the Office of Public Works) in building an access road through the boggy slopes to the summit of Kippure, situated on the far northern sector of the Wicklow Mountains. Due to its height of 757 meters and its positioning over Dublin city, this was the site chosen for the first transmitter for the newly established Irish television station. I remember Uncle Joe driving me up 'his road' to witness its construction.

Telefís Éireann broadcast its first live transmission at seven pm on New Year's Eve, 1961. My father, like so many others, bought his first television set and had the necessary roof-mounted aerial installed in order to receive that much-anticipated broadcast. By that time, TV screens had become a little larger and the wooden encasements had been largely replaced by plastic surrounds. I recall watching eagerly to see those historic black and white pictures on the original 405-line VHF system originating from the Montrose Studios in Donnybrook and transmitted via the mast on Kippure. I thought of Uncle Joe and 'his road' that evening. Kippure was the first of the original five Telefís Éireann transmitters to come into service.

Now, on my wide-screen TV, I see crystal clear colour pictures transmitted live from many parts of the world. I watch, once again intrigued, but this time my fascination is from seeing how my four-year-old granddaughter can so adeptly select her favourite channels using the remote control. How technology has advanced!

[A previous version of this story was published in The Irish Times, Friday, October 5, 2018.]

My Mother's Wish

'What can I be when I grow up, Mama?' It is a question most young children ask their parents at some stage of their lives. I suppose I was about five years old when I remember putting that question to my mother. I was disappointed at not getting a definite answer. I was told I was a little too young to make up my mind. I should just continue to work hard at school. Good advice at the time.

I began to think of the world around me. What could I do in that world? Could I invent or discover something? I felt that if I had lived in the 1400s, I would have owned a large ship and sailed westwards across the Atlantic Ocean and discovered the Americas before Christopher Columbus did. What a pity! If I had lived in the early 1800s, I would have invented the first steam locomotive to carry passengers on a railway line before Stephenson did. Indeed, I might even have patented the incandescent electric bulb before Thomas Edison did. What a shame! And if I had lived in the late 1800s, I'd have definitely produced the Model T motor car before Henry Ford got around to doing it. It seemed that all of these famous people had got there before me. Was there anything useful left for me to do, to invent or discover? Could I still become famous? I was again encouraged by my mother to work hard at school and then think about a job to earn a living. In time, perhaps, this might allow me to fulfil my dreams, whatever they might be at that time.

I needed to plan for a job. Soon I thought of a few possibilities, straightforward ones to start with. First and foremost was to become a tram driver. I envied those uniformed men commanding those large double decker monsters, filled with people, moving effortlessly along their tracks through the busy Dublin streets. With an air of authority, they would ring their bells to clear the streets in front of them. We had to get out of their way. That seemed like the job for me. Then to my disappointment, trams began to disappear from our streets when I was about seven years old. Such a shame! They were being replaced by double decker diesel buses. So, I turned my attention to becoming a bus driver. That provided the additional challenge of having to steer those big machines through the traffic. And I could drive even where there were no tram tracks or overhead wires. I would have liked that important job. 'Work hard,' my mother told me, 'and your dreams, whatever they are, will come true. The best satisfaction comes when you get what you want by your own hard work.' That was her constant wish for me.

Then sometime in the 1950s, a drive with my parents to Collinstown Aerodrome (later to become Dublin Airport) in north County Dublin changed my mind. My father parked his Hillman Minx near the perimeter from where I could view those impressive Dakota DC3s with their sleek silver bodies and noisy propeller engines. To see them trundle along the runway as they gathered speed and then magically lift themselves into the sky was so exciting. I watched as they disappeared into the clouds on their way to mysterious far off destinations. To pilot one of those amazing flying machines must surely be the ultimate experience. I definitely wanted to be a pilot. 'Work diligently', my mother told me, 'be positive, be yourself and you'll be happy when you succeed at whatever you want – that's my wish for you'.

However, my aptitude for building bridges and other mechanical constructions with my Meccano set put the idea of becoming an engineer into my mind. The challenges of using my imagination to construct such edifices in full scale eventually became foremost in my ambitions. You'll have to go to university for that, I was told. And so I did. But by that stage my liking for the rapidly advancing wonders of science took over. The structure of the mysterious atom had been deduced. X-rays had been discovered. Nuclear energy had been experimented with. Satellites were beginning to orbit the earth. The microchip and the laser had just been invented. Discoveries in all branches of the sciences were promising to turn the world into a better place for mankind. Surely that was where the future lay. And for me, it was the way forward. That's where I could achieve. And so I put my efforts into the fields of science. My dreams of tram driver, bus driver, pilot or even engineer had dissipated, as did my aspirations of becoming somebody famous. I recalled another piece of my mother's advice: don't do anything just for prestige or status, do it because you want to accomplish it for its own sake and it is within your ability to do it; do it because you gain the satisfaction of knowing it is the right thing to do, something that is good for both you and for others. And encourage others to do likewise.

Years went by and I never forgot the work ethic that my mother taught me. I needed to strive diligently to succeed and, by doing so, to acquire self-fulfilment. That is more important than fame. It is the realistic sense of achievement, within my limitations, that has propelled me over the years. She reminded me that the road to success and achievement may not always be the straightest or the easiest. If success becomes elusive, continued diligent effort would achieve it eventually. Nothing I gained was without effort. Life is what you make of it, and you must strive to make something of it. And, no matter what the outcome, you'll have the satisfaction of knowing that you tried your best. Those were the wise and pragmatic guidelines she herself lived by and her wish was that I would follow them.

Now in my retirement years, the nature of my activities and efforts has changed. And, in many respects, I also have changed. My personality is fluid and ever-growing. I am no longer the young boy for whom my mother's wishes were initially intended to apply, yet I am tethered to that boy by my very nature, by some invisible thread of sensibility created by time. Hence, I believe my mother's message continues to be relevant for me today. She undoubtedly meant it to apply to all of my life's tasks, irrespective of my age or responsibilities. I would like to think I have succeeded and continue to succeed in fulfilling my mother's wish, spurred by the work ethic she imparted to me. It gives me pleasure to share her inspirational thoughts with my children and grandchildren in the hope that those same thoughts will also help them acquire fulfilment in life.

I vaguely remembered my mother putting in writing her advice and her wish for my success in life. However, it was only recently that I discovered a short poem, scribbled with many amendments, in one of her old diaries. She had composed it some years before she passed away, her way of recording her wish for me in words that shine through the years with warm and inspirational wisdom. I treasure the poem and its simple and meaningful message, a final and valuable gift from my mother.

To My Son

I would not wish that you would stand and stare
Or shout to urge or hinder those who run,
But I would have you pant with muscles bare
And share with men the shadow or the sun.

I would not have your way 'neath sheltered trees
To follow blindly where the pathway led,
But I would have you face the storm or breeze
And clearly choose each step that you would tread.

I would not have you placed in Life's Great Race
Nor have you wear another's hard won crown;
But I would see you make a steady pace
To earn your seal of honour or renown.

by Eileen Nangle R.I.P.

The Royal Hospital Kilmainham

My foot caught in something partially hidden beneath the thick undergrowth. It was a small marble headstone, no more than a foot high. On scraping the years of undisturbed moss and grime away with my fingernails, I could barely decipher the inscription:

> *Hanlon, Christopher, 63*
> *Pte in 13th Hussars*
> *Died 15/02/1890*

I had been playing with two of my cousins in Bully's Acre, Dublin's oldest collection of graveyards. As a seven-year-old boy, I was unaware of the wealth of history hidden beneath that thick undergrowth and deep within the soil below. These graveyards are situated in the lands of the Royal Hospital, an iconic landmark in Kilmainham in the south west outskirts of Dublin City. This was an institution built in 1679 during the reign of Charles II as a home for old and infirm soldiers who had served in the British Army. It was inspired by the famous *Les Invalides* in Paris, inaugurated by Louis XIV.

The Royal Hospital lands harbour a very remarkable history, dating probably from the seventh century when it is thought that the Kilmainham Estate was first established as the site of Saint Maignend's monastery. During the following centuries, the area was occupied by the Knights Templar, the Knights Hospitaller and other military and religious groups. Buried in the part known as Bully's Acre are the remains of the citizenry of Dublin of all creeds and classes, united now in death – monks, princes, criminals, celebrities and soldiers. But for me, Bully's Acre was simply a place of childhood adventure, a place of some mystique, enhanced by my discovery of Private Hanlon's headstone.

Most of the headstones were not readily visible, being covered by uncontrolled vegetation. It was a place exuding a certain eeriness, the sunlight being obscured by a canopy of large oak trees. At dusk, the harsh croaks of the rooks in those dark branches seemed to be warning me to stay away. Were they speaking the language of the dead? And with the approach of darkness, the greenish-blue light of the gas fuelled lamps on the avenue outside would enhance the ghostly atmosphere of the entrance gates and stone walls. I would venture behind those large black gates only in daylight and when accompanied by my young cousins or school friends. I felt the need of having other living beings with me in this place of the dead. When leaving, I would always glance over my shoulder, wondering if one of the old soldiers' ghosts might be following me.

Private Christopher E. Hanlon, as I was to find out much later, received medals for bravery in the Crimean and Turkish wars and was discharged from the army, carrying significant battle wounds, in 1861 after twenty-four years of honourable service. As an inmate of the Royal Hospital, he received a pension of eleven pence per week. Now he lies in the Pensioners' Burial Ground at the northern end of Bully's Acre, where the remains of over three hundred ex-soldiers lie.

As a young boy, I entered the Royal Hospital graveyards only occasionally, preferring to play in other areas of the forty-eight-acre grounds. The impressive old building itself, rectangular in structure with an octagonal steeple-like clock tower on its north side and a large inner courtyard, was then the Headquarters of An Garda Síochána. My father was Garda Duty Officer and occupied an official residence in the estate, sandwiched between the Board of Works buildings and the original British Adjutant General's Quarters, now long vacated. That modest three-story dwelling was my home for the first nine years of my life. The upper story windows at the rear afforded an impressive view over the roof tops to the extensive Guinness brewery buildings in the James Street area of the city. The large hall of the Adjutant General's Quarters, accessible from our hallway, was an uninviting and dark area. Its domed skylights were blacked-out, a precaution taken during the Second World War, which was still raging in Europe during my early years.

The Royal Hospital was a busy place while the Garda day staff was present. Garda cars, large black Fords, would frequently swing past our house. But in the evenings and on weekends, I had the grounds virtually to myself. The hospital building was not accessible to me but I had little interest in its interior. I was unaware of the wealth of paintings, armour and other historical valuables displayed within its highly ornate Great Hall and Chapel, much of it having been transferred from the Tower of London in the early 1800s. The only significant item I could see from the outside was a large bronze statue of Queen Victoria peering coldly out through one of the ornate windows below the clock tower. Her gaze seemed to be fixed on the large beautifully maintained Master's Garden bordering the northern side of the estate. We knew it as *Rollens's Garden*, named after the head gardener.

But I was more interested in playing in my father's private garden. I would enter via a small green painted wooden gate in the north-eastern corner near what was known as the Guard Room (the original hospital Deputy Master's house). I was attracted by the swing my father had hung from a stout tree branch or perhaps by the inviting smell of tomato vines in his small greenhouse. It was his pleasure growing a variety of vegetables there for his family and seeing his meticulously planted flower beds add a touch of colour to the garden, whatever the season.

It was in the Royal Hospital grounds that I learned to

ride a bicycle. When I received my first bike, I would often cycle down the lengthy Western Avenue. This originated close to the Garda Commissioner's Office (originally the hospital Master's Quarters), with an Irish tricolour flying from a large pole on the lawn close by. On the way, I would pass on my left the allotments, or 'plots', as they were called, where Garda families would grow their vegetables. Cycling quickly past the forbidding gates of Bully's Acre, its large rooky oaks staring at me from behind the cemetery wall on my right, I would reach the impressive Richmond Gate, or the *Tower Gate*, which was our name for it. If the public bench facing Kilmainham Gaol on the roadside below were occupied, it was hard to resist letting a few small pebbles fall from the gate's small parapet onto the hats or preferably bare heads of the unsuspecting occupants, while quickly ducking back to avoid detection. The simple joys of boyhood!

We would normally enter the grounds via the rear and more frequently used entrance with its short driveway, opposite the two tall Garda radio masts on the lawns. This entrance, close to Kingsbridge (now Heuston) Railway Station, had a large austere looking suit of armour standing sentinel-like on each of the gate's two stone columns. I used to wonder if ghosts of the departed soldiers, perhaps including the spirit of Private Hanlon, might still be hiding within the dark coloured suits, staring at me through their slotted visors as I entered. They looked so human-like. Inside the gate, the small wooden Garda sentry box was always occupied. Yellow flowered shrubs lined the footpath on the right. To the left of the driveway, a small path lead to the blacksmith's forge, hot and smoky during weekdays when the clanging sounds of the hard-worked anvil would attract my attention. There I would watch, intrigued, as Harry Murphy, the Board of Works' blacksmith, bedecked in thick leather apron, shod one of the Board's horses or perhaps fixed or fabricated some other piece of ironwork.

Most exciting, however, were my visits to the Garda firing range on those days when Special Branch Gardaí were being trained in the use of firearms. This was on the west end of the large tarmac rectangle in front of our house. I would crouch behind the line of Gardaí, covering my ears and peeping to see how accurately the paper target on the end wall was hit with each deafening round. At the termination of the firing practice, I would collect the empty cartridge shells and use them to make toy armies of tiny brassy soldiers on the kitchen floor, warning my tolerant mother not to disturb their elaborate military formations.

But those childhood experiences abruptly came to an end in 1950. Dry rot was discovered in the hospital's old oak beams and the building was vacated by the Garda, which had used it as its Headquarters since 1930. This necessitated our relocation to the Garda Depôt on the other side of the River Liffey in the Phoenix Park. This was already serving as the Garda Administration Centre. There, my father was assigned a smaller house with no garden and the Phoenix Park became my new playground. The old Royal Hospital lay derelict for several years while extensive repairs and renovations were performed.

I revisited the Royal Hospital recently after an absence of almost seventy years, thus nostalgically reversing the passage of time. As I entered the estate, the façade of the large building with its green-topped chapel steeple had a very familiar and friendly countenance. It was a sight which had etched itself into my memory as a child and which now seemed to be welcoming me back. Now the home of the Irish Museum of Modern Art with a large conference centre, the old building has been given a new purpose. Of course, the place has changed substantially since my young days there in the 1940s. The suits of armour on the back-gate columns have been removed and the entrance doubled in width with a third stone column incorporated. While the yellow flowered shrubs are still there (though with fewer flowers), sadly my father's lovingly tended garden has disappeared under newly erected buildings. Harry Murphy's forge has also gone since the Board of Works, now the Office of Public Works, no longer depends on the power of horses. The Garda firing range and allotments have been subsumed into a large car park. And Queen Victoria has disappeared from her window seat, gazing out instead over the buildings of Sydney in far off Australia.

The gas lamps throughout the estate have been replaced by ornate electric lights. Bully's Acre incorporating the Privates' Burial Ground is still there, of course, hidden behind those same stark iron gates that used to discourage my entry but to where my curiosity drew me again during my recent visit. The thick undergrowth and much of the foliage has been assiduously removed by the OPW to reveal many more of the small headstones, their simple inscriptions now readily visible. The widening of busy Saint John's Road West required part of the high boundary wall to be moved and some of the graves to be relocated. The entire graveyard area, with its now tidy walkways, no longer exudes that eeriness I had associated with it in the 1940s, but it still retains an air of peaceful reverence. After some searching, I found what I was looking for – Private Hanlon's headstone. Something prompted me to say a silent prayer for that courageous soldier and for all his buried comrades.

Over the course of the years, the Royal Hospital has seen significant changes in its function, from army hospital and nursing home to police headquarters to museum and conference centre. But the soul of the majestic old building and its extensive grounds has remained unchanged, impervious to the passage of time. I left the graveyard of brave remains, feeling I had been reunited with Private

Hanlon. I quietly closed the black cemetery gates behind me. Was it a lingering childhood habit that made me glance over my shoulder as I exited?

The Oil

As we started to walk away towards the harbour, I heard her shouting something after us. It sounded like '*Vous aimerez l'huile*'.

'What was that about?' I asked Suzanne, puzzled.

'What do you mean?' She replied. 'She simply said "*Vous aimerez l'île*". Remember, I told her we were heading for Sardinia tomorrow and she was just telling us we'd love the island.'

'Oh, sorry - I thought she said we'd love the oil, *l'huile*.'

Suzanne laughed. 'Well, that would be stupid! Anyway, I suppose it could have sounded a little like that because of her Tunisian accent. To be honest, I was glad to get away – she just wanted money to tell us our fortunes and you know I don't believe in that sort of thing. Did you notice the sign over her little stall? It said: '*Diseuse de Bonne Aventure*'? That means 'Fortune Teller'.' I hadn't noticed.

While the predominant language was Arabic, our interaction with the people resulted invariably in responses in French spoken with that characteristic Tunisian accent. We moved through the Place Bouchacha, a vast market area with its many stalls, all tempting the visitor with everything imaginable, and all at prices surprisingly low compared to those we were accustomed to in the South of France. Our small supply of Tunisian Dinars seemed to last a long time. That final day we had spent strolling through the old part of Bizerte with its narrow streets and alleyways with their colourful displays of local crafts of all types. Exotic aromas assailed us from all quarters. The *adhan*, or call to prayer, sounding five times a day from the city's many minaret-mounted loudspeakers, reminded us that we were in a predominantly Muslim country. At times, we felt we were navigating a time warp where Bizerte's vibrant present and its past centuries of diverse civilizations were each vying for our attention. However, the smiles greeting us around every corner dispelled any feelings of being strangers.

As the darkness of the hot summer night approached, we arrived with our purchases at our motor cruiser *Bacchanal.* She was lying in her mooring in the *Port de Plaisence,* situated at the eastern outskirts of the city on the north coast of Tunisia. We had an early night. Just before sunrise the following morning, we made our final preparations for departure for the Italian island of Sardinia. In keeping with maritime etiquette, I changed the courtesy ensign on our radar arch from the red Tunisian flag with its white and red emblem to the Italian tricolour. Somehow, such small rituals always instilled a little sense of adventure. We cast off our lines and eased *Bacchanal* out of her berth past the broad entrance to Bizerte's canal and into the open sea. The air was fresh, the heat of the day not yet having taken its powerful grip. Heading northwards, we left an awakening Bizerte on our port side with its background of distant hills and the faint echoes of the first *adhan* of the day. We were retracing our route back to the South of France after an enjoyable two weeks in that fascinating North African country. Early morning usually provides the best weather for Mediterranean cruising. The marine forecast was good and a calm sea and light breeze promised a smooth crossing for our first leg of the voyage back to Europe. That was to the port of Villasimius on the south eastern tip of Sardinia. Having set our autopilot, we relaxed at the lower helm to enjoy the voyage.

Our GPS indicated a six-hour trip at our cruising speed of around 23 knots. After the first hour, the few fishing boats operating off the Tunisian coast, with their accompanying flocks of flapping sea birds, were left behind. The flat coastline of white buildings, now blushing red in the sunrise, was slowly disappearing beyond the horizon. Soon we had a cloudless blue sky as our canopy and no land in sight in any direction. We were in a sea of rippling sunlight with its millions of dazzling sparkles. Our long white frothy wake, stretching far into the distance behind us, was like our personal history, showing our path through the past. In front of us stretched vast waters, which, like our future, lay as yet undisturbed by our presence. These were the waters over which Phoenician and Roman galleys, propelled by oars, had traversed to explore and conquer lands around two thousand years ago. For the Romans, *Mare Nostrum,* as they called it, was the centre of the known world and served as their gateway to expanding their empire. In the Middle Ages, these waves were crossed by Arab trading vessels with their iconic lateen sails. This sea had also carried over one million European slaves to their fate in Northwest Africa at the hands of the infamous Barbary pirates during the fifteen and sixteen hundreds. And the last century saw conflict between modern battleships on these same waves. We wondered what wrecked remnants of those turbulent years might lie scattered some 1,500 meters below our small and insignificant craft. We were cruising over centuries of history that had changed the face of Europe.

Now in more tranquil times, *Bacchanal* was alone in the vastness of the ocean, a place now devoid of human activity. It was an experience we enjoyed and somehow I liked to feel that our boat was enjoying it too, her thirteen-meter planing hull riding gracefully over the gentle Mediterranean swells. There was a feeling of oneness with our trusty craft. Together we were forging through this endless expanse, filled with nature's extraordinary emptiness. Like a lone migrating bird, we were traversing that deserted space between continents.

We sat and talked about our experiences in Tunisia while enjoying some fresh dates from the Place Bouchacha market. We discussed the initial worrying encounter with two customs officers who coyly requested payment for clearing our boat for entry into the country. We reported this illegal practice to the *Capitainerie* and the two officers never approached us again. Apart from that incident, the friendliness of all those we met was impressive. One memorable example was that of the attendant at the marina fuel depôt. We chatted with him, a man of no more than thirty, while *Bacchanal* was being re-fuelled with diesel costing an amazing one third of that in France. We were taken aback when, on hearing that we had voyaged from mainland Europe on our first visit to Tunisia, the attendant offered to bring us some special Tunisian couscous made by his wife. We were highly impressed when, later that evening, he arrived at our boat with a substantial couscous meal and refused to take any payment. Indeed, the exceptionally enjoyable and inexpensive food in all parts of the city remained a lasting memory.

Another example of the eagerness of people to assist us was when I questioned the young girl in the *Capitainerie* about the darker colour of the marina's diesel compared to that in France. To my surprise, she had her uncle, who was a Quality Assurance Manager at the local refinery, phone me to detail his product control tests and thus satisfy me of the fuel's compatibility with *Bacchanal's* engines for our long trip home. We had a lot to reminisce about.

As the sun rose higher in the clear sky, we lapsed into contented silence, lulled by the hum of the twin turbo diesels and the gentle motion of the boat. Turning my attention from the placid sea, I noticed two blips appearing on our radar screen, a large one some five nautical miles off our starboard bow, a smaller one somewhat closer on our starboard quarter. We were no longer alone. Soon, both vessels were becoming visible to the eye. The large blip, which I identified as an oil tanker, was moving steadily on a course which would bring her across our route. The smaller blip, an unidentifiable motor craft, was moving somewhat erratically in our general direction. As the minutes passed, it became apparent that we were on a near collision course with the tanker. No more relaxation. While considering my options, Suzanne, using binoculars, drew my attention to a black dinghy being launched from the smaller craft. Much to our concern, it started to head directly towards us with three men in dark uniforms or overalls on board. If they were police or customs officers, surely they would have radioed us on the standard Channel 16 and identified themselves with a request to stop. Our VHF radio was silent on all channels. While piracy in that part of the Mediterranean was rare, it was not unknown. Instinctively, I opened full throttles on both engines, increasing speed up to our maximum of around 29 knots. *Bacchanal's* ride became unpleasantly rough as she lunged over each wave. The dinghy was a high-speed rigid inflatable approaching us at probably around 40 knots. I knew we could not outrun it. My pulse was racing as if matching *Bacchanal's* increased engine speeds.

By this time, we were within a few hundred meters of the tanker and on an imminent collision course. She was a vessel of probably about two hundred thousand tonnes deadweight. I judged that, with our increased speed, I could now pass in front of her bow, but only just. That was a manoeuvre I did not want to risk taking – any engine failure at the critical moment of passing under her gigantic bow could be disastrous. Prudence dictated that I alter course a few degrees to starboard and pass around her stern. By so doing, however, I had allowed the dinghy to gain a little more on us. Then, at the last moment, I noticed that the tanker was discharging oil. Its high freeboard indicated that its tanks were empty and it was purging the tanks with sea water, resulting in their oily residues being jettisoned. This procedure was contrary to The International Convention for the Prevention of Pollution from Ships (MARPOL). However, it is a method sometimes employed by unscrupulous tankers when far out to sea, where the risk of detection is minimal, as it saves the time and expense of cleaning their tanks when in port. I had traversed some small oily slicks before but this one, I realised, was different – it was apparently a type of bunker oil, a very crude and high viscosity liquid. Its large thick globules, each like part of a broken sea-turtle shell, were forming an almost constant and broad stream emanating from the stern of the tanker. My immediate concern was the possibility that the globules would block our sea water intake filters or choke the impellers, thus causing the engines to overheat and stall. The intake filters were located on the bottom of the hull but, at fast planing speeds, they would be close to the contaminated sea surface. Should I turn back? The dinghy was now closing in rapidly and almost within shouting distance. My head was pounding. So much was happening so quickly. I had to make a quick decision. I headed in through the thick oil. After a few agonising moments, *Bacchanal* reached uncontaminated water on the other side. The engines were still running at full speed, close to 2,700 rpm. Monitoring the temperature gauges indicated no sign of overheating. We had succeeded.

Looking back, we realised that the dinghy had turned away and had disappeared behind the tanker. Apparently, its crew had feared that their much smaller engine's sea water cooling system could not cope with the thick oil. We continued at full speed for some time, watching the sea to our stern. For our pursuers to alter course to overtake the tanker and pass through the uncontaminated water in front of her bow would by then have taken them a significant amount of time. To our great relief, they had turned back to re-join their mother ship, now a considerable distance away. We were no longer being followed and we found ourselves once again alone in the broad expanse of sea.

I eased the engines back to a more comfortable cruising speed and reset the autopilot. Soon, the island of Sardinia appeared on the horizon, our welcome destination. With our shattered nerves now calming, we gradually relaxed again and enjoyed a couple of cold drinks from the 'fridge. Even *Bacchanal* seemed to have regained her composure as she triumphantly approached the coast, as if pleased with her performance in the challenging encounter. We realised how fortunate we probably were. It was only then that I thought of *Madame Diseuse de Bonne Aventure*. Maybe I had heard her correctly after all…

The Quarry

My surroundings are peaceful. Rock climbers and dog walkers have departed for the evening. The sweet-throated birds have settled into their secluded nests. The sun, having dutifully traversed the heavens for the past several hours, is now dipping peacefully into her slumbers. Her disappearing face is assuming a spectacular orange-reddish glow, her way of bidding us a majestic goodnight. The few faint clouds in the once clear blue sky are magically stealing some of the sun's marvellous hue, as if eager to clutch onto the disappearing remnants of the daylight. I'm alone in this vastness of solitude.

I slowly turn my back to the sunset and gaze at the quarry face above me. It too has taken on that extraordinary hue, now deepening in intensity as the moments pass. And even the bright yellow of the gorse is being transposed into something unique. I am transfixed by the scene. I stand and contemplate on the great mystery of time and its significant relevance to the spectacle I am now witnessing:

Several million years since photons, those quanta of electromagnetic radiation destined to become sunlight, were created in the sun's hot core.

Hundreds of thousands of years, perhaps even millions, since that quarry of granite was formed from molten magma under the earth's crust.

About eight minutes since those sunlight photons departed from the sun's surface and, refracted by the earth's atmosphere, arrived here to bathe the granite in their magnificent colour.

And finally, one hundredth of a second – the time my smartphone takes to digitally record this breath-taking convergence of sunlight and granite – an insignificantly brief moment in the infinite and incomprehensible space time continuum...

Such astounding time contrasts represent stepping stones on that imponderable pathway between the ephemeral and the eternal, between the scale on which we humans live out our brief lives and the vast cosmic scale of the universe, part of that enigma termed infinity. I find it hard to keep in mind that this complex universe was formed from the multitude of interactions between simple primordial chemical elements. I marvel at the part that time plays in that universe and, significantly, in creating and maintaining the wonders of the natural world that we are blessed to inhabit. Nature's timekeeping, as evidenced by its reassuring clockwork-like predictability, dictates that the sun's radiant face will appear again in the east in just twelve hours' time. Daylight will return and, with it, the boisterous birds, the rock climbers and dog walkers.

But for now, I wait and gaze at the spectacular scene, slowly transitioning into twilight. Is this miracle really the consequence of random chance, funnelled over time through nature's laws? I stand and wonder…

[A shorter version was published in Dalkey Community Council Newsletter, June 2016, Dalkey, County Dublin.]

The Rare Ould Times

The strains of that well-loved song 'The Rare Ould Times' drifted towards me as I walked down Dublin's Kildare Street one summer's evening. The tune, mingled with the sounds of merriment, was issuing from a pub on a side street. As I walked on, the melody continued to wrap itself around my mind like some gentle ethereal record, conveying me into a Dublin of the past.

The words of that song by The Dubliners seem to resonate with me all the more as I grow older since and, in many ways, they mirror my own memories of my native city. I never lived in the city centre, but it was rarely more than a short distance away, and my childhood days were always enhanced by a visit to that magical metropolis.

And what magic it was for me, as a young boy, to witness the sights and sounds of city life in the 1940s and '50s, to enjoy those things named with nostalgia in the song – to walk under Clery's clock and climb to the top of Nelson's Pillar, where my mother would bring me to absorb the unique view, and feel the slow but definite pulse of a city in motion far below; together with my parents, to enjoy Jimmy O'Dea and Maureen Potter, and Tommy Dando on the organ, performing in the old Theatre Royal on Hawkins Street; to see the crowds lining up outside the Metropole, or the *Met*, as that large and exclusive cinema next to the General Post Office was popularly known. All the memories recounted in the song have meaning for me.

As I walked, Ronnie Drew's voice continued to float around in my head. I found myself seeing the old Dublin in my mind – the noisy cars weaving their way between the trams, the horse drawn carts and the many cyclists and pedestrians on the grimy cobblestoned streets with large metal water troughs here and there for the thirsty horses; the

Guinness barges on the River Liffey with their cargoes of wooden barrels, plying between the company's wharf at Victoria Quay by Kingsbridge and their ships on Custom House Quay, while lowering their funnels as they passed under each bridge along the way; the puffing and whistling of the occasional CIE steam train rattling across Butt Bridge by the Custom's House. Further down river, where the larger vessels were tied up, I could always detect that distinct odour from the huge grey gasometer, which dominated the city's eastern skyline. The car horns, tram bells, the cries of the newspaper boys, the smell of exhaust fumes and horse dung – for me, all of these gave the city its unique living character.

A little further from the city centre, I would stand on the banks of the Grand Canal at Portobello and watch the horse drawn barges arriving from the Midlands laden with turf for the fires of Dublin's households. I marvelled at the helmsman's ability to keep the barge in the centre of the waterway, despite the horse at the end of a long rope pulling from one of the banks. I also recall my fascination at seeing the air raid shelter in James's Street, one of the final remnants of World War II, being demolished by a large lead ball swinging from a crane.

But it was the trams, those double decker monsters, that seemed to dominate the city centre streets, trundling along on their tracks under their cobweb-like cables. I have faint recollections of climbing the curved stairs with my mother to the upper deck of one of those trams waiting at Nelson's Pillar. It had a large number '8' high up on the front. I was a little disappointed that the deck was enclosed – I would have preferred being on one of those open top trams. It was an exciting trip southward out of the city and along the coast to the end of the line – a quiet village named Dalkey. The two castles are the only things I can remember about the village, the tram itself being of greater interest to me, as an eight-year-old boy. I recall asking my mother how they were going to turn the tram around in the yard for its return trip to the busy city. 'They don't turn it', she told me. 'Just watch!' There was a clatter as the conductor rotated the backs of all the slatted wooden seats to accommodate passengers facing in the opposite direction. And the driver, with a cord hanging from the long spindle of the trolley, unhooked it from the overhead electric cable and swung it around to be pulled along the wire in the opposite direction. I was intrigued. That's when I made up my mind – I wanted to be a tram driver.

But I have more recent memories also, memories from the 1960s, memories of Dublin with my then girlfriend, now my wife of over fifty years – enjoying tea, fairy cakes and chatter in the Paradiso on Westmoreland Street and in the original Bewley's on Grafton Street; viewing the CinemaScope blockbusters in the Ambassador Cinema on Parnell Square; and, best of all, dancing to Dicky Rock and the Miami Showband at the Science Hops in the Crystal Ballroom on South Anne Street. (I think that's how I won her heart.) All these venues have long since gone, drowned in the vast ocean of time. I also recall bringing her up the 168 steps of the interior spiral stairway to the top of Nelson's Pillar, her first visit there, just as my mother had brought me almost twenty years previously, and looking down on the rooftops and busy streets of a somewhat more modern city with a slightly faster pulse.

Just four months after our ascent of the Pillar, Lord Horatio Nelson was unceremoniously toppled from his proud perch, from which he had looked down on a slowly changing Dublin for the previous 157 years, when the pillar was blown up by the IRA in 1966. That unique view from the top is gone forever. And in 1949, also about four months after my first and only tram ride to Dalkey, that line was closed down and, sadly, the old Number 8 tram was scrapped, to be replaced, as all the trams of the 1900s were, by those polluting diesel busses. Is it because such things are gone forever that they become precious to our minds?

It is said that time flies but memories last forever. While we cannot retrieve the past, perhaps in one sense, we are reversing time by bringing back electrically driven transport in the city in the form of the DART and more recently the Luas, winding its way through streets broad and narrow. But I have my own way of reversing that fast-flowing torrent of time – by reliving my memories. Whenever I hear the strains of that song by The Dubliners, a tiny cloud of nostalgia descends. While I never did become a tram driver, that ambition eventually died – like the trams themselves and much besides that have now evaporated into memories.

Yes, I remember Dublin in 'The Rare Ould Times'.

He is Here

As the chimes of the old grandfather clock struck four, I stood with Roy, her black cocker spaniel, in the hotel hallway, as we often did, waiting for Aunt Kitty to arrive home from Loughlinstown Hospital in County Dublin. She worked there as a physiotherapist. That drive on those winding roads to Wicklow Town normally took almost an hour in her old black 'Baby Ford'. Roy was usually the first to greet her with his welcoming leaps. As a seven your old, I would look forward to my little hug. But that day was different. As she stepped through the doorway, Aunt Kitty's face turned pale. She stared unseeingly over my head into the distance. Neither Roy nor I got our customary greeting. My mother was coming down the stairs carrying a tray. She was helping out temporarily in the family hotel business.

'Father is out there,' Aunt Kitty exclaimed. 'I just realised what I saw.' My mother stopped on the bottom step and stared at her sister.

'What do you mean, Kitty?' she asked.

'Father is out there on the bridge – he just waved to me,' Aunt Kitty said in a trembling voice. She turned and hastily stepped back outside followed by my mother. Roy and I also followed, not knowing what to expect. Aunt Kitty was pointing to a spot by the low stone wall on the right-hand side of the bridge just about twenty yards away.

'He waved to me with his walking stick as I got out of the car, just the way he always did when I'd arrive home.' We stood and looked. Of course, there was nobody there. My Grandfather had passed away just a year earlier.

The two sisters were silent for a moment as they continued to stare at the spot.

'Sit down and have a cup of tea, Kitty,' my mother urged gently as she linked her sister and brought her back inside. They sat and talked quietly together in the drawing room. I stayed by the door.

'Perhaps that's Father's way of telling us he's happy where he is,' my mother suggested pensively. Aunt Kitty nodded.

'Sadly, Father isn't here, Kitty.' I could hear my mother say in a voice hoarse with emotion. 'Perhaps he was just saying goodbye.' Their father had passed away suddenly during a weekend visit to Dundrum and the sisters were not afforded the opportunity to say their final farewells. There were some tears as they briefly embraced.

But now, over sixty years later, I wonder if perhaps my Grandfather *is* here. Of course, he's not here in person, but I feel he's here in spirit. As I sit now in the corner of the little snug he used to occupy in the bar attached to the Bridge Tavern, I can sense his presence. When not serving at the bar, this was where Grandfather, as hotel proprietor, chatted with his guests, both locals and mariners from faraway places. Many of his visitors arrived on merchant ships under sail – Wicklow was a vibrant trading port in the early 1900s and The Bridge Tavern, a prominent three-storey building, was situated close to the harbour. And in August each year, Grandfather would also be host to the many jubilant yachtsmen taking part in the annual sailing regatta, one of the oldest regattas in the country. He relished those social occasions.

I look around the snug. Of course, it has changed considerably since Grandfather's time. Interior walls have been broken down making the place look much larger and brighter. Newly installed tiled floors have replaced the old uneven stone floor on which Grandfather would liberally sprinkle sawdust to soak up the inevitable puddles of spilled Guinness and the occasional deposits of saliva, contributed casually by his happy guests. Yes, this was a pub for the ordinary people, the loyal townsfolk and the sailors of that time. I can still recall the mixed odours of tobacco and stout together with the sounds of laughter emanating from that smoky snug. The large *'Players Please'* and *'Sweet Afton'* signs have long since gone, together with the mosaic of picture postcards pinned neatly to the walls, each one portraying appreciation for the hospitality bestowed by my grandfather to a sailor from some distant land. Yes, inevitably much has changed visually, all in the name of 'modernisation'. But I still find myself trying to detect some aspect of the interior that is familiar to me, something that my memory can latch onto. My gaze is drawn to a small framed document mounted on the wall in a corner. It is a memorandum dated 18th June 1907 from John Power & Son Limited, Distillers, confirming the delivery of one quarter cask of whiskey to Thomas Murphy, my great grandfather, who purchased the hotel in 1903 for his daughter and his son-in-law, my grandfather. That seemingly insignificant document now gives the old building a tangible and welcome link with my past, a visual connection with my family.

The 300-year-old Bridge Tavern has witnessed a lot over time. I recall being intrigued by my Grandfather's stories of the past, related in his own engaging style. There were stories of pirates and smugglers who, during the 1700s, were said to enter the courtyard, unseen, via the old wooden gate leading from the hotel's small stone wharf on the adjoining river. I was intrigued when he showed me the rusting iron ring embedded in the wharf to which, he assured me, they used to tie their boats. True or not, they were intriguing stories for my young ears. He also told me stories of the Halpin Family, owners of the hotel during the 1800s, and their famous son, Robert, who was born here in 1836. I'm sitting now in that same snug in which Robert, as a boy, listened to tales of far off lands and adventures on the oceans narrated by visiting sailors, just as Grandfather did years later – stories that obviously whetted the young Robert's appetite for a life at sea. His was a life which became famous due primarily to his laying the first functional trans-Atlantic telegraph cable as captain of that magnificent ship, *The Great Eastern*. What fascinating stories! And what fascinating history was witnessed by the old building.

But the hotel has also witnessed the story of Grandfather himself, who ran a thriving business here for almost half a century, a period far longer than the first eleven years of Captain Robert Halpin's life that were spent here. Born in Tullow, County Carlow, in 1865, my Grandfather emigrated to Bristol at the age of fourteen. He worked there for the next nineteen years learning the hospitality trade and, while in the UK, became an active member of the Irish National League. Through this, he was involved with several British politicians in his attempts to further the cause of Irish independence. During these interactions he developed a lasting friendship with Prime Minister Gladstone. Then, in the early 1900s, he returned to Ireland and became proprietor of the Bridge Hotel. While he occasionally spoke with sadness of his brothers, twins Ben and Michael, who were killed while serving in the British Army in the First World War, my Grandfather habitually exuded an air of quiet joviality. He probably felt that life was too unpredictable not be enjoyed to the fullest. I always recall him having a smile on his face and a mischievous twinkle in his eye. He loved entertaining his hotel guests with his almost endless repertoire of jokes.

My Grandfather may not have been as famous as Captain Halpin – his career wasn't played out on the world stage, as was Robert's – but in the much smaller setting of Wicklow Town, his life was perhaps just as accomplished in its own modest way. He was Chairman of the Town Council for a period and was an active member of the Harbour

Board and Regatta Committee. He took an exceptionally active role in the political and social life of the town. He was the man who, good humouredly, defied the Sunday drinking ban by ringing a large bell outside the hotel door on Sunday mornings to remind the thirsty locals that drinks would be served as usual; his popularity was such that the local Gardaí chose, wisely I think, to ignore his actions. But above all, William Martin Byrne was a dedicated family man, loved and admired by his six children and his many grandchildren. Yes, every stone in the old building has witnessed, even absorbed, his very being over such a long period; so long a period, in fact, that I can still sense his presence here.

I walk outside and look again at the old stone bridge. Of course, he is not there. I hadn't expected to see him. I turn my gaze for the last time at the old hotel. Its façade has changed little over the years. Apart from newly applied decor, it's the way I remember it and probably the way my grandfather would have remembered it. There is a plaque there now, a reminder that this was Captain Halpin's birthplace. As the first stop in the so-called 'Halpin Trail', tourists come from afar to visit the old Bridge Tavern to see the birthplace of that world-famous mariner. But *I* came for a different reason – I came to reflect on my Grandfather, his many captivating stories, his life; to feel his presence. Because, for me, he is here.

The Whistle

From the moment he stepped off the train onto the rain-soaked platform, he sensed something was not right. The crowd were dispersing hurriedly, seemingly anxious to vacate the station, as if fearful. He stood and brushed the creases out of his sergeant's uniform and donned his cap. Just twenty-three years old, he was a big man, close to six-foot-tall, with a generous crop of dark brown hair and alert blue eyes. Five other members of the Civic Guard, his subordinates, were alighting from the train. Each carried a large bag of personal belongings. They were prepared for a lengthy stay in this remote part of Ireland.

The misty Kerry air felt refreshing after the long and tiring trip from Dublin, during which he had tried not to let his deep feelings of apprehension show. He had forced himself to participate in casual conversation, mostly remarking on the passing scenery. He did not want to cause any anxiety among his recently trained young men. While he could sense their eagerness to do their duty, they lacked practical experience and would be looking to him for guidance and reassurance. He knew that a difficult and perilous task lay ahead. Having completed his police training in Dublin just over two years earlier, this was his first assignment after being promoted to his present rank. He had been specially selected for this dangerous mission as he was known for his leadership qualities and his steadfast sense of discipline. His previous experience as Officer in Charge of a company of men in the Old Irish Republican Army had honed these attributes.

The recent Anglo-Irish Treaty that Michael Collins had signed in London, which granted independence to twenty six of the thirty-two counties of Ireland after seven hundred years of British rule, was the basis for the formation of the Irish Free State government. But that Treaty was the catalyst for a bitter civil war now raging throughout the country as many people wanted immediate independence for the whole of Ireland. Nowhere was that hostility to the Free State government greater than in the south and west of the country and the newly formed Civic Guard was seen as representatives of that government. A member of the Civic Guard had been shot dead by anti-Treaty forces just a few months earlier in Mullinahone in County Tipperary. The sergeant knew that County Kerry was a particularly strong anti-Treaty region and he was on his way to open the first Civic Guard station in the small town of Rathmore in the east of that county.

Now on the platform, he and his men were attracting many glances. In itself, this was probably not surprising as they were the only uniformed passengers there. A young boy nearby was staring at them:

'Look, Mammy. Policemen!'

'Come on. Let's go. Quick,' responded his mother, hurriedly pulling him away by the arm. The engine hissed loudly as it discharged its head of steam, as if breathing a great sign of relief after its long journey. But, for the sergeant, there was a sense of unease as he surveyed his new surroundings. A white sign some distance along the platform read *Slí Amach*, marking the exit near where a few mailbags had been thrown from the guard's van. The platform had now cleared, apart from a group of six or eight men who were approaching. They stopped and formed a line directly in front of him and his men. He stiffened as he observed that most were carrying firearms, a selection of both rifles and revolvers. While most wore civilian clothes, their orderly line looked like a quasi-military formation. One member of the group, a tall man, probably in his late twenties, stepped forward and confronted the sergeant, distinguishable by the three silver stripes on his right sleeve. The man was wearing what looked like an old army jacket with several buttons missing and a Sam Brown belt with shoulder strap. His bushy red hair was protruding from under his cap. He held a revolver in his hand. There was a determined look on his face:

'Now listen to me', he said in a loud voice. 'You'd better understand *we're* in charge here. You and your feckin' Free Staters are not wanted. So, if you value your lives, you'd be well advised, you and your young boys, to get back on that train and take yourselves back to Dublin right now. D'ya hear?' He brandished the revolver threateningly. While the man didn't identify himself, it was obvious to the sergeant that he and the men belonged to the so-called *'Irregulars'*, part of the well organised and armed group who were in the forefront of the escalating anti-Treaty violence. The sergeant and his men had just arrived in this hot bed of anti-Treaty country and the resentment to their presence was already being made forcefully. He had not expected such an immediate and hostile confrontation. Their arrival had obviously been anticipated.

There was no doubt that the men now lined up in front of him were serious in their intent. Their guns were at the ready. They were waiting for an order from their leader. The sergeant had to think quickly. His pulse was quickening and he could sense the tension building in his men. His life and possibly the lives of his small group were being threatened. Their only weapons were their wooden truncheons, no match for the firearms confronting them. But in a situation such as this, his devotion to duty was paramount.

He took one step forward, his face now within inches of that of the leader of the threatening group. 'Now, it's your turn to listen,' he said in a voice which embodied both confidence and determination. 'We're here to enforce law and order, to ensure the safety of the entire community, irrespective of their political views.' He raised his finger and pointed directly at the man. 'And that includes the safety of you and your families. Our loyalty is to Ireland and we are here to guard the peace.'

Flushed in the face, the leader held his revolver aloft and shouted mockingly:

'You're here to guard the peace?' He spat defiantly on the ground. 'Well, show us your arms then, Mister Policeman, you feckin' guardian of the peace!'

'We are unarmed,' the sergeant responded in steady, measured tones. 'We will keep the peace, not by force of arms, but by our moral authority as servants of the entire Irish people.' With these words, he was paraphrasing what the Civic Guard commissioner had stated in justifying the establishment of a non-armed police force. Without waiting for a response, which he knew was likely to enhance the confrontation to an even more critical level, the sergeant pulled his official whistle from his breast pocket by its chain and placed it between his lips. The man facing him winced as the shrill sound was directed into his face. He looked startled. Before he could react, the sergeant turned, waved his arm at his men who, at a second blast from the whistle, quickly formed a line. Taking his place at the head, he shouted:

'Quick march!' and he led the small party past the line of Irregulars and along the platform towards the exit. No shots were fired. The only sounds were the rhythmic clip of their marching boots on the cobblestoned platform. They marched out of the station.

Later, the sergeant's actions were hailed as a remarkable act of courage. In his mind, however, he regarded his whistle as instrumental in the resolution of that dangerous situation. In taking those threatening him by surprise, that whistle had averted an overt and imminent threat to their lives.

Those were politically confused and troubled times. The previous police force, the British-instituted and much-hated Royal Irish Constabulary, an armed force, had been formally disbanded, leaving a lawless country in its wake. It was the sergeant's task to establish the new police presence in the vacated RIC barracks in the town. But that initial encounter with the Irregulars was a cogent warning of the difficulties he had yet to face in this small community. This was reinforced by the news, some weeks later, that a second member of the Civic Guard had been murdered during a raid by the Irregulars on the Guard's station in Scartaglin, another small village in County Kerry. More murders were to follow as more Civic Guard stations were ruthlessly attacked.

Against this background, attempting to enforce law and order was both difficult and highly dangerous in a country wracked by civil war, which raged from June 1922 to April 1923. The Civic Guard, now officially renamed *An Garda Síochána na hÉireann*, increasingly found itself cast in the role of the State's security force, a hazardous assignment for which its members were woefully under-equipped. For the safety of his men, and ignoring directions from his superiors in Dublin, the sergeant did not instigate any night patrols for several weeks. When he eventually did, he and his men were armed with nothing but their truncheons. However, he always carried his faithful whistle, which he had cause to use on many occasions in efforts to enforce law and order.

The years passed and Ireland transitioned into a relatively peaceful land. That man, who opened the first Garda Síochána station in Rathmore, advanced through the ranks and was assigned duties in various locations throughout the country. He received at least two awards for 'Exemplary Service'. When eventually he hung up his uniform for the last time, he removed his whistle from the breast pocket. It and the badge from his Garda cap were the only mementos of his forty-three eventful years of service that he took with him into retirement. It's a solid metal whistle, that tiny symbol of moral authority, with a ring on top for the chain, and the words *An Garda Síochána* engraved on it. I keep it in my father's memory.

FICTIONS

Short stories are tiny windows into other worlds and other minds and other dreams. They are journeys you can make to the far side of the universe and still be back in time for dinner.

NEIL GAIMAN

The Lighthouse

He had lied. He had told Bill the boatman that he was very experienced in sailing. He wanted to rent a small sailing dinghy for the afternoon. It was Mike's first visit to Ireland since his childhood and he was anxious to see as much as he could of the fascinating countryside before his return to Chicago. His doctor had told him to take a break from his ceaseless work schedule. 'You're only forty-two, Mike,' the doctor reminded him, 'but you'll be dead in another ten years at the rate you're going in that high-pressure environment.' Somewhat reluctantly, he agreed to take a short vacation. So here he was, an over-weight scantily haired man, in the land of his ancestors, hoping to revive some of his childhood memories.

The friendly hotel receptionist advised him that the best view of the wild coastline of the Burren was from the sea. 'You can rent a boat from old Bill down on the pier,' she suggested. Faint happy memories of sailing along the coast with his grandfather flashed through Mike's mind. Yes, he would go sailing, he would recreate those childhood memories. He would do it in memory of his grandfather. But in fact, Mike had little sailing experience. His busy father had taken him sailing on Lake Michigan on a few occasions when he was young. But his father had always insisted on handling the boat himself while Mike sat and enjoyed the view of the impressive shoreline of the city he had come to call home. His father had left his home in County Clare many years previously when Mike's mother died, and he had taken the young boy, his only child, with him. Mike was just six years old then. The only family member left behind in Clare was his grandfather. Mike's faint memories of the old man were those of a tall slim figure always in a dark blue uniform, sporting a small neatly trimmed moustache over a loving smile.

Bill the boatman, a swarthy individual in black knitted sweater and with a weather-beaten face, warned him about the possibility of the weather changing. 'Try to stay within sight of this pier,' he advised. The tiny pier was marked with a hand inscribed 'X' on a tattered marine chart pinned to the wall of Bill's small wooden office. 'That's quite an antique you have there,' Mike commented as he noted the chart was marked '*London, Published at the Admiralty, 31st December 1883, price 15s 0d*'. Perceiving his interest, Bill explained: 'Yes, it's a very an old chart. It was given to me by an old lighthouse keeper many years ago and I like to keep it there in his memory. He was a stubborn old man who refused to retire from his post.'

'Well, that's nice,' said Mike, 'but we wouldn't use maps that old in Chicago. Things can change a lot.'

'Well, nothing much has changed around here since that map was printed,' Bill replied, 'that is, apart from the new lighthouse up on Blackhead, much further north.' He pointed with a work-worn finger to another 'X', the only mark showing the location of the new lighthouse. 'Apart from the Blackhead beach and this pier here, there are very few safe places to bring a boat ashore. I wouldn't recommend the tiny beach just under to the *old* lighthouse.' He pointed to the printed symbol of a lighthouse on the chart. 'Much too dangerous! That's why you shouldn't go too far out to sea. And do watch the weather.'

With a feeling of elation, Mike cast off from the little pier in the small sailing dinghy under Bill's watchful eye. Despite Bill's warnings and his own limited experience, he was determined to make this sightseeing trip work. Aided by a firm breeze, he made rapid headway away from the coast hoping to get a panoramic view of those spectacular cliffs. But before long the Atlantic was throwing up waves the like of which he had never experienced on Lake Michigan. He struggled with the sails trying to turn the boat around and set a course back towards the small pier he had left. But the strengthening wind had other ideas in mind for him. Despite his best efforts, his small craft was being blown northwards. He regretted his lack of experience. He felt that Father Neptune, that irascible God of the Sea, was punishing him for his foolhardiness. The determined Sea God was battering the small craft mercilessly with his powerful waves while whistling mockingly through the rigging and defiantly spitting salty spray into Mike's pale face. Frantically, Mike tried to tack back and forth, trying to recall his father's techniques. But as the boom swung repeatedly, the boat would tend to turn broadside to the waves, seething angrily around him. He tightened his life jacket belt, fearing that the boat would capsize. Those large Atlantic waves periodically swept over the gunwale, threatening to swamp the small craft as it pitched and rolled violently. The sky was darkening as rainclouds rolled in and evening started to merge into night.

Mike's fear heightened as the shoreline became fainter behind a squall of rain. At times he could see nothing but the frothy waves threatening the small boat continuously. A feeling of total helplessness overcame him, grasping tightly at him like a snake twined around his neck. He had never experienced this before. Was his life about to end here somewhere off the rugged coast of Ireland? Was this his destiny? Was this really him in this small boat? As CEO of his major international company based in Chicago, he would sit in his large office near the top of the Wrigley Building on Michigan Avenue enjoying that intoxicating feeling of power. With confidence, he exercised full control of his large worldwide enterprise as his staff diligently followed his instructions. But what was the true meaning behind those relentless activities where he felt pressured through every minute of time? Yes, he was making money, lots of it, but was that all there was in his life? Was there really a meaning to those days he spent chairing endless business meetings in his expensively furnished boardroom? And then there was the stress of having to report to the demanding board of directors who always wanted more. Did he really enjoy those lengthy evenings when he had to be polite to prospective clients he didn't really care about? And what about those endless social gatherings when he probably bored his so-called friends by boasting about his business successes? But now, out in this small dinghy, exposed to the awesome power of nature, he felt like a small, insignificant, utterly powerless figure.

He continued to struggle as horizontal bursts of rain drenched him. The cliff-lined shore, spectacular and ominous, now less than about half a mile away, was visible only at intervals, with no definite landmark discernible. He decided it was no use trying to navigate back to the pier now. His only hope was to find a safe place to bring the boat ashore. But between him and the shore lay a mass of low-lying rocks, their menacing tops disappearing and reappearing as each wave swept over them.

Through the encroaching darkness, he saw a flash of light somewhere further north along the coast. It was repeated at intervals. It was obviously one of the lighthouses that Bill had mentioned. But he knew he couldn't make it that far. The rocky shore was rapidly getting closer. He was desperate. Then, as he continued to struggle with both tiller and sails, another light flashed through the darkness, this time much closer. It was faint and for a moment he wondered if he had imagined it. Perhaps it was the headlights of a car somewhere above the cliffs. Then he detected further faint flashes, which seemed to occur at regular intervals. It might be the old lighthouse, he surmised, the one closer with the small but dangerous beach beside it. He tried to focus on those flashes coming from somewhere atop those black foreboding cliffs. Was it just his stressed and exhausted state that made him feel that the light was beckoning him? This was his only chance. Firmly grasping the tiller and tightening his hold on the mainsheet, he managed to steer the boat in the general direction of the faint recurring light. Rocks were breaking the surface on either side of the craft but he tried to put the imminent danger out of his mind as he concentrated on his difficult task. It was an agonizing fight against the elements, all the while guided by the faint intermittent light. Then the light disappeared behind a ridge just as his centreboard grated along the bottom. He quickly retracted it and started to lower the sails as a huge wave, like some gigantic monster from Neptune's cave, hit the transom and carried the craft onto the small shingle beach between the cliffs. It was the Sea God's parting blow. He jumped waist deep into the frothing water and dragged the boat ashore. He was overwhelmed with relief and experienced a brief sense of triumph. He had made it!

Exhausted, Mike collapsed onto the shingles, panting and gasping for breath. Then, with an effort, he struggled to his feet and made his way up a slippery slope, shoes squelching with every step, trying to get reception on his mobile phone in order to contact Bill.

'My God, you put the heart sideways in me,' exclaimed Bill. 'I was waiting here at the pier and I was just about to phone the lifeboat. Where on earth are you?' Mike told him he was in the small creek just under the lighthouse, the more southerly one. 'You mean the *old* lighthouse?' exclaimed Bill. 'Good God! Just stay there and I'll be with you in twenty minutes.'

Mike leaned against a rock and slowly lowered his wet and aching frame to the ground. He held his head in his hands. He had a moment to reflect. He shouldn't have been so foolish as to put himself in such danger. And he had also put Bill through a lot of anguish. He removed his cumbersome life jacket and sat still, his back against the cold wet rock. He was known to be headstrong and stubborn, but those traits that had brought him business successes in Chicago had now threatened to bring his life to an end. And would anyone have really cared? What if his so-called friends could see him now, sitting in the dark on the hard ground, alone, dishevelled, cold, wet to the skin, and far away from anywhere. There was something utterly surreal about it. He took a deep breath. Slowly he began to realise he was truly inhabiting his own presence for the first time. The terrifying experience was awakening something inside him, something that was struggling in a plurality of discordant voices within. It was as if some dormant inner being was asking to be set free. A feeling of enlightenment was slowly breaking through that protective veneer of artificiality. He began to see his life in a different perspective. He tried to control his thoughts. He reminded himself that he was in the land of his birth, near where his forefathers had striven for a better life. He fingered the gritty soil beneath him, the soil of his forbears, the soil they had worked in order to derive a livelihood and the opportunity to give hope to future generations. He wiped his grit coated fingers in his shirt and smiled. For the first time in his life, he experienced a strong connection with the real world around him, a mysterious oneness with nature in all its raw reality. He raised his head and, strangely, he found himself laughing out loud at the sheer absurdity of his situation. This, he felt, was a homecoming to his true self. The rain had almost stopped and the moon was making furtive appearances between the scudding clouds.

'Mike! Are you there?' His thoughts were interrupted by a shout. Bill, brandishing a flashlight, was coming towards him down the steep incline. 'Thank God you're alive and well. I'll drive you back to your hotel now and I'll retrieve the boat in the morning.' Together they pulled the dinghy further up the shingle beach to a more secure location. As they walked up the path towards the road in the faint moonlight, Bill commented 'It must have taken some skill to navigate around the rocks on your way in. Even the local fishermen who know the whole area try to avoid that piece of coast. You must be a very experienced sailor. How on earth did you find your way to that beach in the dark?'

'I simply steered towards the light from that lighthouse,' Mike explained. 'It was the only light anywhere close and you told me about the small beach just under it. It was that light that saved me.' Bill looked at him.

'No, the light must have been from the *other* lighthouse, the one at Blackhead, further up the coast. That's the only light around here. There's no light from *this* lighthouse. It's not used anymore.' Mike was taken aback. He was sure the light had come from the lighthouse they were now walking past. He stopped and looked for a moment at the building. It stood sentinel like, a tall cylindrical structure, tapering slightly towards the top as it curved inwards at a gentle gradient. It was built from rough stone which carried the remnants of black paint at the lower and upper parts and white in the centre. The circular glass top housing the lantern remained totally dark. 'I told you, there has never been any light from that old lighthouse since it was abandoned many years ago,' said Bill. Somewhat mystified, Mike continued to accompany Bill slowly up along the path. Could he really have been imagining the light? 'You see', explained Bill, 'I remember the old lighthouse keeper when I was a lot younger. He was known by everyone simply as *The Lighthouse Man*. And a lovely old man he was, always proud to wear his Irish Lights uniform. I never saw him without it. He was the one who gave me that old marine chart you saw on the wall of my office. Then they built that new lighthouse up north of here where the lamp is powered by electricity. The old lighthouse was still using paraffin. When they closed it down, the Lighthouse Man was supposed to retire – he was at retirement age anyway. But he couldn't leave the old job he'd been doing for the previous fifty years or so. I remember him telling me 'They can't throw me out, Bill. I still have the key. And even if I have to steal the paraffin, I'll keep that light going until my grandson returns from America.' Those were his very words. Sadly, they found him dead up at his light about twenty years ago, poor man, and no one has entered the building ever since.' They arrived at Bill's car. 'Get in, Mike,' said Bill. Mike paused.

'Might his name have been Michael O'Shaughnessy?' Bill stared at Mike across the bonnet.

'How did you know that?'

Mike walked back down the path and then up the slight grassy incline to the base of the old lighthouse, the moon, now bright, lighting his way. The strong metal door was secured with a large bolt and a rusting padlock. Pressing against the cold wet metal with the palm of his hand, he looked up at the dark lens high above and whispered, 'Thank you, Grandfather.'

The Castle

'Nobody knows what happened.' The young couple, seated on their barstools, stared at the bearded bartender, leaning across the counter towards them.

'You say he fell from the castle battlements?' Sophia murmured. Her pretty face, framed in long blonde hair, was creased in a frown of disbelief.

'Yes. Onto the rocks below. Poor man. He was the priest here in my parents' time. A nice man. Everyone in the parish was shocked.'

'But what was he doing in the castle?' asked Dermot. The bartender leaned further across the counter, adopting a posture of intimacy.

'Well, in those days, it was said the castle was haunted. You must have passed near to it as you drove here. It's just a little way off the road outside the village. It was occupied by a small garrison of soldiers during the Cromwellian wars in the 17th century. People were dragged in there for very trivial offences and some were murdered by the soldiers. There were all sorts of stories about the place, stories about ghosts and the like. The local landowner claimed he would see figures moving around on the battlements at night, even when he knew there was nobody in the castle. He and his family were so disturbed that he asked the priest if he would exorcise the place.'

'So, what happened to the poor priest? Was anyone with him?' asked Sophia.

'Nobody. He went into the castle on his own. Nobody else would dare enter the place because of the rumours. He was in his long black soutane carrying a vessel of Holy Water. After a while, someone saw him up on the battlements and the next thing was he fell to the rocks below.' The barman paused to let the intended impact of his words sink in. The couple looked at one another in silence as they sipped their drinks. They were thirsty after their long drive from Dublin.

'That's a very sad story,' said Dermot.

'Indeed, it is,' said the bartender. 'They locked the castle permanently after that.' He leaned even closer and lowered his voice, even though there were no others in the small bar to hear him. 'Now, listen. The strange thing is this. The priest's ghost is still there. You can see him walking around the castle, maybe even up on the battlements, and falling over.' Sophia raised her eyebrows. Dermot shook his head.

'Sorry, but I really don't believe in ghosts.' His bar stool creaked as he swivelled around, hoping to put an end to a conversation that was getting too unreal for his liking. Now in his late twenties, he had taken a week off his accountancy job in the city for this trip. But he hadn't brought his new girlfriend all the way to this small village, far away from anywhere, just to talk with a stranger about ghosts. It was getting late and they just wanted to relax quietly by themselves. He tried to suffocate a yawn. They both finished their drinks as the barman continued:

'Yes, it's true. His ghost appears there at exactly midnight every time there's a full moon. I've seen it myself.' Dermot put down his empty glass with determination and placed a ten euro note on the bar.

'Well, we're a little tired now – maybe we'll visit the castle tomorrow. Thanks for the drinks.'

'All right then, please yourselves,' continued the barman, drawing his portly frame back across the bar, 'but just remember, there's a full moon tonight...'

'This is a bit stupid!' said Dermot as they trudged over the boggy rock-strewn field up the hill towards the castle later that night: 'Why on earth did we decide to do this, to come here in the darkness? I'm glad we brought our jackets.'

'Well, I suppose it's my fault for suggesting it', replied Sophia. 'I was just a little curious, that's all. I didn't realise it would be such a difficult climb. From the road, the castle didn't look too far away.' They continued walking.

'You really didn't believe that barman, did you?' asked Dermot eventually.

'Well, not really. Anyway, the walk in the fresh air will do us good after that long drive. And we need to stretch our legs, don't we? It's not too dark – look, the moon is bright.' Despite the pale moon light, they continuously stumbled over rocks partially covered with undergrowth.

'Did you know there's a lot of superstition about the *sceach*?' said Dermot, pointing to a stunted hawthorn bush, which emerged out of the darkness in front of them. 'That's the Irish name for it.' Its twisted branches pointed at them like witches' fingers. Sophia slowed her pace. Then Dermot stopped abruptly as he exclaimed: 'Look! There, beside the bush See the dark shadow? Look, Sophia! It's moving!'

'Oh my God!', exclaimed Sophia, grasping Dermot's arm as she stared in the direction of the bush. 'Where is it? It isn't the priest's ghost, is it, Dermot?'

Dermot felt her cold skin as her arm pressed against his.

'Just joking,' he chuckled. 'Look – there's nothing there.'

Sophia released her grasp. 'Oh, please don't do that, Dermot. You had me scared. My heart was jumping.' She gave him a friendly dig in his ribs. 'You love teasing me, don't you?'

'Sorry, but I just wanted to prove that you *do* believe in ghosts.'

'Well, maybe I do, sort of….' They continued trudging uphill.

'You know what I think?' said Dermot after a further

few minutes: 'I think we're making right eejits of ourselves.'

'Well, console yourself,' said Sophia, 'because there's no one else here to see us eejits. But anyway, it's not much further, Dermot. Let's just get as far as the castle and then go back.'

They continued walking in silence. After a further five minutes' climb, they stopped to draw their breaths. They could see the tall ghostly looking castle, now only about thirty metres away. Its austere grey stone walls were faintly illuminated by the moon light. It was a domineering rectangular structure, seemingly in good condition for its age, with a rounded tower at one corner and undulating battlements along the top. The rocks at its base sloped steeply away on all sides, disappearing into clumps of nettles.

'So that's it,' commented Dermot. 'Now we've seen it. It's just a castle. It must be close to midnight now and I don't see any ghost.' They stood in silence for a moment, holding hands. Sophia tightened her scarf against a slight breeze.

'OK, I suppose we should make our way back now,' she conceded as she turned.

'Well, I've got news for you.' said Dermot, his interest suddenly revived. 'There *is* someone else here besides us eejits, someone or something – look over there at the side of the castle.'

'Dermot, for God's sake. I asked you not to frighten me again with that sort of joke. You know there's nothing there.'

'Actually, Sophia, there is.' They tried to focus their eyes on a dark figure close to one of the castle walls illuminated by the moonlight.

'My God, you're right,' said Sophia in hushed tones, as she grabbed Dermot's arm again. 'Could it be the ghost of the priest? It looks like he's in his long black soutane.' They continued to stare, transfixed. The ghostlike figure in black was moving slowly and silently across the sloping rocks near the base of the wall.

'That's probably where the barman said the priest fell to his death,' whispered Sophia, tightening her scarf a little more against the chilly breeze. 'Let's not go any closer, Dermot. It's really creepy.' She gripped Dermot more tightly. 'Maybe the barman wasn't fooling after all. Do you think it really might be the ghost?' Dermot stared more intently at the figure.

'Well, I'm not too sure about that. But I'd really like to find out, ghost or no ghost.' Freeing himself from Sophia's grip, he ran quickly up the remainder of the hill towards the dark figure. As he did, the figure started to move away from him into the shadows around the side of the castle. There was a shout as the figure tripped in his long black gown and Dermot grabbed him by the arm.

'He's no ghost!' Dermot called out triumphantly as he looked at the young man, probably in his late teens, raising himself from the ground. 'What on earth are you doing here, dressed like that?'

'Sorry if I scared you!' the lad admitted sheepishly. 'It's just that my uncle in the bar got me to do this. He says he's hoping the story of a local ghost will attract more visitors.'

'Well, I think that's a bit stupid,' commented Dermot, as he released his grip on the young man.

'But gosh, you *did* have us fooled for a moment,' admitted Sophia, arriving at the scene. 'From a distance, you actually looked very ghost-like in the moon light. Didn't he Dermot?'

'Yes, maybe, but I thought the real ghost was supposed to jump from the battlements,' taunted Dermot, as the young man took off his cumbersome black gown. 'It would have been much more realistic if you'd done that.'

'Well, I suppose so. But I didn't want to kill myself,' said the youth, grinning, 'not even for my uncle. And anyway, the castle is all blocked up – no one can ever get inside.' He rolled his black gown up tightly.

'We can give you a lift back to the village,' suggested Dermot.

The three chatted as they walked back down the hillside, cautiously picking their way between the myriads of small rocks and heathers. A rabbit scurried out of their way in the undergrowth. Sophia couldn't help glancing nervously at the *sceach* as they passed it. Through the still air, the faint chimes of a distant church bell signalled midnight. No one looked back at the old castle with the full moon shining its milky light over it from a clear black sky sprinkled with stars. No one noticed the shadowy figure hovering on the high battlements. No one saw it falling silently to the rocks below...

Robert

A half-used candle, unlit, stands erect in its ornate brass holder on the mahogany bedside table like a sentinel, guarding her brown medicine bottle. Brigid, the nurse, had administered the prescribed dose earlier and left her for the night. Now the large house is quiet. Very quiet.

The room is kept spotlessly clean – I had always insisted on that. It remains the same. Of course, I know it well. I designed the room myself and furnished it many years ago – the majestic marble fireplace imported from Italy, the oak floor carefully selected in London, the high corniced ceiling. The walls still display those commissioned family portraits with faces from numerous generations peering out of the distant past, many pastoral scenes of Wicklow's hills and the county's most familiar seascapes, the paintings now losing some of their lustre. With advancing age, she gathered as many of these memories as she could around her in her large bedroom. The faint odour of medication disturbs the air. A china vase containing a few wilting bluebells, their purple heads drooping dolefully, graces a small stand in the corner near her bed. The heavy floor-length curtains are almost fully drawn now and the American pitch pine shutters, designed specially to match the ornate architraves, are closed. A thin shaft of the fading evening sunlight struggles to find its way through a chink in the shutters to cut pencil-like through the darkness.

All is still.

She slowly opens her sunken eyes to look at me, trying to focus in the dark room. A faint smile spreads on her lips.

'Do sit on the bed beside me, Robert,' she says in a hoarse whisper. 'I'm always touched by your presence, dear.' She says that every time. I smile back and lower myself onto the edge of the four-poster bed with its coiled wooden columns and thick hanging canopy. Her long grey curls tumble across the pillow and around the laced top of her white bed jacket.

'Talk to me, Robert, my dear. Tell me about Newfoundland. Tell me about Grace Harbour. Is my family all right? Are they still there?'

I've told her so often before.

'Yes, your family is fine,' I tell her. She ponders for a moment. Her eyes move slowly back and forth.

'Have you been there recently?' she asks. She knows I haven't.

'No, Jessie, not since 1873, the year we were married. I've been here with you ever since, Jessie'. There is a long silence. She struggles with her thoughts, then she asks,

'I hope our apple trees are being well tended.' I assure her they are.

'And all our vegetables? We should really give away what we can't use. Why don't you tell one of the gardeners to take them or perhaps to bring them to some of the local people around Rethrew?'

I tell her I will. More silence. Her breathing is laboured. With some effort, she turns her head slightly.

'Robert, please bring me the newspaper.' I know what she wants although she hasn't asked me for it before – it's that old edition of *The Wicklow Newsletter* dated Monday 22nd January 1894, its creased and well-thumbed pages now fading into aged yellowness. She has preserved it for the last twenty odd years. I take it from the large Burmese mahogany cupboard containing all her valuables in the far corner of the bedroom. I gently lay it on the bed beside her. Of course, she can't read it in the darkness – she just runs her feeble fingers up and down the front page.

'But tell me more, Robert. Did you ever see *The Great Eastern* since you were her captain? You were so famous, Robert, so famous. Have you seen that great iron ship recently?' She should know the answer.

'No, Jessie. *The Great Eastern* was scrapped on the River Mersey many years ago. That was her sad end.' Silence again. A long silence.

'Come closer, Robert. Let me see you.' Her eyes strain again to see me in the dimness.

'Yes, you can see me,' I reply. 'Remember, I'm always here in the house with you, Jessie. Always.' A faint smile crosses her lips. Again, a lengthy silence.

'Hold my hand, Robert,' she says quietly, as she extends her frail right hand across the thickly embroidered quilt and gently touches mine: 'Your hand is very cold, Robert, my dear.' She says that each time. More silence. She stares up at the overhanging bed canopy. Her breathing is becoming heavier.

'Robert, tell me about Newfoundland. I often think about it. Is it still so beautiful? Tell me, Robert.' Her words are barely audible. I quietly tell her again. But her eyes are closed. She's asleep. I lean over and gently kiss her lips. I know it's the last time. The shaft of sunlight has faded, surrendering to the darkness. I wait in the shadows.

When morning comes, it brings with it the anticipated commotion in the household. She looks so peaceful lying there as the sun streams in between the open curtains. By the time the doctor arrives, *rigor mortis* is setting in. There are the usual hushed conversations about the arrangements. I watch as Brigid starts to prepare the room. She stops and stares at the newspaper lying beside Jessie. She knows it wasn't there when she left her last night – I know she hadn't wanted Jessie to get her hands on it in case it might rekindle sad memories. I watch her move pensively over to the cupboard where the old paper was always kept along with other memorabilia from a long life, a life with very many memories for both of us. It's still locked securely. She knows

Jessie doesn't have the key. I see her puzzled expression as she turns and looks around the room. I think she senses I am here. She knew how close Jessie and I were. Surely she would know I would return to comfort my beloved Jessie in her last moments of life.

Brigid picks up the paper and checks the date – yes, it's just as she thought. Instinctively, she turns to page ten, the Obituaries, and looks at the entry neatly marked by Jessie's pen many years earlier. I know Jessie had shown it to her so often before. I watch her face as she reads the first line once again:

'Captain Robert Halpin passed away peacefully two days ago at his Tinakilly home....'

Now Jessie joins my world. My visit is over.

The Brooch

She couldn't help herself. Now it was too late. She realised she had already said too much, excited as she was about the possibility of making a little money, but now she felt she had better tell her the full story.

'Listen, Mother, I shouldn't have told you anything. Then you'd be none the wiser – you'd think it was *really* stolen during the break-in last week.'

'So, it *wasn't* really stolen, then?' enquired her elderly mother, looking quizzically at her through her thin rimmed spectacles. She leaned forward in her creaking chair, its fading upholstery showing its age.

'No! I already told you it wasn't. We're just saying that to the insurance people.'

'Really?' exclaimed her mother, with a look of horror creeping over her wrinkled face.

'Yes,' replied Kate earnestly, leaning over to her mother and gripping her frail arm. 'So just promise me you won't tell anyone. You know you're old and you get all confused and you might just say the wrong thing.'

'Well, all right then. But I *do* have my moments of clarity, you know.' The old lady tapped the arm of her chair defiantly.

'Well, I hope you have one of those moments if the insurance people come and ask you anything.' Her mother thought for a moment.

'So, it *wasn't* stolen!' she repeated, knitting her brow.

'No, it wasn't, but for God's sake don't say that!' insisted Kate, as she rose and turned to leave the room.

'That brooch is worth a fortune, you know,' her mother called after her. 'It's in delicate jade with platinum gold and diamonds, a real antique – you wouldn't get the likes nowadays. And it has great sentimental value for me –

it was my dear Brian, your devoted father, who gave it to me on our wedding day all those years ago.' Kate looked back at her mother and sighed:

'Yes, I know, Mother. You told me that so many times. But I only borrowed it for a little while, that's all.'

'But you didn't need to borrow it at all, Kate.' Her mother's countenance was turning sour.

'It was only to show it to my friends. And anyway, if I left it with you, I was afraid you'd lose it. You know how you lose things, Mother.'

Her mother's eyebrows knitted in a faint scowl.

'A little while,' reiterated her mother with a hint of sarcasm in her voice. 'You said a little while. But that was a long time ago, Kate.' Kate ignored the comment and was closing the door to the downstairs bedroom behind her when her mother called out:

'But remind me again what I'm *not* supposed to tell anyone. You see, if they ask me, I might get a little nervous, you know. Don't forget I'm old.'

'Oh my God,' Kate replied, now raising her voice as she re-entered the room. 'Just *don't* tell them it *wasn't* stolen.' The old lady looked a little confused.

'Well, does that mean tell them it *was* stolen?'

'Yes! It *was* stolen. That's all you have to say. Now, don't forget that in case they ask you. OK?'

'Yes, I'll try to remember that – it *was* stolen. I'll practice saying that in case I forget. It *was* stolen.'

'Stupid old woman,' muttered Kate, exasperated, as she finally closed the door firmly to her mother's bedroom. That door was her barrier against all that confusion.

Kate remembered the difficulties she had previously experienced in convincing her mother to move out of her old bedroom upstairs into that downstairs room.

'But it's *my* house,' her mother had protested. 'I occupied that room with your dear father for over forty years, Kate, ever since you were born. When you're old, you'll know what it's like.' Why was her mother always so difficult, Kate wondered? Even though she knew it was because her mother's mind was becoming feebler, she found it hard to be patient with her. Kate's ruminating was interrupted by her husband's voice:

'Kate, I've already informed the insurance company. Now all we have to do is hide it somewhere really safe in case they come. Where did you put it?'

'I already told you,' she said impatiently, still trying to calm herself after the frustrating exchanges with her mother. 'It's in my small red handbag with my rings and things hidden at the back of the closet shelf – all the stuff that *wasn't* stolen in the break-in. We're so lucky they didn't find *that* bag. That brooch is very valuable, you know.'

'Yes, I know. But I looked there already, Kate. You must have put it somewhere else.'

'No, I didn't. Are you sure you looked properly? Maybe you missed it – remember it's a small brooch, small enough to fit easily in the palm of your hand. I know I saw it there last week and I haven't touched that bag since.' There was silence for a moment.

'Well, let's look in that bag again. And in *all* your other handbags. You have so many damn handbags, Kate, and you don't use half of them. Let's look everywhere.' Lengthy frantic searches followed. Bags and drawers were searched, their contents scattered. No brooch was found. They stood for a moment and looked at one another. The realisation was hitting them both.

'My God!' said Kate, standing in the centre of the room as she held her head in her hands, 'it really *was* stolen. It must have been in the other handbag after all, the light grey one with the shoulder strap, the one they took. Those damn wretches! I feel like screaming.' She stamped her foot on the floor in frustration. 'I could have sworn I had that brooch in that red handbag.'

'Well, you were obviously mistaken. It just isn't here, Kate. It isn't in the house.' Kate tried to calm herself. Then they both slumped onto the sofa and stared blankly at the walls for a while and then again at one another. Their clever plan had been thwarted. Their feelings of being in control of a potentially lucrative exploit had suddenly evaporated. They were victims.

'Well, maybe it serves us right for wanting to be dishonest,' ventured Kate eventually, vainly trying to disguise her disappointment; 'I thought we were on to a good thing, but I suppose I really didn't feel comfortable telling that lie. And then, just suppose they found out...' Dave pondered for a moment and then nodded slowly.

'Well, I think you're probably right. To be honest, Kate, I never felt too happy about it either. I thought it was an easy way to make a few bob. But now your poor old mother will be very sad when she knows it's gone.'

Kate nodded slowly.

'Anyway,' Dave continued, 'let's go for a walk to clear our minds. Will your mother be OK on her own for a while? You should keep an eye on her, you know.' As they prepared to leave, Kate opened the door slightly to her mother's room to check on her. The old lady looked up from her book.

'It *was* stolen,' she said quietly, as if to reassure her daughter that she knew what to say and also to proudly demonstrate a moment of mental clarity. Kate hesitated momentarily. No, she wasn't going to go through that whole issue again with her dithering old mother to correct the story that she'd already told her; at least the old lady was now unknowingly telling the truth about what had actually happened. Kate just smiled, nodded approvingly and left the room.

When all was quiet, the old lady chuckled softly to herself

for a few moments as she left her book aside and settled herself in her chair. Then she sighed as she whispered:

'At last I have you next to me again, my darling Brian.' She slowly pulled the brooch up from deep within her bosom and placed it against her heart.

The Lady Mystery

'Look Grandad! Our footprints are the only ones in the sand.' In her yellow t-shirt and white shorts, my six-year-old granddaughter was enjoying the feel of the fine sand on her bare feet as she skipped along beside me on the broad deserted beach. 'Big footprints from you, Grandad; little ones from me.' It was our first time visiting that remote beach and Julie wanted to explore. Then, after a few more little skips she said: 'I think we're going to see something strange today, Grandad.'

'Really?' I said.

'Yes, we are. I know it.' Not for the first time, I wondered if Julie had a sixth sense. I recalled similar predictions in the past, many of them accurate.

It was a partially overcast Autumn day with a mild sea breeze, ideal for walking in the salty sea air and absorbing the vastness of nature. We were accompanied only by the gentle sound of the waves as each one washed up onto the sand and disappeared into tiny residues of froth. Some pebbles and small shells were deposited by the tide. A couple of curious seagulls wheeled overhead, announcing their presence with their cat-like cries.

'Would there be any crabs in that old wreck, Grandad?' Julie asked. She was pointing at the abandoned hulk of a small merchant ship, probably about thirty metres long. It was resting not far away on the sand, its dark hull contrasting with the green sea and white tipped waves behind it.

'Well, probably not, Julie,' I replied, 'but let's take a closer look at it anyway and see if we could go inside. Old ships can be very interesting, you know.'

'Well, not if there aren't any crabs inside. We've only caught one so far, Grandad,' the little girl reminded me. She held up her small pink plastic bucket with a tiny crab trying unsuccessfully to hide under a stone she had placed in the sea water at the bottom.

'Well, we'll hunt for more crabs in those rocks in a moment,' I assured her, 'but let's just take a quick look at that old shipwreck first.' Having some interest in old ships, I was curious. The battered metal hull was now almost fully above water as the tide was low. It was obvious that its sea going days were long over. Its bow was raised slightly, as if, like some extinct monster, it was lifting its head to show some remnant of its former pride. Its name, once carried proudly on the prow, was now weathered to illegibility. In my mind, I could see that bow surging gallantly through adventurous seas off distant lands. There must be a lot of history embedded in that old ship.

Julie agreed to take my hand as we waded to the wreck through some shallow puddles in the sand. Having donned our flip-flops to protect our feet, we climbed easily over the ship's low side onto the slanting deck.

'Now don't get any dirt on your nice clean clothes,' I warned Julie, 'or your Mummy will kill me.'

'No, I'll be careful, Grandad. I'm always careful.' A small broken mast lay diagonally across the foredeck. I again took Julie's hand and we threaded carefully past the few rusting cables that were strewn around.

'There's the wheel-house,' I told her, in an effort to make the visit a little more interesting for her. I pointed to the small enclosure on the aft deck. 'That's where the captain used to steer the ship.' A seagull was perched sentinel-like on the wheel-house roof. It slowly stretched its wings and launched itself into the air with a harsh cry, signalling its disapproval of our intrusion into its domain.

'Any crabs in the wheel-house?' Julie asked.

'No, it's too high above the water for crabs. But let's take a quick look below deck – you'd never know what we might find there.' A deck hatch was open, its cover missing. Carefully, I descended a short ladder, lifting Julie down after me. As our eyes became used to the dim light, the true extent of the gaping hole near the starboard bow, which must have doomed the vessel, became apparent. Apart from some stones and sand, the hold was empty, its contents having been plundered long ago. Treading carefully past the barnacle encrusted ribs and bulkheads, we made our way aft to the small dark engine room. Julie stayed at the entrance at my suggestion. I cautiously waded through some bilge water, past the remains of an open coal-blackened furnace and boiler. A few tiny fish scuttled swiftly away from my intruding feet. I stepped onto the centre floor plates. There was a cold and eerie feel about the place. Dominating the room was the rusting remains of a small marine steam engine. Its cylinders, shafts and trunnions suggested it was of a type dating from the early 1900s. I stood there for a moment gazing at its gaunt form in its present sad and silent state, a neglected relic of its former hot and hissing self. I wondered to what far off places it had dutifully propelled the ship during its working life. How it must have been admired in its early days, an engineering marvel, the exciting successor to sail, the future of marine propulsion. Looking at the old engine, I was relishing a fascinating mental excursion into the past, into another world, the bygone days of early propeller driven steam ships.

'It's cold in here, Grandad. And I don't see any crabs.' Julie's tiny voice brought me instantly back to the present. Her diminishing interest in the engine room and its contents suggested that we shouldn't remain there any longer. We made our way up and jumped off the deck into the puddles, causing a slurry of sandy water to coat our lower legs. Julie giggled as she threw off her flip-flops and continued to splash in the puddles. 'I'm splashing you, Grandad,' she laughed.

'Come on, the tide is coming in,' I said. 'It's time to go back up to the drier part of the beach.' The rising waters were beginning to swirl around the wreck, embracing it as they had done countless times over the years. It was as if the sea was stretching out its arms, trying vainly to reclaim its long-lost treasure. We paddled through the now flowing rivulets, just keeping ahead of the advancing wavelets, each with its frothy tip.

'Look, Grandad, the waves are wiping away our footprints behind us,' Julie commented. 'Now nobody would ever know we were there. It's a little like the way Mummy smooths the icing on the top of her cakes.' Once on drier sand, we started to walk towards the nearby rocks at the edge of the long strand. Julie was walking more quickly, now buoyed up by the expectation of finding more crabs.

'I think they hide in the pools between the rocks, Grandad, don't they?' She glanced again at her only catch hiding in the bucket. 'He must be a baby. Maybe I'll let him go if we catch a bigger one.' She flicked a strand of hair that had escaped from her ponytail away from her forehead. Then, after some moments, she added thoughtfully:

'See, Grandad, I told you we were going to see something strange today. I just knew it.'

'Yes,' I said, 'That's amazing. You were so right, Julie. That was a very strange old ship indeed. I hadn't expected that.'

'No, not the ship, I mean the man, Grandad.'

'What man?' I asked.

'That strange looking man on the ship. He'll have to get off the ship soon if the tide is coming in, won't he?' Julie glanced back at the lonely looking wreck. I looked at her.

'What man?' I asked again. 'There was no one else on board the ship except you and me, Julie.'

'Yes, there *was*, Grandad! I'm talking about that man

with dark skin standing beside you in the engine room,' she continued quite assertively. 'He seemed very strange. Don't you remember? He had dirty clothes and it looked like one of his arms was missing.' I stopped and stared at her, puzzled. There had been no one else on board. I was on the point of insisting that there was no such man and that she must have been imagining it, when suddenly she shouted:

'Look, Grandad! A huge crab! He's running sideways for the rocks – let's catch him! Quick!'

Later that day, I sat at the bar in the small local pub with its worn wooden furniture and sipped a welcome glass of cool beer. The few remaining customers had just left, taking their laughter with them. It was quiet, apart from the shuffling of the bartender. As I recalled the day's events, I ventured to ask him:

'Tell me – what's the story with that old wreck down on the strand? She's an interesting old ship.'

'Oh, that's *The Lady Mist*,' he replied, seeming glad to have someone to talk to. 'That was her proper name, but the locals here call her *The Lady Mystery*, as nobody knows much about her.' I listened with increasing interest as I fondled my glass. After a moment, he leaned against the bar, his soiled apron caressing his bulging stomach, and continued. 'Yes, a strange boat. Around here, she's looked on with a bit of superstition. She was a foreign registered vessel – I forget where she was originally from. Anyway, she was wrecked one night about seventy years ago in a ferocious storm. Supposedly the engine failed, just off the coast here. Thankfully, the small crew got off safely – all, that is, except the captain. Some of the survivors, all foreign lads, told the locals about him. They said he was down in the engine room trying to fix the engine when the ship hit the rocks off the headland there. He was never found, poor man.' I took another sip of my beer as I reflected on what I had just heard. The bartender reached over and started to dry some recently washed glasses. After a pause, he continued in softer tones:

'However, one of the survivors, they say, told a somewhat different story – he said there had been a mutiny on board and the captain, a Moroccan fellow I think, had been murdered by some of the crew. So, without the captain in control, the crew, all inexperienced lads, couldn't handle the ship in the storm. Of course, you really wouldn't know what to believe. It all happened such a long time ago.' He paused as he continued to use his small towel dexterously on the wet glasses. 'Over the years, the old ship has been pushed farther up onto the sand by the winds and the tides, and there she'll rest, no doubt. Nobody will ever know the true story of exactly what happened. That's why we call her *The Lady Mystery.*'

'That's really sad, but very interesting.' I replied. The barman turned to place the dried glasses one by one in a neat array on the shelf behind him. I stared for a long while into the last sup of beer remaining in my glass.

'Tell me', I said. 'That Moroccan captain you mentioned – might he have been a one-armed man?' The bartender turned slowly and looked at me.

'Yes, they said he had only one arm. How did you know?' I pondered for a further few moments, a further few *long* moments. I pointed to a bottle of vintage whiskey on a shelf behind the bar. 'I'll have a glass of that, please. And make it a large one!'

The Cottage

'Damn it! I can't find my wallet.' He was standing close to their few pieces of luggage, already partially packed for their return flight to Boston.

'Oh no!' exclaimed Ellen. 'So what are you going to do, Rick? You can't leave Ireland without your wallet.'

The young man thought for a moment. 'You know something, it must have fallen out when I took off my wet jacket in the cottage last night. It has to be there. So, don't worry, honey. We'll ask your uncle to swing round there when he's taking us to Shannon Airport – it's probably not too far out of our way.'

'Gee, I hope nobody steals it in the meantime,' commented Ellen as she folded away her slacks.

'Not a chance! There was nobody there except that old lady I told you about – she seemed a little strange but I'm sure she's honest enough.'

He had been out walking the previous evening, taking a last stroll on that boggy Irish hillside. The slanting rays of the sun, edging towards the Atlantic horizon, illuminated the occasional tuft of purple heather and white-headed bog cotton. He wanted to savour the tranquil scene, to enjoy the beauty of nature the Irish way. His contemplation was interrupted when the sky suddenly darkened and a squall of rain hit him. *You can't trust this Irish weather,* he thought. *The forecast said it would be a fine evening.* Having had only a light jacket, he looked to see where he could take shelter. The hillside was almost bare of trees with just a few scraggy hawthorn bushes visible, their gaunt shapes bent in reverence to the prevailing wind. *No shelter there,* he thought. A bird rose from the undergrowth in front of him with a shrill whistle and disappeared into the rain.

He trudged onwards and the rain, now attacking him horizontally, penetrated through to his skin. The way things were going, he figured, he could be returning to the United States with an unwanted Irish cold. But, in a strange way, he was enjoying the soggy desolation around him, which he found both austere and beautiful. As he plodded on, a small dolmen appeared through the blinding rain. *What a lovely touch of ancient Ireland,* he thought. *I've read about these things.* He paused, trying to convince himself that he could shelter under its large top stone. But after a few moments, he abandoned that fruitless effort and continued trudging, his flimsy canvas shoes now squelching water with each muddy step.

Then he saw it – not far from the dolmen, a small rough stone cottage with thatched roof. It looked like the type of dwelling he had seen in picture postcards of rural Ireland in bygone days. It had an abandoned look about it, but he still hoped there might be someone there. *Maybe I'll put Irish hospitality to the test,* he thought. Between two tiny windows was a half door, typical of Irish country cottages in the past. There was no reply to his polite knocks on the decaying wood. Perhaps the house was uninhabited after all. To his surprise, the door creaked open easily when he pushed on the rusty latch. He stooped to enter through the low opening and felt relieved to get out of the downpour at last.

When his eyes got used to the rather dark interior, he found himself in a small room, sparsely furnished. But before he could fully take in his surroundings, his gaze was drawn to a figure standing next to a door on the other side of the room. It was a frail looking woman, her face faintly visible beneath a long black shawl.

'Oh, excuse me,' Rick stammered. The woman stood motionless and said nothing. He smiled somewhat awkwardly but got no reaction. The rain was blowing in through a broken windowpane and the sound of the wind was almost deafening. He took off his wet jacket and threw it over his arm. The old lady didn't display the typical Irish welcome he had been led to expect, but maybe he had disturbed her. He stood uncomfortably, his clothes dripping onto the uneven stone floor, and looked around. The interior was quite dilapidated. Then, after a few moments, the rain stopped just as suddenly as it had started, and the feeble rays of the setting sun streamed through the small window. Rick looked again in the direction of the woman. In the faint reddish glow, he could make out her piercing green eyes, sunken deeply into her wrinkled face. Her cold gaze seemed to look right through him. She slowly turned and started to withdraw into a darkened room at the back, probably the only other room in the cottage.

'I'll go now,' he muttered, not knowing if the old lady was hearing him. 'Thank you for allowing me to take shelter, Ma'am.' He left, slightly perturbed, but thankful that the Irish rain had stopped at last. He quickly made his way back to the guest house as the last of the sun's rays gave way to the encroaching dusk.

'Tell me where to stop, Rick.' Ellen's Uncle Pat manoeuvred his old Ford Cortina up the winding road the following morning through the almost deserted West Clare countryside. 'Can you remember where it was?' The Atlantic mists were rolling over the barren fields and the salty wind was again getting stronger.

'The Irish scenery is awesome,' commented Ellen. 'How my grandparents would have loved to know I came back to see all of their beautiful countryside.'

'But your roads are certainly not great,' said Rick, as Uncle Pat changed to a lower gear and swung round a sharp bend. 'In the States, we'd call this a dirt track. Anyway, we're coming close now. Look – it's the small cottage on the hillside, close to the dolmen over there.' Uncle Pat slowed down and surveyed the scene.

'But I don't think you mean *that* cottage, Rick – that one's not inhabited and nobody ever goes there.'

'But I was there last evening – I know it was *that* cottage.' said Rick, a little puzzled, pointing to the small stone cottage he plainly remembered. It looked even more derelict in the daylight.

'Well, Rick, if you want, I'll stop here and you can take a look. But I think you'll find you're mistaken.'

'I know this is the cottage,' insisted Rick as he was getting out of the car. 'By the way, what do you mean when you say nobody ever goes there?'

Uncle Pat hesitated. 'Well, I'll tell you – it's said the place has certain superstitions associated with it.' Rick stopped momentarily and laughed.

'Superstitions? Well, superstitions or not, I'm going to get my wallet.' He closed the car door and started to make his way up the short rocky path towards the cottage.

'What do you mean, Uncle Pat?', enquired Helen from the rear seat.

'Well, it's a long story,' continued her uncle as he turned towards his niece. 'There was a young couple living there at the time of the Famine – that's about 170 years ago now – and the man left for America to seek a better life. His young wife, Máire Glas, waited all her life for him to return but he never did. She became a recluse. Sad to say, many years later, they found her dead in the cottage, poor soul. They think she starved herself to death, but nobody wanted to speak about it. No one lives there nowadays and nobody wants to visit it. It was my grandfather, Pat Murphy senior, who told me the story when I was just a small *garsún*.'

'That's very sad,' said Ellen. 'Poor woman! What a tragedy that famine caused. I've heard a lot about it.'

'Yes, it was indeed a terrible tragedy, Ellen.' He

paused for a moment, turning to observe Rick approaching the cottage, then added quietly: 'I really shouldn't tell you this but it's said anyone who goes in there will suffer bad health for one whole year.'

'Oh my God!' exclaimed Ellen. 'You native Irish have some weird superstitions. I'm glad Rick didn't hear that. Anyway, I don't think he'd let it worry him.' She paused to look again at the cottage. 'By the way, you said the lady's name was 'Máire Glas' – is 'Glas' a common Irish surname?'

'Oh no, Ellen. 'Glas' means 'green' in the Irish language. Your grandparents would have known the language well before they emigrated. The lady was called 'Máire Glas' by the locals because of her very green eyes – a little unusual around here.'

Meanwhile, Rick had reached the cottage door and knocked. There was no reply. As before, the door swung open easily to his push. He could see the interior a little more clearly than he had the previous evening. The overcast sky was just visible through a hole where part of the thatched roof had collapsed. The wind was blowing through the broken windows. There was an open hearth containing the remains of what once was a turf fire, the ashes scattered around by years of rain falling through the chimney. A small wooden table and chair stood close to one wall and a dresser with two broken shelves leaned precariously against another. A picture of the Sacred Heart hung sideways on the wall over the table, its glass broken and the picture itself torn in half. An open door lead to another room. There was no sign of the old woman he had seen the previous evening. In fact, he wondered now how such a dilapidated dwelling could have been inhabited.

To his relief, Rick spotted his leather wallet, lying there on the dirt covered floor, exactly where it had fallen. Its clean appearance seemed out of place in its surroundings, even a little surreal. He picked it up and turned hurriedly to leave. Forgetting the low height of the door, his head struck the top of the opening with a sharp blow. He fell backwards.

'Oh my God!' cried Ellen, who observed the incident from the car. 'I hope he's all right.'

'It's the curse!' exclaimed her uncle, as they got out and ran up to help Rick. 'it's definitely the curse.'

'What curse?' said Rick as he staggered to his feet and came out, rubbing his head. 'There's no curse. I just hit my head, that's all. I'm fine. And the good news is I found my wallet.'

Later that morning, as they got out of the car at Shannon Airport, Uncle Pat enquired about Rick's head.

'Shucks, I'm just fine.' Rick assured him. 'That little fall was nothing, nothing at all. I've often had a lot worse on the baseball pitch. Anyhow, thanks a lot. I don't know what I'd have done if you hadn't helped me out.' He shook Uncle Pat's hand warmly.

'We've had a really wonderful time in Ireland', whispered Ellen as she kissed her uncle goodbye. 'The whole trip was really awesome, something we'll always remember. Thanks so much, Uncle Pat. And, by the way, there's no such thing as that stupid curse. As you can see, Rick's just fine.'

'Yes, I'm sure you're right, Ellen,' replied her uncle. 'It's just a silly story. Anyway, Rick, I'm glad you found your wallet but I'm sorry you had to tolerate a little bit of typical West of Ireland weather yesterday. Of course, we're used to it here. Good luck to you both and safe flight home.'

Several months later, the postman smiled as he handed Uncle Pat a letter.

'It's from the United States. It's not often you hear from your relatives over there these days, is it Pat?'

The opening paragraph in Ellen's neat handwriting startled the old man:

'*Dear Uncle Pat, I know I should have written a lot sooner to thank you for all you did for us during our lovely vacation in Ireland just twelve months ago. But, unfortunately, Rick came down with an unusual illness. He started to see double when we boarded the flight for home as his eye muscles became weak. Then the weakness slowly spread to other muscles making him unable to walk or even stand up, and he's been laid up ever since. This rare and highly debilitating condition was eventually diagnosed as Myasthenia Gravis, which the doctors refer to simply as MG…*'

Uncle Pat stopped reading and slowly lowered the letter onto the table and whispered:

'MG … Máire Glas…'

The Wall

Whenever he entered a room for the first time, any room, he always looked out of the window. It was a habit, perhaps to give him a sense of orientation. And he did it on the first day of his new job, as he was ushered into the small room that was to be his office on the first floor. Through the dusty panes supported by that rusting iron frame, he could look out on a small part of the city's inner suburbs. The view was not impressive – the railroad sidings with their entanglement of tracks, mostly disused, the jumble of shabby warehouses with their corrugated roofs, and, in the distance, a tall grey wall obscuring any further view eastwards.

Leaving his small briefcase on the wooden floor, he surveyed his immediate surroundings. It was uninspiring – just a small metal desk near the single window, a metal chair facing the desk and a grey filing cabinet against one of the walls. Pasted at an angle on another wall was a bumper sticker reading 'If guns are outlawed, then only outlaws will have guns – support the NRA'. The desktop was bare apart from a black telephone. With the back of his hand, he wiped the dust away. He opened one of the drawers. In addition to a collection of pens, pencils, erasers and paperclips, there were some personal belongings, including a baseball cap and a pair of sunglasses.

'Those belonged to Steve,' Jim, his new boss, told him later. 'Steve left a little hurriedly. He didn't say why. Just toss all those things in the garbage.'

At just twenty-four years old, Chuck had that vitality of youth. And he was eager. He regarded himself as fortunate to have been appointed Shipping Clerk for a small trading company on the south-west side of Chicago. It was his first full-time job. Due a slight eyesight impediment, he had not been drafted into the army, and thereby avoided fighting in the protracted Vietnam war. The company was situated in an old but functional three-storey building in a somewhat run-down area north of I-55, a district that was not escaping the effects of the ongoing race riots. While he was not overly impressed with his new situation, he regarded it as a good start. He badly needed the money and he convinced himself that he could advance in the company – there seemed to be some scope.

His first day went well. He had met some of the other employees and was greeted with the customary 'welcome aboard'. The people seemed pleasant but his boss, a small gruff-mannered guy, had little time to brief him on the details of his work.

'It's pretty simple really – you'll learn as you go,' he said. So, Chuck enthusiastically settled into his small office and embraced his new responsibilities. He quickly found out that the work was indeed relatively simple and generally routine in nature – mostly arranging small shipments of various goods as instructed, many of them to and from overseas destinations. This entailed preparing and signing the relevant paperwork for transport companies and customs authorities, and making and receiving related phone calls. There was little supervision and he took some pleasure in organising his work himself. He soon learned what he had to do and mastered his daily tasks. In time, however, he began to find the days getting quite monotonous – the same shipments, the same destinations, the same forms, the same contacts. But he would work hard, he told himself, and get a promotion giving him more money and perhaps he could acquire a larger office upstairs. Even a bigger office with a better view would be a nice promotion in itself. But for now, he had to settle for this small bleak room with that equally bleak and uninspiring view.

Then he received that phone call. 'Hi. Am I speaking to the Shipping Clerk?' The voice was husky. Chuck assured the caller that he was the Shipping Clerk.

'So, you're new, yes? We used to deal with Steve. Did you know him?' Such queries were not uncommon from some of the company's customers who hadn't made recent contact.

'No, not personally, but I'm sure I can help you. Who am I speaking with?' There was a slight pause.

'Well, my name is Bob.'

'OK, Bob. I'm Chuck. What's your company's name? Do you have an account with us?'

'No, not really.' The caller hesitated for a moment. 'But maybe you can help. Eh, it's a little difficult to discuss on the phone, Chuck. If you meet me somewhere after work we can talk.' Chuck was suspicious. Meeting potential clients outside the office wasn't the way the company did business, and certainly not outside working hours.

'Sorry,' he replied. 'You'll have to come to the office or at least give me some more information about the nature of your business.' The caller hung up.

Chuck was a little perplexed by that call but tried to put it out of his mind by paying one of his frequent visits to the coffee machine at the end of the corridor next to the washrooms.

Chuck's work rarely provided him with an opportunity to interact socially with the few other company employees. His boss disapproved of any prolonged gatherings around the coffee area. Indeed, the short supply of the coffee-stained mugs, displaying motifs such as 'Chicago Cubs' and 'Vote for Nixon', didn't encourage lingering there. Neither did the acidic tasting coffee left percolating all day. Chuck spent most of his time in his office, which was sandwiched between two small storerooms. He distracted himself from the boredom of his work by gazing out through the window and imagining better times to come. It was his only respite. The railroad sidings, some with empty freight cars, put him in mind of travel. Where did those tracks lead to besides the city's stockyards? When he could afford it, he would take a train across the country, maybe to California and the west coast. He'd never been west of Illinois. And those warehouses, he wondered what they might contain. They were probably stocked with all sorts of goods, perhaps expensive items, the like of which he could purchase when he had the money. For a start, he'd love to carry an expensive watch on his wrist, then maybe get a sharp suit and eventually, a larger car, one of those big V8s. Yes, that would be cool – perhaps an Oldsmobile Cutlass Coupé or a Pontiac GTO Convertible or, better still, a Cadillac de Ville Convertible. That would really impress Cindy. Then in due course, having his own apartment, maybe together with Cindy, would be a dream come true. There were so many things he would like to have.

He continued to gaze through the window. As for that high grey wall in the distance, it didn't inspire him in any way. But perhaps from an office on the upper floor, he could see over it. He'd also look forward to that. Perhaps he could then see all the way to the city skyscrapers, to Chicago's Loop, Michigan Avenue, perhaps the Wrigley Building or the 'Top of the Rock', and all the expensive downtown restaurants where he'd like to bring Cindy. They could go to the Playboy Club – he had heard there was an inner room there for the more affluent guests. Yes, that would really be living. He knew she'd like that. She was pretty and was Assistant Floor Manager in Walmart's on South Ashland Avenue, just a few blocks west of I-94. That's where he'd met her. During their first few dates, he discovered she had quite expensive tastes. He couldn't cater for those just yet. But he would in time – he just had to earn money quickly. And time was passing. That old rusting window was becoming a frame through which he could imagine that exciting future. It seemed that the distant wall, defining the limit of his view, was a barrier between him and that future.

Having worked diligently for nine months in the company, he decided he should approach Jim, his boss, about the possibility of advancement. He was met with the response: 'I'm busy. Just keep doing what you're doing.' And so he did. He sat in his office and continued to do what he was supposed to do. The air conditioner inserted into the upper part of the window frame whined annoyingly during that hot Chicago summer. He tried to get used to it, but it continued to grate on his nerves. Some days later, another call came from the husky voiced man named Bob. He was pushing hard for a private meeting with Chuck. But Chuck gave him the same reply, even though his curiosity was further aroused.

Time passed. During the cold Chicago winter which followed, the large iron radiator against the wall hissed and groaned unceasingly, as it sporadically deposited droplets on the linoleum floor. But even when interior mist or exterior frost on the windowpanes obscured the outside world from his eyes, Chuck could still see that view in his mind, all the way to the wall. That wall seemed to be staring at him constantly, defying him, almost mocking him. He continued to tell himself that he was going to be successful and enjoy what life had to offer beyond that wall. But when would his dreams materialise? Cindy wouldn't wait forever.

He registered for a night course in Management Studies in a city institute. Surely that would enhance his chances of advancement. He was not a good student but he completed the course and achieved a low-grade pass certificate. Armed with this, he approached Jim again only to be told that they didn't want any more managers in the company. He had wasted his time and money. He returned to his desk, dejected. The days, weeks and months were slowly passing. His work was becoming unbearably monotonous. Indeed, despite his imaginings, even the view was becoming boring. He was folding in on himself. He decided it was time to start looking for a job in another company that would appreciate his talents. His first two applications did not result in interviews but he would keep trying.

One morning his black telephone brought a further call from Bob. 'Chuck, just to remind you we did great business with Steve. And we'd like to do the same with you. We'll really make it worth your while.' He paused. 'Meet me in the burger joint on Kedzie at six this evening – that's just two blocks north from you. I'll explain everything. There'll be no problem, pal, trust me. I'll be sitting near the door in a black sweater and a Cubs' baseball cap.' There was another pause. Chuck stayed silent. 'I'm telling you: we'll make it worth your while, Chuck,' the husky voiced Bob reassured him. 'Just be there and you'll see.' Bob hung up.

Chuck thought about that conversation for a long while that day. What was he getting himself into? Should he discuss it with difficult Jim? On the other hand, if Bob used to deal with Steve, his predecessor, then maybe it was OK. Chuck couldn't suppress his curiosity, particularly when considering Bob's final assurance. Despite his suspicions, anything that made it worthwhile for him seemed attractive. And, at least, a little distraction might alleviate the wretched boredom.

He met the man named Bob as arranged: a dark-haired man, a little older than himself with deep sunken eyes set into a sallow face. Bob was smoking incessantly. Initially, Chuck was apprehensive as he sat down at the table opposite the stranger, but Bob had a confident and reassuring manner. Chuck accepted the offer of a burger and Coke. They talked about the baseball game scheduled for the following week. The Cubs were doing well that season.

Chuck began to feel at ease. Bob then told him he had a few simple requests and assured Bill there would be no problems in complying with them. It was straightforward and nothing would go wrong. He explained what he wanted. They continued to talk for a while.

Thereafter began further frequent meetings, with specific instructions Chuck had to follow when one of his company's regular shipment of miscellaneous goods was expected to arrive into the country. Bob would alert him as to which shipment to look out for. Chuck signed the required forms, as normal. There were the meetings with Jessie, the junior customs agent at O'Hare International Airport's Cargo Section, but only at the appointed times when her superiors were taking their breaks. She'd clear the shipments after a cursory check and give Chuck a knowing smile. She had a Latino appearance and Chuck found her an attractive young girl, but Bob had instructed him not to have any conversation with her. She already knew what to do. Chuck would then separate that special package from the rest of the consignment. He never asked what it contained – he preferred not to know. Later he would pass it over to Bob, usually meeting him in the evening at one of those warehouses he could see from his office window. The meeting places changed by arrangement after each delivery. In exchange, he'd receive a bulging brown envelope.

After the first such meeting, he felt elated as he opened the envelope while sitting in his car. He knew he must be participating in something illegal, but any feelings of guilt were swept aside by the satisfaction of handling so many crisp one hundred-dollar bills and thoughts of what they might bring him. As he drove home in his noisy eighteen-year-old Ford Fairlane, thoughts of seeing Cindy's expression when he'd pick her up from her Oak Ridge apartment in a bright red Cadillac de Ville Convertible, while wearing his tailored suit and flashy Rolex, surged through his mind. But to benefit to the extent he was dreaming about, these interactions with Jessie and Bob would have to continue for some time longer. And they did. He never argued about the contents of the brown envelopes – he needed the cash, whatever the amount. He also knew Bob and his associates, whoever they were, needed him and wanted to keep him happy. He was obviously a key player in their little operation. His position in the company was valuable to them, as apparently Steve's had been in the past. It was a mutually beneficial arrangement.

Despite Chuck's occasional feelings of unease, all went smoothly. Indeed, after the first few deliveries, it started to become routine, the system working like clockwork. He was fulfilling his responsibilities for the company in arranging for the receipt of those routine shipments flown into O'Hare. As Bob had assured him, nothing could go wrong. And his little personal nest egg was mounting all the time. Meanwhile, however, his few attempts to ask Cindy out were met with excuses. Perhaps she had another boyfriend. But he convinced himself that with sufficient money, he could win her back. He could take her on a trip to California, or maybe even to Europe, and he could buy all those expensive items he knew she'd like. Of course, he would leave his boring job. He would take delight in telling that wretched boss Jim a thing or two. And he would not have to look at that dismal view anymore. For a start, however, he would enjoy the exciting life beyond the wall, that wretched grey wall. Yes, life was beginning to look good, really good. Just a few more shipments, that's all...

Yes, I remember it well. That young innocent man has grown into the man I am today, an older, wiser man; yes, a lot wiser. I wish I could have had good advice then. But would I have listened? Perhaps not. I was too busy imagining what I could do if I had money, imagining what my future might bring, trying to take some flimsy inspiration from that view from my office. Now I don't have that view anymore, that boring view. I don't have to look at those railroad sidings or those ugly warehouses and wondering what life was like beyond the wall. My view is different now, very different. But I'm still looking at that high grey wall, that damn wall. Now, of course, I view it, like my life, from a very different perspective…

The guard is taking the roll call:

'Prisoner 3138?'

I answer 'Here!'.

Jacinta

'Can I have this book, please?' Jacinta asked, picking up a notebook with a hand painted primrose on the plain white cover.

'No, Jacinta,' her mother Rita replied, 'let's wait and divide all the books after we've had a chance to look through them later.'

'But I really like that painting of a primrose', the six-year-old girl insisted. Before Rita could respond, Grandmother Lily interjected.

'Of course, you can have it, Jacinta dear. It's only an old notebook. Your Grandad used to keep it beside him whenever he wanted to reflect and to draw flowers. I'm sure there's nothing important in it. And the primrose was your Grandad's favourite flower. He always referred to it by its Irish name – *sabhaircín*. Each year, he'd watch for the first *sabhaircín* to appear shortly after Saint Bridget's Day, the first day of February.' Rita smiled. Perhaps the notebook might keep the young girl, her only child, busy for a while. Jacinta beamed and embraced the book warmly, as if it were a new teddy bear.

Rita and her sister Vera had come at their mother's request to her small cottage in the Carlow countryside to take away some of their late father's belongings.

'I want to clear the place out before I become too old,' she had said. 'I don't want you girls to have to go through all of this stuff after I've gone, so I've kept only a few small mementos for myself, like his watch and other little personal items and, of course, our old photo albums.'

Rita and Vera were faced with a formidable task. There was a vast miscellany of items, many no longer of any practical use, most from a bygone era – stacks of well-worn books, some with covers missing, tattered and yellowing newspapers in piles, rolls of ancient maps, torn lamp shades, decorative ashtrays, a small snuff box, a brass candlestick, a pipe rack, a small coffee table with a leg missing, an old radio with no knobs, a variety of artists' paint brushes, dried paint tubes and small canvas paintings... the list seemed endless.

'Your father was a great man for collecting things, all sorts of odds and ends,' Grandmother Lily said. 'I could never get him to throw anything away. He was just too sentimental.' She continued to reminisce as her daughters sorted through the items. Jacinta was listening intently. 'He was quite an artist. He'd paint all sorts of flowers, especially the *sabhaircín,* which he said was a special flower, blessed by Saint Bridget herself, he claimed. He was also quite an unusual man, you know. He developed a sixth sense – he could tell you very strange things at times, almost predicting the future. Sometimes I thought he might have a little psychic streak in him. I think his mother was a bit like that too. In fact, he claimed he would receive little messages from his late mother when looking at the *sabhaircín*, even gazing at a drawing of it. It's a very special flower, you know. The ancient Irish always maintained the *sabhaircín* possessed strange powers.' While the old lady talked about the past, Rita and Vera paid little attention, concentrating instead on what was a somewhat emotional task. Many of the items brought back childhood memories, and the girls found themselves pausing to recall family events associated with a lot of them. While they wanted to oblige their mother by removing all of the unwanted stuff, they knew that they had to cast sentimentality aside.

Eventually the cars were loaded. Standing in the November cold, Jacinta kissed her grandmother goodbye and thanked her for the notebook. 'I love the paintings, Granny,' she said.

'I'm so glad, Jacinta. And remember what I told you about your Grandad and the primrose.' Jacinta smiled and nodded. Rita and Vera promised their mother they'd come to see her again in the near future. While Vera headed for Galway, Rita set off for her home in Dublin with Jacinta in the back seat. She decided to take a different route back, in an effort to avoid the traffic. She knew the road well. Through her rear-view mirror, she observed that the little girl was engrossed in her Grandfather's notebook. She couldn't help admiring her daughter's pretty face framed by her long brown hair. She was usually top of her class at school and although she was of a quiet disposition and a little shy, she had plenty of good friends about her own age. Rita was happy that her daughter was apparently cherishing something belonging to her Grandfather. Just then, Jacinta raised her head abruptly and, looking out through the side window, said:

'Look Mummy. That's where you used to live.' They were driving past a large grey brick two-storey house amid grass covered fields a little distance up a driveway from the roadway. Rita was surprised as she had never taken her daughter on the long drive from Dublin to visit the house.

'Yes, you're right – that's where I used to live with your Grandad and Granny when I was a little girl, dear. But you weren't even born when your Grandad died and that's when we moved out of the house.' Jacinta was silent as she turned to look back at the house disappearing into the distance. Rita asked:

'Tell me, how did you know that was where I used to live?' Jacinta scrunched up her face as she thought for a moment.

'Well, I'm not sure, Mummy. But I just knew it. I think Grandad told me.' Rita was about to remind the girl once again that she had never met her Grandad but she decided not to pursue the conversation. Let the little girl believe it if she wanted to.

As Rita put Jacinta to bed that night, the young girl

pulled her Grandad's notebook into the bed with her.

'So, is it a nice book?' Rita asked. 'Did Grandad write something in it? Are there any stories in it?'

'I can't tell you, Mummy,' she replied. 'It's a secret between me and Grandad. He has put things in his book just for me.' Rita didn't persist. Whatever was in the book, let the child imagine she shared a little secret with her Grandfather. That was a pleasant thought. She kissed her daughter good night.

Later that night, Rita mentioned Jacinta's comment about her parents' old home to her husband, Tony. It had been on her mind.

'Perhaps she saw a photo of the old house,' Tony suggested. 'Remember, you had an old photo album once. Our Jacinta is a very observant little girl, you know. She looks at all sorts of things she sees lying around and she remembers everything.' Rita knew she had no photos of that house. She had to attribute Jacinta's comment to a very strange coincidence.

Some days later, as Rita was picking up Jacinta after school, the little girl said casually, 'Mummy, I think Grandad has a few more things to give you.'

'What do you mean, dear?' Rita asked. 'What sort of things? We already took everything.'

'Just some things, I don't know what.' Jacinta was silent for a moment. 'I think there's something for keeping time.'

'You mean an old clock or watch?' Rita asked, intrigued.

'No, not a clock or watch, but something else that keeps time.'

Rita was a little puzzled but disregarded the remark. Perhaps her daughter was just hoping that another visit to her Granny's house might yield more items of interest for her. However, she was taken aback when, as they arrived home, she received a phone call from her mother saying that she had discovered another box of her father's belongings in the shed. Another trip to Carlow was requested. 'There are a few things you might like, including an old metronome, which is still working. It could be useful for Jacinta's piano lessons.' A further very strange coincidence, Rita wondered.

Over the following couple of weeks, Rita's thoughts on her father were brought into focus as she sorted through more of the memorabilia of his life. It was a nostalgic exercise. She began to feel a little guilty that she had not visited his grave back in Tullow for quite a long time. She thought of bringing Jacinta along for what would have been the child's first visit but, upon reflection, she felt it might be a little too sad for her daughter at such a young age. That night when she entered Jacinta's room to tuck her into bed, she found the little girl studying her grandfather's notebook. She looked up at her mother and said:

'Mummy, I'd like to say a little prayer for Grandad at his grave.' Rita was taken aback. Had her daughter read her mind? Maybe she should take her to the grave after all.

'Yes, that's a lovely thought, dear. Maybe we'll go sometime soon then. How about next week?'

'No, Mummy, not next week,' said Jacinta, 'let's wait until the primroses on his grave are in bloom. I was looking at the primrose paintings in his book and I know that's what Grandad would want.' Rita recalled that there had been no primroses or flowers of any kind growing on her father's grave when she had visited it by herself about a year ago. Strange, she thought. She hoped Jacinta wouldn't be disappointed to find no primroses there.

'Well, we'll have to wait until Spring then, after Saint Bridget's Day,' she said. 'That's another few months away.' Inwardly she felt that might be better timing as Jacinta would be a little older then and perhaps more able to cope with what might be a somewhat sad visit. Jacinta smiled and nodded, as she quietly turned the pages of her Grandad's notebook. Then she added:

'Mummy, I know Grandad wants me to bring my little sister along when we visit him.' Rita was startled. She knew she couldn't have any more children. She had explained to Jacinta already that she shouldn't expect any little brother or sister. Obviously, this was one prediction in which she knew her daughter was definitely and sadly mistaken. She would find it a little difficult to have to tell her once again, so she decided to say nothing at that time. With a sad smile, she nodded and kissed her daughter good night.

The following day, after Rita had driven Jacinta to school, she found herself pondering on her daughter's occasional strange comments and predictions. Was she a little like her Grandfather who had some feelings about things in the future? She became curious about that little notebook that Jacinta kept referring to. She felt this was her opportunity. She entered Jacinta's bedroom and took the notebook with the primrose painting on the cover from under the little girl's pillow. She guessed Jacinta had hidden it there. Siting on the edge of the bed, she opened it, turning the pages one by one. They were filled with paintings and pencil drawings of spring flowers – daffodils, crocuses, foxgloves, and even the humble daisies, but mostly primroses with the word s*abhaircín* in her father's fine calligraphy beneath each drawing. There were certainly a lot of colourful paintings to hold the little girl's attention. Her father certainly had a fascination with primroses. But was there something else about Jacinta's attraction to that notebook, especially her interest in the primroses? Was it related to her mysterious predictions? Were her mother's comments about her father's communication with his dead mother of relevance? She returned the notebook to its hiding place as she pondered on her daughter's unexplainable predictions…

*

The snows of Winter had melted into the warmth of Spring as Saint Bridget's Day passed. The air was fresh as Nature was awakening and the earth was breathing new life. Tony and Rita gazed at the primroses raising their fresh green leaves and delicate yellow flowers above the soil of a grave in a Tullow cemetery, while Jacinta cradled her new Labrador puppy in her arms and whispered:

'Meet my new baby sister, Grandad.'

Red Lady

'Women will never be allowed to succeed in this company.'

Anna found herself almost shouting at the young Asian girl in front of her in the lobby of Lawson Shipping. She knew she appeared flushed, both with anger and from the effort of rushing to their Southampton headquarters. She suddenly felt quite embarrassed both at her inappropriate comment and at her appearance. Her red face was probably matching her crumpled red t-shirt and red slacks that she hadn't changed since leaving Trinidad the previous night. She knew she had to control herself, to quell the indignation that had been simmering within her all night long during the trans-Atlantic flight and that had now exploded into those ill-chosen words. That wasn't like her. She was normally calm and collected but the knowledge that she was being brought here to the company headquarters to be dismissed was something she couldn't accept.

She had done nothing wrong. She had acted on her professional judgement. She had every right to do so in the circumstances but it did not meet with the approval of George Lawson, the company director. He didn't like women in any position of responsibility in his company. She had witnessed examples of his overtly misogynistic behaviour before. Now in her late twenties, she was a qualified senior skipper, the only female with that qualification in the company. She was also as experienced in handling the company's superyachts as any of the male skippers, yet she was always given the least attractive assignments. Her male colleagues captained the company's boats to the more exotic locations in the Mediterranean and the Caribbean. They were privileged to bring the more affluent clients on cruises to places like St. Tropez, Elba and the Italian coast. They also skippered the superyachts to the more sought-after Caribbean destinations, like Barbados and St. Lucia. And the substantial gratuities they received from satisfied clients on those multi-day voyages added considerably to their earnings. Meanwhile she was given local one-day cruises along the English coast and occasionally to the Channel Islands, with no tips of any consequence. Even her male colleagues regarded Lawson as a bully and few of them liked him.

Anna had been disappointed once again just the previous week when assigned the task of transferring one of the company's super yachts from Gibraltar to Tortola in the British Virgin Islands. This boring trans-Atlantic crossing of several days brought with it the ever-present risk of adverse weather conditions creating an unpleasantly rough crossing. On such a transfer, she would have no passengers on board, just herself and a small crew. The vessel was required in the BVI to start the **company's winter schedule of Caribbean cruises. Anna had completed similar** transfers previously so she was familiar with what was involved and she was not looking forward to it.

She joined the vessel, a sixty-metre motor yacht named *Astrid*, in Gibraltar as arranged, and was a little surprised to find an elderly Chinese couple already on board.

'We are Mr. and Mrs. Tang,' they told her. Having introduced herself, Anna checked their passports and radioed base to enquire if they were authorised to come on this crossing. After some time, she received the reply: *'Mr. and Mrs. Tang are authorised to accompany you'*.

Anna made the usual preparations for departure, running through her check list. With the paperwork in order, she checked all safety equipment and confirmed that both standard and auxiliary fuel tanks, together with water tanks, were full for the lengthy voyage. All operational equipment had been checked by the engineer and the three other crew mcmbers had taken care of the remaining essentials. The weather forecast was reasonably good. There was a warning of a tropical storm developing in the Atlantic, but no concerns were indicated for *Astra's* planned route.

Piloting from the open flybridge, Anna eased the white hulled multi-deck vessel out of its mooring in Marina Bay in Gibraltar. The anticipated small crowd of onlookers lined the pier. Anna wondered if some might be surprised to see a young pony-tailed female at the helm – *they shouldn't be,* she thought. Superyachts always attracted attention. Having navigated through the busy shipping lanes, Anna retreated to the enclosed lower helm and set the GPS and autopilot for the port of Road Harbour in Tortola, some 3,200 nautical miles away. *Astrid* was capable of maintaining a comfortable cruising speed of around seventeen knots, which meant that the voyage should take a little over nine days. Anna divided the piloting duties into shifts involving herself and the two junior skippers. She made sure that all on board were comfortable and prepared for the lengthy passage. As the voyage progressed, Anna observed that Mr. and Mrs. Tang liked to sit in the forward saloon behind the lower helm and look out at the sea. Anna took the opportunity to chat to the pleasant couple occasionally. They were from Shanghai, had not been long in Europe and were looking forward to their first trans-Atlantic crossing. Their English was not fluent and conversation was somewhat limited. Anna always invited them to join her and members of the crew at mealtimes in the main saloon.

With the tropical storm warning in mind, Anna kept a close eye on the forecast. Over the first couple of days, the risk of encountering Irma, as the storm was now named, continued to appear minimal. With her twin diesel engines and generator humming below the aft deck, *Astra* moved effortlessly over the long Atlantic swells with a gentle motion. Despite her impressive size when in port, she was now a tiny speck in a vast and empty ocean. But by day five there was a real danger that Irma, which was intensifying rapidly into a Category 3 hurricane, might come close to their path. Later that day, it became apparent that it was heading for the vicinity of the British Virgin Islands. Anna radioed Head Office in Southampton in the hope of getting more detailed weather information. She was told that Irma should not pose a threat to her and that she should continue on her course to the BVI. *'Astrid is urgently required in BVI,'* she was informed. *'You should arrive before the hurricane gets close'.* She suspected that Larson himself had dictated that message. But by day seven, Anna felt increasingly uncomfortable with what she was gleaning from the forecast. Irma was continuing to strengthen in an area south east of her present position. In fact, it was becoming apparent that it might not be safe to proceed to the BVI. *Astrid* was already beginning to pitch and roll excessively as the craft encountered Irma's outer fringes. Incessant surges of heavy spray blocked any view forward requiring sole dependence on radar, even during daylight hours. Waves of six to eight metres surged over the bow and thundered onto the foredeck. Her anemometer was recording wind speeds between Force 6 and Gale Force 8. *Astra's* radio was alive with hurricane warnings.

Anna contacted George Lawson directly by satellite phone. 'Get *Astra* to the BVI,' he shouted. 'I need her there. Our Caribbean winter season, starting in three days' time, depends on it. We'll lose thousands if that has to be postponed.' Then in a softer voice, he continued 'If you get her there, Anna, you can have the pick of the company's cruises from now on, and a good salary increase as well, let's say 20%. I just want Astra in the BVI. I hope I've made that quite clear.' He put down the phone.

Lawson's offers were tempting. It would enhance her career path substantially. That was what she always wanted.

Anna had piloted through storms before and she knew she had the skills to do so now. She also knew that *Astra* could take the pounding, assuming the conditions did not deteriorate further. Could she outrun the hurricane? But she also knew if any system failures developed in the craft, whether mechanical, electrical or electronic, *Astra* could be left totally at Irma's mercy in an area far from any possibility of assistance. Safety must be her first priority. She knew the crew respected her and trusted her.

She made her decision. Having confirmed that she had the extra fuel needed, she altered course for Trinidad, re-setting her GPS and autopilot for Boca Grande off its north west tip. Trinidad, the southern-most island in the West Indies, lay south of the predicted hurricane path. In fact, it was known that the island rarely received any hurricanes' direct hits. She increased her speed to twenty knots, close to *Astra's* safe maximum in those deteriorating sea conditions. She informed her crew and Mr. and Mrs. Tang of her decision. She could observe that the Chinese couple were both suffering from sea sickness. But they continued to smile as they clung to any fixtures to steady themselves against the wild rocking motions. She advised them to lie in their cabin.

The highly unpleasant conditions continued. Cooking meals was impossible and even dining was a test of skill with food, utensils and cutlery and any other lose items being thrown around with the violent motions of the craft. Then, after what seemed an eternity of endurance, Anna felt a sense of accomplishment when day nine saw *Astrid* safely berthed in the yacht harbour just north of Port of Spain, Trinidad.

When Anna contacted HQ, George Lawson's texted response was terse:

'You know I wanted Astra in BVI, not in Trinidad. You have disobeyed instructions. If I could, I would fire you immediately.

Await further instructions.'

Anna was enraged. She, as skipper, had made a professional decision based on available information and in due consideration of the safety of the vessel and those on board. That decision should be respected. She felt sure that if one of her male colleagues had made the same decision, he would have been complimented, not threatened with dismissal. She had had enough of this unfair treatment. She returned to her cabin, took off her company uniform comprising a white blouse with the company emblem and black shorts, and grabbed whatever garments first came to hand – an old red t-shirt and a worn red pants. Glancing at herself in the mirror, she felt that perhaps the colour red was appropriate – it matched her mood. She was aware that changing out of her uniform while still in command of the vessel was against company policy. But she didn't care. Shortly afterwards, she received a further text message:

'Leave the ship and crew and fly back to Southampton immediately.'

All right, thought Anna, *when I get there, I'll tender my resignation before Lawson has a chance to fire me.*

She packed her bag and said goodbye to her crew and to the pleasant Chinese couple. Mr. and Mrs. Tang nodded and smiled politely, thus giving Anna some reassurance that their rough voyage hadn't been too uncomfortable. Then to her surprise, the elderly lady said

'You're a Rooster, aren't you?'

Anna stared for a moment, puzzled.

Mrs. Tank continued. 'I've been observing you. What year were you born in?' Anna told her.

The old lady nodded knowingly to her husband, saying something in Chinese. She turned to Anna. 'I knew it. Your Chinese sign is the Rooster and this is the year of the Rooster. That means your hard work will be rewarded eventually with brilliant success, my dear.' Then, pointing to

Anna's red t-shirt and pants she added 'Red is a lucky colour in Chinese. It will fan the Rooster fire within you and bring you good luck in Southampton.' Anna smiled back.

'Thank you, I hope you're right,' she replied politely. Little did they know what she would be facing the following day in Southampton. Obviously, one can't believe those Chinese superstitions.

Now here she was in the Lawson Shipping Company HQ, glaring at the petite Asian girl in a neat navy-blue blazer and knee-length skirt. Anna hadn't seen her in the company previously – she was obviously a newcomer, perhaps a secretary. Lawson was always hiring and firing his female office staff. Having heard Anna's initial outburst about women not being allowed to succeed in the company, the girl stared at her for a moment and then smiled.

'You must be Anna, the skipper who took *Astrid* to Trinidad.' *So, the news has spread quickly,* Anna thought.

'Please follow me,' the girl said and led her straight to Mr. Lawson's office. Lawson wasn't there but entering through that doorway brought back sudden unpleasant memories. In her mind, Anna could picture the odious Lawson's bulky frame sitting smugly behind that large desk with black leather top and leering at her. He could still appear any minute. But she was going to take no nonsense from him this time.

The girl gestured to Anna to sit and, to Anna's surprise, the girl seated herself on the opposite side of the desk in Mr. Lawson's large chair. 'My name is Koh Chang Heung. Thank you for coming so promptly, Anna. Now, we need to talk urgently.' Sitting upright, Anna tensed herself. Her throat was dry. But where was Lawson? Ms. Koh continued: 'First of all, I have to disagree with you, Anna. Let me tell you that women get on very well in this company, otherwise I wouldn't be the managing director.' She smiled.

'My company, Koh Ship Chartering, have acquired ownership of Lawson Shipping. Negotiations have been underway for several days. We let Mr. Lawson go just yesterday.'

Anna was trying to digest all that was being thrown at her. Could this be real? Ms. Koh continued 'I want to compliment you on your professionalism.' She gave Anna a warm smile. *Now this is someone I can work with,* thought Anna, as she found herself starting to smile back. 'You made the right decision to divert away from Tortola,' Ms Koh continued. 'All the boats in the harbour there, including two of ours, were either destroyed or severely damaged. Hurricane Irma devastated the entire harbour. Thankfully, however, no one from our company was injured.' Anna reached with a shaking hand for the glass of water resting on the small table beside her chair. She began to feel a weight lifting from her shoulders. 'The reason I called you here,' continued Ms. Koh in a pleasant and confident tone, 'is that we are taking delivery of a new mega yacht in Hong Kong next week. She's 110 metres long and will be our flagship, the largest in our fleet. I want you to be her skipper, Anna.' Ms. Koh smiled again.

Anna was speechless. Was this really happening? She found herself staring at Ms. Koh in disbelief as the girl continued:

'We'll make arrangements to have you participate in her commissioning and sea trials as soon as possible.' She raised herself, leaned across the desk and extended her hand to Anna. 'Congratulations on your new appointment, Anna. And by the way, thank you for looking after my uncle and aunt on your eventful voyage. They were very pleased with their first ever Atlantic crossing, even though I understand it was very rough at times.' Anna nodded. Words were difficult to find. She relaxed back into the chair. All she could do was to smile broadly and eventually stutter a faint

'Thank you'. She slowly got up to leave, her legs unsteady.

'And by the way,' said Ms. Koh, looking at Anna's attire, 'I see you like the colour red. I should mention that our new mega yacht will be quite spectacular – her hull is totally red. That's a lucky colour, you know, and we're naming her *Red Lady*.'

All Souls

'I need to tell you something very strange,' she began. I was visiting Aunt Lily and we had just sat down to a have a cup of afternoon tea together. That was many years ago. She lived alone in the County Carlow countryside and always seemed glad to have someone to talk to. Wearing her elegantly embroidered blouse, she was sitting on her faded cloth covered sofa in her small darkly lit sitting room. The old-fashioned China teapot with two matching cups sat on a small inlaid mahogany table beside her. Her face, slightly tinted by the flickering flames of the turf fire, bore the proud wrinkles of age but also carried a more serious expression than usual. Her plaited grey hair was curled up on top of her head. She spoke quietly in her usual precise style, taking the time to relate every detail between sips of tea. I listened in the stillness of the room as she explained that, some days previously, she had been cycling along the deserted country road towards the village church.

'It was early that morning, probably around a quarter to six,' she told me. 'I remember wrapping my new scarf more tightly around my neck – there was a clingy early morning mist. You know, I really liked that white woollen scarf. I bought it a few days previously at the market in Tullow and I thought I'd wear it to Mass that morning.'

She mentioned how she had checked herself in the hall mirror before she left the house. She wanted to look tidy. For a moment, the face looking back at her appeared to be that of her late mother. She smiled faintly as she admitted she was beginning to look old. Then, after a pause she continued.

'As I buttoned up my overcoat, I wondered if the white scarf was appropriate for that particular day – you see, it was All Souls' Day, 2nd November. Perhaps something of a subdued colour might be more suitable for a day when our thoughts should be on the souls of the dead. But I eventually convinced myself that Fr. Murphy wouldn't mind. After all, there was some white in his vestments, isn't that right? So, I made the decision – I wore the white scarf.'

Aunt Lily knew the road well, every bend, almost every stone in the undulating surface. She cycled on her old black bicycle to church every Sunday morning and also on the mornings of holy days, as decreed by the church. She was always punctual and checked her progress along the way. She knew she should be past the small crossroads when the first peals of the doleful church bell cut through the morning air for six o'clock Mass. She knew she should be close to the graveyard when the hoarse calls of the rooks in the large oak trees would reach her ears. She was just approaching the cemetery gate that morning, reflecting on the many departed relatives and friends for whom she should pray while at Mass, when it happened. Aunt Lily leaned forward in her sofa and laid her cup gently on the small table. Her gaze was steady but her voice began to tremble slightly as she continued:

'Suddenly, I was jolted back to reality by a figure who emerged from the shadows of the oak trees on my left just a few feet away. It stopped right in front of my bicycle. I gasped. I pulled hard on the brakes but it was too late. I couldn't stop in time. Then, to my amazement, I passed right through the figure without feeling anything, anything that is except a rush of very cold air. There was no sound, no feeling of hitting anything … nothing.'

Aunt Lily paused and looked to see my reaction as she slowly leaned back on her sofa. I looked back at her in amazement. She then described how she fell off her bicycle as it shuddered to a halt. Lying dazed on the ground, she turned her head to look back. There was no one there, she claimed. The road was deserted. She raised herself to her feet and looked all around.

'No one,' she reiterated, 'not a single person. It was still. Only the church bell and the rooks' cries broke the silence. I stumbled over to the ditch where I sat down, trying to recollect myself. I was dazed but thank God I wasn't injured and only slightly hurt. Now, what on earth had happened? I asked myself that question again and again. I was sure I hadn't imagined the incident, quite sure. I could picture the figure very clearly, and I can still picture her – an old woman dressed head to foot in a white garment.'

'That's very strange, Aunt Lily,' I commented. 'Really very frightening. So, what did you do then?'

'Well, I just sat at the edge of the road,' she continued. 'I leaned back and felt the rough cold cemetery wall against my coat. After a moment, the church bell stopped ringing, so I knew that Mass was about to begin. I pulled myself to my feet and, wheeling my bicycle, I walked the short distance to the church gate. I found it difficult to keep my mind on my prayers during Mass. Then, after Mass, I chatted with some of my friends, as usual. They were very sympathetic but they told me I must have been imagining the strange incident. I remember Margaret admiring my new scarf, probably trying to distract me. But I'm sure they could still detect the shock in my face. I couldn't hide it.'

I was aware that Mass in those days brought friends together who might live some distance apart in the Carlow countryside. They always found something to chat about after every Mass, before they went their different ways. And this time it was Aunt Lily's mysterious experience that held their attention. She told me that she was convinced that she hadn't imagined anything that morning – it was so real. She felt it was definitely something supernatural she had witnessed and so she thought she'd mention her strange experience to Fr. Murphy.

'He must be knowledgeable about this sort of thing,

you know,' she said. 'So, when our little conversations were over and the rest of the small congregation had dispersed, I found Fr. Murphy back at the altar, preparing for the later Mass that morning. We sat on the front pew together as he listened quietly to my story. "Well, Lily", he said when I had finished, "that's quite an unusual experience. You may indeed have seen something special. It wouldn't be the first time that the souls of the dead revisit us, and that can be for different reasons. Remember, this is All Souls' Day, a very special day devoted to the souls of those departed. You must have seen a spirit. It might perhaps be the spirit of someone who died in the past or even a spirit from the future. Time does not exist in the afterlife. Perhaps you were even being forewarned about some future event, Lily. I suggest you say a prayer for that soul." That's what he said. I left and felt some relief that he had believed me and even suggested a possible explanation. But of course, I was still a little perturbed. Indeed, to some extent I felt humbled that the spirit had chosen me to appear to. You know, I do pray a lot.' She turned her gaze momentarily to the small wall-mounted crucifix over the door.

It was a bright morning, the early mist having dissipated by the time Aunt Lily left the church. Before she rode home, she entered the graveyard, pushing aside the black iron gates, and made her way up along the soggy moss-lined pathway between the rows of oaks to her mother's grave. The rooks, like guardians of the graves, made their presence felt with occasional squawks. Were their utterances the language of the dead? She remembered the gravestones casting long shadows from the weak autumn sunlight penetrating between the oak branches. She knelt on the dew-damp soil at the foot of the grave and started to pray. But she said it was difficult to concentrate as Fr. Murphy's words were still running through her mind, particularly the possibility that the occurrence might be some sort of sign.

Could it have been her mother's spirit she had seen? She had noticed that the woman in white did bear a resemblance to her late mother, but somehow she doubted it was her mother's spirit. She was alone in the graveyard, most worshippers planning to visit their family graves after the later Mass on that holy day. She got up and left quietly.

As she mounted her bicycle close to the spot where she had encountered the figure in white, she said a further silent prayer, as Fr. Murphy had suggested. Then she tried to put the worrying incident out of her mind. She pedalled homewards, enjoying the fresh morning air caressing her face. She had almost forgotten that it was her birthday. She was sixty-nine years old. She said she rarely bought any new clothes, but the white scarf had been a birthday present to herself. With a wistful smile she mentioned that she had received no other presents. Then she looked directly at me as she said:

'Just think about this – the next time I'll be present for All Souls' Day Mass in that church, I'll be seventy years old.' She tapped her finger gently on the sofa arm to emphasise her words. She said she thanked God that, despite her age, she had the good health to be able to cycle the six miles to Mass and back every week. She knew that many women of her age would not be able to undertake that cycle ride on those rough hilly roads. Many of them were married and had children.

'I sometimes wonder,' she mused as she bent to gently stoke the fire with a long black poker, 'if perhaps I'm healthy because I'm single and childless. But, of course, my health is all in God's good hands.' I smiled. She readily accepted my offer to pour her another cup of tea.

'My hand shakes a little when I try to pour it myself,' she explained. 'It's just my age. But let me finish the story.' I sat back to listen as she continued. 'When I arrived home, I took off my new scarf and held it for a moment, admiring the fine lambs' wool stitching. It was only then that I recalled something quite startling – in addition to the long white dress, the mysterious figure was wearing a white scarf exactly like mine. Now, don't you think that's extraordinary? How can you explain that? Do you think it means something, as Fr. Murphy suggested?' She took a few sips, replaced her cup on the small table and waited quietly in expectation of my reaction.

I put down my cup. 'That's an intriguing story. It's really most amazing. I'm sorry you had such a terrible experience, Aunt Lily. You were obviously very frightened. I can't explain it. But, to be honest, I really don't believe in ghosts.'

I thanked her for the tea.

Fr. Murphy celebrated her funeral Mass. When I saw her lying in the coffin, she was dressed head to toe in a white garment and her favourite white scarf was draped around her neck and shoulders. We thought she'd have liked that. I knew she wanted to be there at Mass on that special day, All Souls' Day. I laid a single red rose from her own garden on her scarf and whispered, 'Happy Birthday, Aunt Lily.'

The Chalet

It was even better than she had hoped. The small timber chalet with slanted snow-covered roof stood alone in a corner of the woods, a short distance from the quiet laneway. Icicles hung delicately at intervals from the edge of the roof like slender lace tassels on a thick white curtain. A picturesque white blanket lay all around, glistening in the afternoon sunlight. The tiny dwelling was embraced on three sides by tall pines with snow laden branches, each guarding sentinel-like the darker snow-free clearings at their feet. A narrow pathway leading across the clearance to the front door was almost hidden. There was a pleasant stillness about the place.

Mary stood still for a moment. It was a fairy tale setting, ideal for her purpose. She had sought a retreat where she could write for a week, undisturbed by the distractions of normal life. She had left it too late to reserve a place in a writers' retreat house where some of her fellow aspiring writers had secluded themselves. She had almost abandoned her search. Then she spotted an advertisement in the newspaper offering a chalet in the Wicklow woods for rent. The idea of a remote location appealed to her.

A slim girl, now in her mid-twenties, Mary always aspired to becoming a writer. She was getting encouragement from her weekly writers' workshops and had gained satisfaction from the few short stories she had composed following her tutor's guidance. But she felt she could do better. She needed more focus. Her tutor had quoted Pulitzer Prize winning poet Mary Oliver: '*Creative work needs solitude.*' Yes, Mary needed productive solitude to feed her inner self and give her the inspiration she craved, that spark that would enlighten her. Having taken a week's vacation from her librarian job in the city, she was determined to embrace the unique opportunity. She had gathered her writing materials and packed her bag with a few old sweaters, jeans, casual shoes, nightclothes, a washbag and a brush for her long brown hair – just the essentials. She would be alone, concentrating solely on her writing. And now she was here, gazing with anticipation at the secluded chalet. This would be her little island at the edge of the world, her contemplative retreat where her inner voices might become audible. Here her mind, unfettered, could soar to heights unknown. Even the majestic pines, those living wonders with their friendly arms stretching upwards towards the heavens, seemed to be inviting her to enter into their thoughtful solitude, to be a part of their silent world, to be inspired.

At that moment, the chalet owner, Frances, arrived as arranged, a pleasant middle-aged lady with a fresh complexion, greying hair and a welcoming smile. As they stepped carefully together up the snow-covered path, Frances mentioned that the chalet had been owned by her grandmother's sister, an elderly lady she called Auntie Avril. She had been a writer and lived there from time to time, apparently enjoying the solitude the location offered. Mary was delighted to hear that.

'I'm a writer too, and it's the quietness here that appeals to me also. Did Auntie Avril publish any of her writings?' Frances was not aware of any publications. Auntie Avril had stopped writing eventually when her fingers became too arthritic.

'That's such a pity,' said Mary.

As Frances stopped and turned towards her, Mary could detect a touch of sadness in her eyes. 'Yes, it is a pity,' she said. 'Some of her writing was quite beautiful. She had a real talent. She would read her children's stories to her young nieces and nephews. She was a big lady with a big heart who never married and loved nature. She would always leave some food out for the foxes and the birds and also for the deer you sometimes see around here.'

'How nice,' said Mary, 'I admire such talent, especially the ability to write engaging children's stories. I'd love to see some of her writings.' Frances turned the key in the front door and sighed.

'I really wish now that I had some of Auntie Avril's lovely stories to remember her by. But unfortunately,' she added, 'before she left the chalet for the last time, she tore all of them up – strangely, she said she didn't want to keep any memories. She was a very shy person. I think perhaps she thought her stories were too intimate, revealing too much of herself. And even though everyone thought they were so beautiful, she insisted they were not good enough. After she passed away, I found a large pile of her writings by her bed in the chalet, with each page torn into pieces. It would have been too arduous to put them all together again. I could retrieve nothing. In fact, I couldn't even find the special silver fountain pen she'd always used for her writing. She said it gave her inspiration. Sadly, I have no keepsakes of Auntie Avril. I miss her a lot.'

'That's really such a pity,' commiserated Mary, as they knocked as much of the snow as they could from their boots and stepped inside. A soft waft of welcoming heat greeted them.

'I put the heater on for you this morning', said Frances, pointing to the small electric heater against the opposite wall. There were only very basic furnishings but, even so, it exuded an air of simple comfort. A small wooden table and chair stood by the window of the main room, a tiny kitchenette in one corner. The small adjoining room contained a single bed with patchwork quilt and a bedside table. Its simplicity delighted Mary.

'I hope you'll have a very comfortable and productive stay,' said Frances as she departed. Mary left her boots on the rubber mat inside the door as they slowly deposited their remaining snow in tiny puddles. She unpacked her bag and emptied the few provisions she had brought into the small fridge. Having had little time to eat that day, she prepared a cheese and tomato sandwich and a cup of hot chocolate which she enjoyed at the table near the small window. Then reaching for her notepad and black ball point pen, she started to think about her writing. That's what she had come here for. She was eager to get started, to find stimulation for a good story. Being too pre-occupied with her trip to the chalet, she had made no journal entries that day. She tried to remember all the guidance from her writers' workshop:

'Write from your personal experience,' Catherine, her tutor, had said. Mary turned her many thoughts over in her mind. What experiences had she had that could be translated into an interesting story? Her mind was unproductive. For what seemed like an hour, she struggled with her thoughts, but only a few scribbled phrases were appearing on the page, disjointed thoughts, nothing worthwhile, nothing that could be developed into a story. Auntie Avril, whose chalet she was inhabiting, would not have been impressed with her performance. Frustration began to grip her like a noose around her neck. With a tissue, she wiped the light film of condensation which had formed on the inside of the windowpane and gazed out. The sun was slowly disappearing behind the pine trees with their snowy tops silhouetted against the last light of the day. Snowflakes, those tiny miracles of beauty, started to descend from the darkening sky. Quietly and gently, they dusted the newly made footprints on the pathway with fresh specks of white. They became more numerous. It was as if nature were lowering a lace curtain and saying good night. Perhaps she should follow nature's lead and close her thoughts for the night. Perhaps one of the Nine Muses, rulers of the arts, would bless her with a little inspiration tomorrow.

Mary laid her notepad on the bare bedside table together with her ballpoint pen. *'Always be prepared,'* Catherine had insisted, *'inspiration can be fleeting.'* She changed her clothes, turned off the heater and, switching off the bedside light, snuggled under the cosy quilt. All was dark. She lay quietly for a while, trying to relax her mind in her new environment. Being a city girl, she was not accustomed to the intense silence which enveloped her, a stillness that seemed to be accentuated by the blanket of snow. This was nature's all-consuming silence of awareness and her mind slowly became immersed in it. She turned over and tried to sleep. Then it struck her. It was so obvious that she wondered why she had not thought of it before. The story was right here, all around her, as if pleading to be told. She herself was the principal character, coming to this secluded chalet in the Wicklow woods surrounded by nature. Frances's Auntie Avril, the writer, had lived alone here seeking seclusion. Could this in itself be an intriguing subject for a story? Mary sat up in bed, turned on the bedside light, took her pen and, placing her notepad on her lap, started to write:

'It was even better than Mary had imagined. The small timber chalet with slanted snow-covered roof stood alone in a corner of the woods, a short distance from the quiet laneway. Icicles hung delicately at intervals from the edge of the roof like slender lace tassels on a thick white curtain. A picturesque white blanket lay all around, glistening in the afternoon sunlight. It was almost mystical....'

The pen was slipping from between her fingers as tiredness overcame her. She left the notepad carefully on the bedside table with her ballpoint pen on top, turned off the light and snuggled back under the quilt. As she tried to sleep, she had to admit that she was not pleased with her effort. She felt that if Auntie Avril were here, she would not have approved of what she had written.

She was not long under the quilt before there was a

sound. It came from the window beside her bed. She stiffened and turned her head. After a few moments, she could see in the moonlight a lump of dislodged snow falling from somewhere above the window outside and landing on the windowsill. Perhaps that's what she had heard. She lay down and tried to relax. Then there was a brief creaking sound from somewhere within the room. She thought for a moment. It must be the warm timbers contracting on contact with the cold snow. She heard the sound again, almost like footsteps on the floorboards. She convinced herself that it was probably stupid to be concerned about these strange sounds. Surely, they could all be explained with a little thought and investigation. Or could they? As her mind drifted towards sleep, she began to wonder if she could feel the presence of the old lady, Auntie Avril, in the chalet. Or was it just her imagination? She had heard of instances where spirits came to dwell in houses they had once inhabited, but she hadn't really believed in those stories. There was no need to be concerned. She drifted off to sleep.

It was still dark when Mary jumped up in bed. Another sound had disturbed her, this time from beside her bed. It was like paper being torn. In her mind, she could see the top page of her notepad lying torn into little pieces on the chalet floor. She switched on the light. She looked on the floor. Nothing there. She slowly realised it was a dream, a very vivid and disturbing one. Her gaze turned to the bedside table. Of course, her notepad was still there on the table with its top page intact, just as she had left it, with her black pen lying on top. She breathed a sigh of relief. *Dreams can seem so real,* she thought, gently rubbing the sleep from her eyes. It was obviously thoughts of Auntie Avril that induced the dream. *In fact,* she thought, *I wonder if the old lady put that dream into my head. After all, she tore up all her own stories. Was she trying to tell me something?* She lay back in bed. It had been such a realistic dream that it took her a few minutes to relax. Was it just her imagination or was she again feeling the presence of the old lady in the chalet? The dream had unnerved her. She couldn't close her eyes. After what seemed hours, the first rays of the sun appeared through the curtains. She got up, dressed and embraced another day with hope.

Mary reviewed the notes she had made. It was a start to a story, but a poor one with little to make it attractive. She continued to scribble. She preferred to write by hand, as her thoughts flowed more naturally without the distractions of a keyboard. Conveying any worthwhile text to her laptop could be accomplished later. By evening, with persistence, she had completed a rough draft of a piece about the old lady living alone in the secluded chalet and writing stories for her grandchildren. But Mary was not satisfied. Her story was not inspiring. It definitely lacked something. It was an attempt that Catherine would surely have torn to shreds, figuratively if not literally. She went to bed that night as a further feeling of frustration overcame her.

It was snowing gently again. She was getting used to the silence. It was that intermediate space between yesterday and tomorrow, the perfect time to let her mind drift and float and then settle softly, like a falling snowflake, into a place of rest. Sleep eventually enveloped her. Then a sound. Something was touching the timber wall. Was it inside or outside? She wasn't sure. Did it come from somewhere near her bed? Her muscles tensed. She strained her ears. She raised her head slowly but couldn't see anything moving in the room. Nothing. She tried to relax. She must have fallen asleep when that dream engulfed her once again – hearing the sound of tearing paper and then seeing her page torn into pieces on the floor. She raised herself and looked, finding difficult to convince herself that it was just a dream. Of course, her pad was still intact on the bedside locker. She again wondered if the dream was inspired by Auntie Avril. She became convinced that the old lady was trying to tell her something. *If so,* she thought, *then please, Auntie Avril, inspire me with the ingredients for a really good story. Give me that spark I need.*

Disturbed by the recurring dreams, she got up early. It was still dark. There were more faint sounds. This time it was from outside the chalet. She tiptoed to the bedroom window. The snow had stopped falling. A half-moon, peeping through a clearance in the clouds, was casting her magical light on a scene worthy of a Christmas card. Then she saw it. A fox was making its way across the clearing, its thick brown fur dotted with sprinkles of snow. It stopped and looked in her direction, one paw slightly raised, its ears erect, probably aware of the movement inside the glass. For a brief moment, Mary saw beauty in those beady eyes. Then it disappeared quickly, leaving only paw prints in the snow now lying thick on the ground. The fox might have made that sound, she thought. She now had a magical experience that she could surely incorporate into her story. She took her pen and notepad and started to write. She didn't finish her story. She remembered another piece of advice from Catherine: *'Always stop writing before the end: that way, you have something to write the next day'.* She put her pen down, contented that she could finesse the sequence later that morning. But she was still not happy with the quality of what she had written. The inclusion of the fox did not mesh smoothly with the rest of the story – it emerged from the pages like an afterthought.

Morning came and Mary's thoughts were still on her writing. It was now her third day in the chalet and she had not succeeded in writing anything worthwhile. How could she incorporate the fox episode appropriately into her story? She thought of Auntie Avril writing children's stories and how she loved animals. What story might the old lady have written? Perhaps, like Auntie Avril, she could write a children's story. It was late afternoon when she sat down at the table with her head in her hands. The fox was still on her mind. If she had been about twenty years younger, she would have loved to read a story about a friendly fox. Then she decided – the fox would become the central part of her story, not an afterthought. It would be a children's story about Mary, a lonely little girl of five years old, living with her Auntie Avril in the chalet, and befriending a fox that she saw in the snow one night. They roamed the woods together and the fox introduced Mary to all his animal friends. They had many exciting adventures and the child was back in her snug bed before the morning. The happy story flowed magically from Mary's pen from beginning to end. She felt sure that it would help children appreciate the abundant beauties of nature that she was experiencing and was now committing to paper as part of her story. By midday, she had completed a children's story that she felt proud of. Did Auntie Avril answer her plea and send that fox to give her the inspiration she so badly needed? A stupid thought, perhaps. But the fox *did* provide a welcome idea, that spark, and at last she had a story.

Satisfied with her achievement, she rested on the bed. Tiny droplets of melting snow fell like magic beads outside her window, illuminated by the evening light. Once again, she thought she heard a faint sound. It was definitely within the room. She couldn't describe it but it was certainly not the sound of pages being torn. She was too tired to look. Indeed, she was no longer surprised to hear sounds and she again convinced herself that they could all be explained rationally. There was no spirit.

She must have fallen asleep briefly. When she awoke, she thought again of her children's story. She was sure that Auntie Avril would have been satisfied with it now.

Whispering aloud she said, 'Thank you Auntie Avril for giving me the idea for a good story.' She suddenly felt embarrassed for whispering to a spirit that didn't exist. How easy it is for such superstitious thoughts to confuse the mind during the unreal world of sleep, *'the death of each day's life'*, as Shakespeare had called it. But now, the reality of full consciousness had enveloped her. Stretching her arms, she yawned and stepped to the window. Through the misty panes she was in time to see an icicle slipping from its perch somewhere on the roof's edge and falling into the snow below. The pine branches were shedding some of their dressings of snow, their dark green foliage reappearing like patchwork through the white. In the evening light, the scene was changing its appearance as a thaw was setting in, but it was still magical – a serene setting of sylvan seclusion. A lone hawk lingered on its outstretched wings high overhead, silhouetted against the still-bright sky. As she turned, something drew her attention to the bedside table. *That's very strange,* she thought. There beside her notepad lay a silver fountain pen.

Arabian Fire

'That's strange tasting coffee. Where did you get this?' Bill's taste buds were struggling to come to terms with the beverage Niamh had prepared for him. He had removed his suit jacket after his day at the office and had sat down at the table in their small kitchen, which was illuminated by a single ceiling light. Niamh was taking off her high-heeled shoes to relax for the evening.

'Well, it's a new brand called *'Arabian Fire'*. It was on special promotion, so I thought we'd try it. Do you not like it? Perhaps a little sugar would help?'

'No, I don't think anything you add would change that taste.' He took another sip from his favourite mug with a *'Best Husband'* motif inscribed on it. 'To be honest, it reminds me of Horrid Harold – sharp and bitter! And I've come to the conclusion that nothing will change him either.'

'That doesn't speak well for the coffee,' Niamh quipped, knowing Bill's boss's reputation. She sat down beside him. 'Did he give you trouble again today?' Bill hesitated as he turned and looked into his wife's brown eyes.

'Well, I shouldn't have mentioned his name, I suppose, as I wasn't going to tell you, but the truth is he did. You see, those clients who were going to finalize the purchase of the house on Carysfort Avenue today told me they wanted to hold off for another week. When I told Harold, he went berserk. "It's your bloody fault, Bill," he shouted. "It's all your fault. You're not pushy enough. When you have a fish on the hook, don't just play around with it. Reel it in! God! You're so stupid!" That's what he said. Of course, as you know well, it wasn't the first time that loud mouthed eejit upset me. Anyway, I told him straight out that I had no control over my clients' wishes and I also told him to stop shouting at me. I'm sure Rachel outside in the main office was hearing everything, not that it mattered much as I know she also can't stand Harold. In fact, she already told me he has upset so many clients with his ugly manner. Nobody likes him, not even our clients. I'm telling you, he's such a brute.'

'That's absolutely terrible behaviour,' Niamh said. 'What did Harold say after you said that to him?'

'Well, as I expected, he reminded me that he was the boss and told me to get out of his office. And he was still shouting.'

'That's dreadful. Poor you, Bill,' Niamh said sympathetically, as she put her hand on his arm. 'Just relax and try to forget about it. You shouldn't be under such pressure at work. It's not good for you. Thank God my part-time job isn't as stressful.' She tied her long brown hair into a ponytail. 'Oh, by the way, this came for you.' She reached over to the table and handed a letter to Bill. 'I saw it's marked *'Private and Confidential'.*'

'Letters like that are rarely good news' muttered Bill as he tore open the envelope. His frown slowly deepened as he read the contents.

'What's the matter?' asked Niamh eventually. 'Is it really bad news? Why can't you tell me?' Bill laid the letter down on the table beside his half empty coffee cup. He was silent for a moment as Niamh waited for a response.

'It's like this.' said Bill eventually. 'It's the bank again. We're overdrawn, Niamh. I mean badly.'

'God, I was afraid you'd say something like that. I don't want to hear any more bad news, Bill. Anyway, that happened before, didn't it? Remember, we cut down on all the spending we could.'

'I know, but this time it's serious, very serious, Niamh. We just can't make ends meet.'

'My God, that's terrible. Are you sure? Maybe we should cancel that week in Italy next summer?' sighed

Niamh. Bill nodded slowly.

'Yes, I'm afraid so.'

Niamh rose to take a ready-made meal out of the fridge. 'Maybe I'll see if I can get a better paying job myself. But that's not easy, you know. I didn't think married life would be like this.' Her eyes were welling up.

'Look, it's not my fault, Niamh. Don't start blaming me.' The newly married couple sat in silence for a while.

As Junior Sales Manager in his late twenties, Bill was on a small fixed salary, most of his income coming from the sale of properties for the real estate company which employed him. Niamh's earnings from her library assistant job didn't amount to much. Bill was staring blankly at the letter on the table. He hesitated to tell Niamh how bad the real estate market really was with house sales plummeting.

'It's really bad,' he eventually blurted out. 'Bad all around. And, incredibly, Horrible Harold is preparing to renovate his own office. He's probably going to spend a lot of money on that. He says it's necessary to impress clients. The problem is he's the one who turns clients off. I don't know how head office can approve such expenditure at this difficult time. I'm sure he hasn't told them the cost yet.'

Niamh nodded. After a light meal, the young couple sat together in gloomy silence for the rest of that evening as Bill prodded the TV remote control repeatedly, vainly trying to concentrate on anything they could find on the screen.

Niamh was always first home from work. The following evening, she watched as Bill arrived. He ignored her, flung his brief case onto the sitting room floor and threw himself down on the couch, staring into the blank TV screen. It was not the time to ask him anything. Instead she waited. After a while, Bill started to talk.

'The couple who said they were going to buy that house on Carysfort Avenue phoned to tell me they had decided on another house. So that's that. I was depending on that sale to allow us to deposit some money into our account. That's the only house left in my portfolio now. Harold, that horrible bully, keeps all the other properties to sell himself as he doesn't want to pay me any commission. I think he's hoping I'll leave.'

'Oh my God, that's terrible!' responded Niamh as she lowered herself gently onto the couch beside him. 'So, what the hell are we going to do now? You must have some ideas.'

There was silence for a while before Bill spoke again.

'Well, there's a good possibility that somebody else will be interested in that house. It's still advertised. In fact, I checked on it on my way home just now to make sure it is still presentable for inspection. It's looking good, so I'm still hopeful, Niamh. Let's keep our fingers crossed.' Then, with his foot, Bill dragged his bulky briefcase towards him along the floor.

'Oh, by the way, as I was checking around the house, I found this tucked into a corner under the stairs,' he said, taking a brown paper package from his case. 'The electricity was switched off so I brought it home to examine it in the light.' He turned the large heavy package over in his hand. 'It's not addressed to anyone – nothing written on it. The previous owners must have forgotten it. I might contact them sometime. It's probably not important anyway.' He threw the package up onto the table whereupon it tore at one end and a small quantity of white powder spilled out.

'What's that?' asked Niamh. With a sigh, Bill rose from his sofa to look. A slight distinctive odour was discernible.

'It might be weed killer. Or something for plastering. I hope it isn't one of those drug things'

'Gosh, maybe it's something illegal,' ventured Niamh as she followed him to the table. 'It's made a mess on the clean table. God, what should we do with it?'

'I doubt it's anything bad. But the truth is I really don't know,' responded Bill, rubbing his finger back and forth through the fine powder. 'Actually, it could be one of those so-called Class A drugs, but I wouldn't know what type.'

'God, don't say that! If it really is something illegal,' said Niamh, 'you should take it to the Garda station.' Bill sniffed at the powder and fingered it again.

'Well, I'd hesitate to do that. I mean, we really don't know what it is. I'd make a right eejit of myself if it happened to be something totally innocuous. And if it isn't, the Guards will ask a lot of questions and I don't want to get the sellers of that house into any sort of unnecessary trouble. They certainly wouldn't thank me for that and could probably take the sale of the house away from me. I wouldn't want that.' He thought for a moment. 'I know, I'll show it to Stewart next door when he returns from his holidays at the end of the week. Remember, his brother is in the Garda Drug Squad and he'd be familiar with anything illegal. In the meantime, let's disturb the package as little as possible. I'll tape it up and leave it back in the Carysfort house tomorrow exactly where I found it, just in case the present owners come back to collect it. At least it'll be out of our house and it can stay there until I discuss it with Stewart.' With a teaspoon, Bill inserted as much as he could of the spilled powder back through the tear in the package. The remainder he scooped up and placed on a saucer. 'That should be enough for Stewart to look at. Now, let's stop worrying about it.' Niamh could detect his reassurance was not genuine as she observed him re-examining the powder in the saucer repeatedly that evening.

Niamh didn't sleep that night. Their dire financial situation was haunting her. How were they going to manage? It was becoming a nightmare. She hated to think her husband was experiencing such an unpleasant working environment.

Also, while she knew the nature of the white powder should be of little concern to her, the thoughts of having a sizeable quantity of something that could possibly be illegal in the house continued to bother her. With some difficulty, she made it through the next day at work. After she arrived home, she waited anxiously for the hall door to open. Her heart jumped when the door eventually burst open suddenly.

'He's coming here to talk to me,' shouted Bill, as he tossed his coat aside and wiped the beads of perspiration from his forehead. 'He tried to talk with me today, that Horrible Harold, but it was too chaotic with all the noise from the renovation in his office, and Rachel was with a potential client in the general office. So, he said he'd call round here to have a serious talk in private with me. I really don't know what to expect but he seemed to be in a really foul mood. I'm not looking forward to it.'

'God, why come here?' Niamh responded. 'This is our home. How dare he?'

But there was no time for discussion. There was a loud persistent knock on the door. Niamh looked at Bill, hesitated, then opened the door. Harold's bulky frame filled the doorway. He offered a curt hello to Niamh. While she had met him only once before, she could detect instantly why her husband always referred to him as 'Horrible Harold'. There was little attractive in his sloppy appearance with stained unbuttoned overcoat and creased shirt. As he shuffled into the living room, his brusque manner and body odour caused her to feel revulsion towards him. Her home had been violated without adequate warning. Most inappropriate. Bill was right – he was definitely horrible, she decided, even revolting.

Niamh politely retreated to the next room but couldn't resist listening at the door. There were muffled voices at first, then some shouting. Niamh's heart raced. She felt like intruding to support her harassed husband but she knew it was not in her place to do so. Eventually she opened the door slightly to peep and to better hear the conversation.

'As I said, you're totally incompetent, Bill.' It was Harold's loud rasping voice. 'You let all your sales slip away. Total lack of any salesmanship whatsoever. No vigour. No drive.' Bill's constant attempts at self-defence were drowned in even louder shouting. 'No capacity to grip a sale and follow it through. No ability to convince the buyer that he should buy. No semblance of persuasiveness. You're just an idiot!' The insults continued unabated while Niamh clenched her fists in anger.

'Now listen to me, Bill, the bottom line is I'm now taking over the sale of the Carysfort house myself. You've shown yourself to be totally incapable of handling it. Just give me the keys right now.' Harold held out his hand. 'I'll have it sold in no time.' Bill fell silent. Niamh sensed that any further argument on his part would have been fruitless. She could see him taking the keys from his work bag and stoically handing them to Harold. 'In fact,' added Harold dangling the keys defiantly in his hand, 'I suggest you should start clearing out your office tomorrow morning, Bill. I've had just about enough of your incompetence. We'll discuss your situation in the morning.' Bill stood motionless and said nothing but Niamh could sense the anger building inside him.

'OK, I'll get out of here now,' said Harold, glancing at his expensive looking watch. 'I've had nothing to eat since breakfast and I need to see a client.' He pushed back his chair noisily and rose to his feet.

'Would you like a cup of coffee before you go?' asked Bill, much to Niamh's surprise, his voice still trembling in suppressed rage. Harold hesitated.

'Well, it's about time that you asked,' grunted Harold. 'That's indicative of the way you mistreat clients. Yes, a quick cup to keep me going. Black, one sugar. When business calls, one must keep going. That's the only way to succeed. You'll never learn that.' There was an uneasy silence while Niamh could hear the kettle coming to a boil and the coffee being prepared and handed over. 'God, that's sharp-tasting coffee!' growled Harold. 'Disgusting, in fact. Have you nothing better?'

'That's a very special brand called *'Arabian Fire'*. It's expensive and very exclusive. True coffee connoisseurs really appreciate it,' retorted Bill truculently. 'Would you like more sugar in it?'

'No thanks. No time,' replied Harold. 'Actually, now that I get the real taste, I can appreciate it better. Yes, really exclusive, I'd say. Quite tasty, in fact.' Niamh felt sick at Harold's feeble attempt to portray himself as a coffee connoisseur. She was sure he was a connoisseur of nothing. Then, as Harold gulped down the last sup, Bill received the only compliment he had ever got from his objectionable boss: 'Useless and all as you are, Bill, at least you have good taste in coffee.' Harold put down the empty cup. 'See you in the morning, bright and early. I'll let myself out.' The hall door closed roughly behind him.

They heard it on the news the next day. A man had died in a single car accident late the night before. There was no one else in the car. Later came the news that an autopsy showed a high level of a Class A drug in the driver's blood and a packet of the drug was located in a house in Carysfort Avenue, the keys for which were found on the deceased.

A few days later, Bill arrived home smiling wryly.

'Don't cancel that holiday in Italy,' he announced proudly. 'The UK director has appointed me manager of the Dublin branch to replace Harold.' Niamh's heart jumped.

'Fantastic!' she screamed, as she embraced her husband and gave him a big congratulatory kiss.

'And, incidentally,' Bill added smugly, 'the job carries

a very substantial salary increase.'

Later that same evening, Niamh found herself staring thoughtfully into a glass of red wine as they relaxed together on the couch before a glowing fire.

'By the way', she asked, 'what eventually happened to the rest of the white stuff you took from that package, Bill?'

'Oh that?' He hesitated for a moment as he gently swirled the wine in his glass. 'Well, I disposed of it appropriately.' Niamh looked at him for a moment, then turned her gaze back to the wine, as it transformed the flickering flames of the fire into an array of magical colours in her glass. They never talked about it again.

My Window

My chair creaks as I turn to look out through my window. My small room offers very little else to interest me. I'm tired of looking at the patterned wallpaper all around and the darkly coloured painting of some bleak landscape. But framed in my window I can see the sea – a panoramic view the blue Mediterranean. It's always there to greet my gaze as I look down over the tops of the yellow speckled mimosas. That wide majestic expanse of water is framed by lush green headlands dotted with Provence-style russet roofed villas. I can see the islands in the distance, shimmering in the heat haze. There is something mystical about that horizon, like the horizon of my life. It's the border between me and another world lying somewhere beyond.

There's my boat waiting for me as she rides peacefully in the bay, swinging gently on her mooring buoy as she responds to the light summer breeze. She's tethered, like me, and yearning to explore again that vast expanse of water and to sail far beyond that horizon. I have such fond memories. The bright sun is reflecting off her polished hull. There are a couple of other boats, both sailing and motor, riding at anchor, keeping her company. I can sense the happy sounds outside – the waves caressing the shore, the birds serenading the mimosas, perhaps some children's laughter…. But inside my room there's silence, except for the ticking of the white-faced clock on the wall, watching me stoically, as its hands move ever so slowly through the minutes, through the hours.

I hear a floorboard creaking outside my door, followed by a quiet knock. My daughter, Ruth, and my four-year-old granddaughter, Mary, come in. I greet their smiles with a hug and a kiss. This refreshing contact with the outside world brightens my day. Their visits always impart renewed interest to my life. They take off their coats and drape them across the bed. Ruth always looks well for a working mother in her thirties. She keeps herself trim. She's in her usual knitted green sweater and blue jeans. Her hint of perfume brings a freshness to the room. She sits on the only other chair. Mary does a little twirl to show me her new pink and yellow dress, her two blonde pigtails swinging outwards as she turns. I tell her the dress is very pretty. She responds with a loving smile that warms my heart. She sits on the edge of the bed. Ruth has brought me a magazine. Mary presents me with a painting she has done of a giraffe. I tell her I like the colours and I place it upright on my bedside table. We talk for a while. They tell me how the rest of the family are and what they're doing. I like to hear the news. I'm glad everyone is well.

After a while, I turn my gaze back to my window. 'Look,' I tell them. 'Look at the ferry on its way to Corsica. Do you remember when we took my boat to Corsica and beyond?' They listen in silence as I continue. 'You were all sunbathing on the aft seat. I was at the helm, in control as we crossed the vast ocean. Remember taking pictures of the pod of dolphins, five or six of them, rising repeatedly, up and down in unison across our wake? Such happy memories, aren't they? And we're going to do it all again.' The room is quiet. I turn my eyes back to Ruth. I wonder why she looks a little sad. 'Are you alright', I ask.

'Of course,' she answers, gently placing her hand on my arm. 'I'm fine, Dad.'

I continue to look through the window. The ferry is crossing between the islands and the mainland. It takes this more sheltered route when high winds are expected. The sea is already becoming a little rough.

'Do you see the white horses?' I ask Mary.

'I can't see any horses,' Mary responds, giggling softly. I tell her that's the term for the white crests that appear on the wave tips when the wind becomes stronger. 'Here in France they're called '*les moutons*', meaning 'the sheep'.' Mary smiles. 'That's funny! But I don't see any sheep either.' We all laugh. Then after a pause, she adds:

'Grandad, when I look through *my* bedroom window, I can see a unicorn.'

'Really?' I reply.

'Yes, she's all white with a pearly horn and a silver mane and a long fluffy tail. I see her every morning when I wake up and I wave her goodbye before I go to school.' I tell her that's so nice.

'Say "Hi" to the unicorn for me.' Ruth smiles at her daughter.

Seeing that the wind is increasing, I ask Ruth if the inflatable dinghy is secure where I tied it down on the beach. I came ashore in it from my boat. She assures me it is and tells me not to worry about it. That's good.

'Can you open the window a little?' I ask. 'I just want to get that fresh salty smell of the sea again?'

'No,' Ruth tells me firmly, 'you'd only catch a cold.' I don't know why she always says that.

We chat for a while about other things. Eventually Ruth says:

'You must be tired, Dad.' They stand up and take their coats. I tell them there's no need to hurry. Mary shows me her new pink gloves.

'Mum bought them for me yesterday', she says as she proudly pulls them over her tiny fingers. Ruth looks at her watch.

'I think we just might catch the 6.10 DART back to Dalkey.' I kiss them both goodbye. 'Keep yourself warm, Dad. It's cold outside.' I watch the door closing behind them. I hear the floorboard creaking under their feet, then stillness.

*

I'm on my own again now in the solitude of the small room. I continue to gaze at the plain wooden door with its brass knob, that barrier between the world outside and my tiny world in here. My dark grey overcoat is hanging limply on the single coat hook, waiting. Within its folds are memories of better days but also promises of good days to come, days to be lived, days to be hoped for. A noise just outside my window attracts my attention and I turn in my chair. It's the maintenance man, dressed in his thick grey overalls, taking some tools from the wooden shed in the small yard adjoining my window. The red coloured shed blends perfectly with the tall red brick walls encompassing the yard. The small patch of concrete hasn't completely lost its white covering of frost from the previous night. The sunlight never reaches over the high walls and rarely enters my room. The patch of sky within my sight is gradually darkening now as another day slowly comes to an end. The room is dim, colourless.

The nurse opens the door. 'It's time for your night medicine.' She's a pleasant lady, small in stature and always attentive. She switches on the light and deftly draws the patterned curtains closed. The daylight is gone. I'm tired. Soon I'll settle down for the night, another night. There is silence again except for the soft relentless ticking of the white-faced clock. Maybe tomorrow I'll watch the blue Mediterranean once more through my window.

Charity

'A worthless sod! So that's what she called me?'

'Well, yes, but I wasn't sure if I should tell you as I think she really didn't mean it, Bob. Aunt Gertrude probably liked you beneath it all.'

'That's not true, Lisa. The old bitch hated me. You know that. She was always nagging me about not getting what she called a "proper job". She was at me about it any time we'd see her. As if it was any of her business.'

'Well, she was right, Bob. I wish you'd get a proper job too,' snapped Lisa.

'Now, don't *you* start that, Lisa.' Bob was raising his voice. 'I'll do whatever work I like. The unemployment benefits are doing me just fine for the moment.' The couple opened the door to the small apartment as Bob continued: 'Anyway, what about all your aunt's money? She must have got a lot from the sale of her big house. Maybe a couple of million. This little apartment didn't cost much to rent. I'm sure she has a lot stashed away somewhere. That's all we're interested in right now. Remember, John already checked out the place. He said there's nothing of value here and he'd know. So, it's just the money we're looking for.' They stood in the centre of the small sparsely furnished sitting room, wincing as they tolerated the musty odour and the faint smell of artists' paint. Lisa looked around and asked sceptically:

'Bob, how do you know that John knows the value of anything? He's probably just saying that to give you the impression he's an expert at something.'

'Of course he knows values, Lisa. He was a driver for some auctioneer for a few weeks last year, so he'd know the value of things – furniture, paintings, everything. He knows a lot more than you or me anyway.' Bob walked over to a pile of miscellaneous items in the corner. 'Just look at all these messy paints and bits of canvas and scraps of paper everywhere – all rubbish,' he continued. 'And this broken easel…'

'Well, you know, before Aunt Gertrude became ill, she used to paint a lot. She was an amateur artist.'

'Very amateur, if you ask me.' He tossed aside a pile of paintings, many canvasses displaying partially finished paintings, and many completed paintings in frames. There were also a couple hanging on the wall. 'Flowers! How many times can you paint flowers? Flowers in a vase, flowers in a garden, flowers on a lake shore – all stupid rubbish. Who wants paintings of flowers?' He threw some small brushes, tubes of artists' paint and a few paint-stained rags on the pile. 'What did she say when you visited her before she died.'

'Bob, she just said she was going to make a will and leave everything to charity. She was certain about that. I tried to discuss it gently with her but there was no point. She always got her way. She looked at me with her usual determined stare. Even as I was leaving her, she repeated it in her stern voice: "My money will go to charity. You wait and see."'

'In that case, we're just lucky she didn't get around to making a will stating that, Lisa. You're her only living relative and by right everything should go to you. That's what the lawyer said. And by the way, let me tell you something – when we find her money, not a cent of it is going to charity.'

'But Bob, maybe just some of it. After all, I know that was my aunt's dying wish.'

'No, not a cent, Lisa. For once, the old bitch is not going to get her way. But let's find the money first. It's not in her bank and Raymond, her solicitor, says he's not aware of her giving any of it away. Anyway, who else would she have given it to? She didn't like anyone, no one, except perhaps you, Lisa.'

'Well, maybe. It's such a pity the bank can't locate all

her old account statements – they might have revealed where the money went. She spent a lot of time in France since she sold her big house. She could have spent the money over there in so many different ways.'

'Maybe. But let's have another good look around – it could be hidden somewhere. I bet it's in cash. You know the way old people hide bundles of bank notes in all sorts of secret places.'

Lisa joined Bob in sorting through every item in the room, throwing everything on the floor. They furtively pulled what seemed like hundreds of books from the bookshelf. 'Nothing hidden here,' murmured Bob.

'She was an avid reader too,' commented Lisa. 'Painting and reading were her only hobbies.' The contents of the dresser drawers and kitchenette cupboards were emptied.

'No money here. All rubbish!' Bob sighed eventually. 'I've arranged with Des to take everything away before the landlord comes. He says he'll dump it for us.'

'Who's Des? You never told me about him?'

'Des is a guy I met in the bookies the other day. He says he can borrow a pickup truck.'

'You mean he's not from a proper disposal company? How do you know Des will dump the stuff responsibly, Bob?'

'Of course he will. He said he knows a good dumping place up the Wicklow Mountains. No worries.'

'What? That doesn't sound like a legal dump to me.'

'Of course it's legal. Des said it was all legal. He's done it before, several times. Does it really matter?'

'But Bob…'

'Lisa, just remember I'm arranging all of this out of the goodness of my heart. So stop asking stupid questions. Anyway, Des will do it real cheap, he told me. The County Council dump is far too expensive. And to be honest, I really don't care where he dumps it. I just want to get rid of all your stupid Aunt Gertrude's stuff.' He paused and scowled. 'She called me a worthless sod. Imagine! I'm telling you, if we find anything, no stupid charity will get their hands on it.' Lisa remained silent as the young couple continued to search the small apartment, adding items to the pile on the centre of the floor.

Wiping his brow, Bob said: 'Are you sure Aunt Gertrude said nothing else to you?'

'Well, before she became cranky and decided on the charity thing, I asked her if she had anything to tell me, and she did say something a little strange. She said: '*Almost nothing need be said when you have eyes*'. She said it's a quote by some writer she liked, somebody called Vesaas, I think. Aunt Gertrude loved to quote famous writers. Anyway, I'm not sure what she meant by that. I think perhaps her mind was rambling a little.'

'That means nothing. If you ask me, Vesaas, or whatever his name was, must have been a right eejit. I have eyes and I still can't see her money or anything of any value here. Let's look again in her bedroom.' They entered the small bedroom with its dark wood furnishings. They emptied the chest of drawers and the wardrobe, throwing bundles of old clothes on the floor. They searched the bedside locker, then pulled the mattress up to check underneath. 'That's where old people hide money,' said Bob. 'But no money there. Nothing.'

'Well,' said Lisa eventually, looking around the room, 'there's another of her paintings on the wall there.'

'More flowers,' murmured Bob. 'This time on a hillside. Well, I'm no expert but it still looks like rubbish to me, just like the rest of her stuff. Very amateurish! It looks just like she was cleaning her brushes on the canvas.' He stretched up and took down the painting. 'Hey, what's this? Look, Lisa! A small wall safe hidden behind it. Say, that's neat!'

'Wow – that's fantastic, Bob. That's what Aunt Gertrude meant. She wanted us to see the painting, the only one in her bedroom, so we could find the safe. Of course, that was before she decided that it should all go to charity. She was clever.'

'I wouldn't call that old woman clever, Lisa. But anyway, I bet her millions are in there, probably all in cash. We'll celebrate tonight.'

'Bob, it's not our money. My aunt's last words keep haunting me: "My money will go to charity." Anyway, let's discuss that again later. First, how do we open the safe? Let's look for the key.'

'Wait!' Bob stared at the safe. 'That's the problem, Lisa. It's a combination lock. We need the code.' They looked at one another.

'Surely Aunt Gertrude mentioned a code to you? Did she say anything at all that might give us a hint?' Lisa slowly shook her head.

'No, nothing. I told you all she said.'

'That stupid old woman!'

'Don't keep saying that about my dead aunt, Bob. I'm sure she meant well by giving us a clue to direct us to the safe. She just forgot about the code, that's all.'

'Well, I call that stupid.'

'OK, so let's think. Maybe we should try some obvious numbers...'

'Like what?'

'Well, let's try her birthday – the eleventh of December – try 1112.' His finger deftly entered the digits.

'No, that did nothing. Think of another obvious number, another date maybe...'

'OK, how about the year she married Uncle Bernard – I know that was 1942. Try that!' His fingers again pressed on the silvery keys in sequence.

'No! It's no use, Lisa. I'm afraid if we try any more wrong numbers, the safe might automatically lock the keypad and shut itself off completely. I believe some safes do that as a security measure.' They looked at one another again.

'So, what can we do then, Bob?'

'Don't know. We may have to get someone to force it open. Des might know someone. He has all sorts of contacts.' Despondently, he picked up the picture he had thrown on its face on the bed.

'Hey, what's this? Look! There're some numbers written on the back. That must be the code. I knew old Aunt Gertrude was not too stupid, despite everything. But they're very faint.'

'Great! What numbers are they?' Lisa took the painting from him and brought it over to the window to get more light. 'Let's see if I can make them out. Yes, four digits...'

'Well, let's try them.' Silently, they held their breaths as the digits were entered cautiously. A satisfying click heralded success.

'Great, Bob.'

'Wait – not so fast, Lisa. Look – there's very little inside. Just a few bank notes, no more than a couple of hundred euros, I'd say.'

'What? You're not serious. There must be more…'

'Look for yourself. That's it.' They looked at one another again.

'Well, that stupid Aunt Gertrude must have either spent or given away her money somehow,' muttered Bob, as he pocketed the cash. 'Nothing here worth giving to any charity, even if we wanted to.' The painting joined the others in the pile in the living room.

'I think we have to admit there's nothing else to see. There's no point in looking any further for any money. Let's just go, it's getting late. I'll meet Des here tomorrow morning to make sure he gets rid of all this mess.' They drove home in silence.

Some weeks later, Lisa spotted a brief article in the daily newspaper under the heading '*Monet painting found in ditch*'. Her heart jumped as she recognised the photo of the painting accompanying the article. The first paragraph read:

> '*An undisclosed amount was paid for a slightly damaged 19th century Monet at auction yesterday. The painting, one of the impressionist's little-known pastoral works, was valued at over two million euros. The anonymous seller claimed she found the painting with other discarded material in a ditch in the Wicklow Mountains while out walking her dog. Extensive enquiries revealed that the painting was last sold by a French art dealer to an anonymous buyer. There were no reports of it having been stolen. Considering the circumstances surrounding her mysterious find, the seller reportedly confirmed she was giving the proceeds of the sale to charity.*'

The Nun

It was emotional for him, standing at his family grave in that small rural cemetery in the west of Ireland. But he needed to be there to pay his respects to his ancestors before his return to Boston the next day. He had spent the previous few days exploring the area where his grandparents had lived and visiting his ancestral home, now in ruins. There were lengthy conversations with locals. The visit to the cemetery was the final commitment of his brief trip to the land of his forebears. As he turned slowly to leave this resting place of the dead, the evening shadows were intensifying with the approach of night. He glanced at his watch. He would catch the bus to Claremorris that passed by the cemetery. It would drop him off at his guest house along the way. The bus, which was due to arrive in ten minutes' time, would be the last one that night.

Sam walked slowly along the rough gravel path between the gravestones, stepping across the protruding roots of the pine trees and the abundant weeds. The occasional twig cracked under his shoes. A light breeze hushed through the branches, as if warning him to be quiet, not to awaken the dead from their slumbers. There were no other sounds. He looked around. No one. He was alone. It was eerie. The gravestones, which had captured his interest with their mossy inscriptions as he had entered, were now changing in character. In the fading light, they were assuming more ominous appearances, resembling gaunt ill-shaped hulks. If he ever were to write a ghost story, this would be the ideal setting. He knew Irish folklore was rich in tales of the supernatural. But surely that was all superstition. It probably went a little way to attracting tourists seeking a touch of the mysterious. But he really didn't believe in anything like that. His scientific training had taught him to accept only what could be proven. During his thirty-five years of life, he had never seen or even heard of any real ghosts. But as he continued along the graveyard path between the lengthening shadows, he couldn't help feeling somewhat uneasy. Every gravestone, every tree, cast a threatening shadow which, with a little help from his imagination, could easily transform into something supernatural. Despite his logical reasoning, he found himself glancing at those shadows, wondering if perhaps one just might move menacingly towards him at any moment. But surely that was being stupid and illogical. There were no ghosts.

Rainclouds were advancing over the darkening sky. As he turned a bend in the path, he saw her, a figure in black, blending into almost invisibility in the shadowy surroundings. For a moment, his heart jumped and his step faltered. But was that because he had allowed his imagination to run wild? He hesitated and strained his eyes. He realised it was a nun in traditional full-length black habit and head covering, her back towards him. She was walking away along the path a short distance in front of him. So, he wasn't alone after all. She was using a walking stick and limping slowly towards the church just beyond the graveyard. This was the small church where, many years earlier, his grandparents had worshipped for most of their lives. Its silhouette was stark against the last glimmer of light in the overcast sky. Was it open at this late hour? He felt slightly ashamed of his thoughts of ghosts as he exited from the graveyard's eeriness. Of course, there were no ghosts.

There was a distant peel of thunder as Sam saw the nun entering the church a short distance ahead. So, the building was accessible. Something seemed to be drawing him to follow her. Was it just curiosity or something deeper? With the gravel crunching under his shoes, he approached the large wooden door and pushed it open. Its creaking was amplified by the empty interior. The faint odour of burned candle wax greeted his nostrils. The only light was the last trickle of daylight coming through the long narrow windows on one side. He walked slowly up along the aisle and looked at the bare altar under the faint red glow of the sanctuary light. Behind was a large stained-glass window, its colours now deadened by the darkness outside. Its three parallel sections reached almost to the top of the arched roof. This must have been the scene so familiar to his grandparents' eyes when they knelt here many years ago to pray for their future. Unfortunately, it was a future that did not bring good fortune for two of his granduncles. They had departed on that huge, supposedly unsinkable ship, the RMS *Titanic*, to seek better lives in America but those lives had ended so tragically in the north Atlantic's icy waters. Feeling nostalgic, Sam stood and said a silent prayer. How his grandparents would have loved to have known that he had returned after all these years to visit their small and intimate parish in the Irish countryside and that he had remembered them in prayer.

Conscious of the time, he blessed himself with the sign of the cross and turned to leave. It was then he noticed the nun standing in the doorway. She was facing him as she leaned on her walking stick. He stopped as he neared her. Her head was lowered, the darkness allowing only a faint glimpse of her wrinkled face. Something about her caused a chill to spread slowly down the length of his spine like a tiny electric current. Why did he feel uneasy facing this nun? She was blocking his way. There was no room for him to pass. She made no attempt to speak and was almost motionless. He wondered what, if anything, he should say. He hesitated, then started to whisper 'excuse me' but his tongue was dry and the words did not form properly. For a few moments he stood looking at her. Why did she not react in some way to his presence? A cold sweat was forming on his forehead.

'I have to go,' he eventually managed to say. But she still did not move. He felt frozen to the spot, almost hypnotised. He wiped the palms of his hands on his coat sleeves. Several minutes must have passed. How should he handle this awkward situation? A sound reached his ears, the sound of a vehicle on the nearby road. He recognised it – it was his bus. He had to get out quickly. To miss that bus would mean to walk back along that long and lonely country road in the dark. A feeling of desperation overcame him. He took a few quick paces forward, uttered a loud 'excuse me' and with his right arm went to move the nun out of his way. To his consternation, he felt nothing as his arm swept through the darkness where she was standing, just a mass of cold air. The figure had evaporated into nothingness. He emitted a muffled scream and stood in the doorway, stiff with shock. Did this really happen? His heart was jumping. She had vanished. Totally. But his bus was still there. With difficulty, he pulled himself to his senses. He could reflect on the occurrence later. He quickly exited the church as heavy drops started to spatter on his face and shoulders. He ran the short distance through the church grounds to the road, only to see the red taillights of the bus disappearing into the darkness. For a moment, he stood in the centre of the road, looking in disbelief after those lights. He glanced back at the church feeling both stupid and annoyed. Something very strange had occurred and he couldn't understand it. Was it just his imagination or was his right arm feeling unusually cold?

He had no jacket and the rain, now heavy, was penetrating through to his skin. After some minutes, the headlights of a car approached, heading in the direction of Claremorris. He moved to the side of the road and, at the last moment, he beckoned for it to stop. He was somewhat surprised when it did. The driver, an elderly gentleman with thick rimmed spectacles and a bulky overcoat, was alone in the small car.

'It's a damp night,' he commented and smiled a welcome. *A typical Irish understatement,* Sam thought, as the rain was now pounding the ground in torrents. Sam quickly took the passenger seat and thanked the driver as the car moved off. Initially he was embarrassed to explain why he had missed the bus. But the incident, racing through his mind, was inhibiting him from having a relaxed conversation with this pleasant looking stranger. Would the driver scoff at him? He decided to tell him. The man listened intently as the car splashed through puddle after puddle on the rough road. When Sam had finished, to his surprise, the man nodded thoughtfully. He told Sam that he knew of an apparition that was seen in the cemetery by several people over the years. A nun, who had a limp, had lived in the local convent many years previously and had been noted for helping the parish community in small practical ways. She had encouraged those less well-off to seek better lives in America and in some instances had even assisted them financially using funds from her religious order. But many of those she persuaded to go had perished when the *Titanic* sank, and her sense of remorse had affected her deeply. She dedicated the rest of her life to helping the relatives of those who had died in the disaster. It was her dying prayer that no other member of those families who had lost loved ones would ever be involved in disasters of any kind.

'And rumour has it,' added the driver, 'that her spirit is still here, continuing that work.'

Sam was silent as he tried to digest what he had heard. He rubbed his left hand down along his cold right sleeve. The wipers clicked back and forth like a metronome as the rain bounced noisily off the windscreen and the tyres splashed through puddles on the uneven road. The engine hummed more loudly as the driver slowed and changed to a lower gear. Through the downpour, a blue flashing light signalled them to stop.

'There's been an accident,' the garda explained. 'The Claremorris bus skidded off the road and capsized into a gully around the next bend. Sadly, there appears to be many fatalities.'

The Leprechaun

'What on earth is that? Where did you get it?' Susie's mother Jane was looking at the small figurine in the child's clutch. It was a carving of a figure, about ten centimetres tall, with a green long-tailed coat, a green waistcoat and trousers, and a large green hat with a shamrock stuck in the hat band.

'It's a leprechaun,' replied Susie excitedly. 'An Irish leprechaun.'

'Yes, I think I could have guessed that. It's pretty obvious,' responded Jane. 'But where on earth did you get it. We're far away from Ireland here.'

'Lucy gave it to me down on the beach just now. She said it brings good luck to whoever owns it. It was her goodbye present to me. They're going back to Ireland early tomorrow morning and she said she wanted me to have it so I'll remember her. She was a good friend.'

'Well that was very sweet of her,' said Jane. 'They're a nice Irish family. I got on well with her parents every time we met them during the past week. I'll go and say goodbye to them myself later today.'

That evening, when Jane met the Irish family, she was told that Lucy, an only child of eight years old, had been diagnosed as having spasmodic dysphonia, a condition which resulted in her having difficulty expressing herself. They happened to meet an old woman in County Kerry who gave Lucy the leprechaun, telling her that the small figurine was very special and that it would bring her good luck: she would meet a girl of her own age with whom she would talk and get better. Lucy's mother said that, just three weeks later, when Lucy started to play with Susie, also eight years old, her speech dramatically improved.

'It was really amazing,' Lucy's mother exclaimed. 'What the old woman said has come true. Lucy is really better now and we attribute it to that leprechaun. So, we want to give it to Susie as a way of saying thanks. Maybe it will bring her good luck also.'

Jane smiled but was naturally sceptical. *The Irish will believe anything,* she thought to herself. She thanked Lucy's mother and wished them a safe trip back to Ireland.

Susie and her family loved the idyllic holiday location. The calm azure blue sea was lapping on the fine white sands only a few meters from their small but comfortable beachside chalet. It was a welcome change from the crowds and bustle of New York. The following morning, they spread their straw mats in the shade of a crop of palm trees by the beach and applied the obligatory sun cream.

'You made an excellent decision to choose this place for an Autumn break,' remarked Jane to her husband, as she surveyed the tranquil scene. 'It really has everything you'd want for a little relaxation.' As Susie sat down, she took the leprechaun out of her beach bag and held it in her hand.

'Don't you think it's a cute present, Mum?' she asked.

'Yes, it is. It's a very Irish present.' As Susie continued to admire her new acquisition, her father's cell phone rang. He let out a swear word that Susie knew she wasn't supposed to use. He reluctantly took up the offending phone.

'That's a call from my company – I told them not to disturb me on vacation. It must be urgent.' He took the call while getting up hurriedly and started to stroll up and down the beach as he listened. A deep frown was spreading on his face as he uttered a further few words that Jane hoped the young girl didn't hear.

'Your poor Dad,' she explained, trying to offer her daughter an excuse for his swearing. 'He never likes having to get involved in his New York business while he's on vacation, especially overseas.' Susie understood, although she sensed that this was something a little unusual. After what seemed a long time, her father re-joined his family.

'I'm sorry,' he said, 'but we're going to have to fly back to the States first thing tomorrow.' Susie let out a small scream of disappointment.

'Oh, no! We're supposed to stay here for another six days. Do we *really* have to go, Dad?'

'Yes, I'm afraid so, darling.'

'Well, that's the worst thing that could happen.' moaned Susie. 'That's not good luck,' she muttered, glaring with disgust at the leprechaun still in her hand.

'But why do we have to go home so soon, dear?' asked Jane.

'Well, a difficult situation has arisen,' her husband explained. 'Remember that penthouse apartment on the 51st floor of the Astor Building on Lexington Avenue that we were selling? Well, the sale has just fallen through. We were depending on that sale to help balance our books for this quarter. And to make matters even worse, Rick, my agent handling the sale, has quit. He left suddenly yesterday. He didn't even have the courtesy to give the usual notice. I need to get back there immediately to try to sort out things.'

'That's terrible, dear,' Jane responded.

Susie asked: 'Well. Can we come back here again after you sort things out, Dad? I really love this place.'

'Well, not immediately, I'm afraid. It will take a while for me to reorganise things.' He picked up his daughter in his arms. 'But maybe we'll come back next year, that's in 2011.' Susie tried to force a smile. But her faith in her good luck leprechaun had already evaporated. She replaced it in her beach bag.

The family arrived at JFK Airport the following morning, after two very lengthy flights. 'I'm so tired. What day is it now?' Susie asked, wearily rubbing the sleep from her eyes. 'It's Monday, October 25,' her mother reminded her.

Susie had taken the leprechaun out of her backpack.

'It's still bad luck that we had to leave Meulaboh so soon,' complained Susie, as she sat on the luggage cart while they waited for their bags. 'My leprechaun has brought us only bad luck since I got it.' She looked up at her Dad hoping to gain a little additional sympathy. But he wasn't listening. He was staring at the large headline on the newspaper he had just picked up:

Massive tsunami hits Sumatra early today – beach resort near Meulaboh totally destroyed – over 500 feared dead...'

Mr. Talbot

'You'll find him in the post office just opposite the church at mid-day. I know he had planned to meet someone there.' The grey-haired landlady was reassuring. 'You'll know him. He's wearing his usual white overcoat.' I had hoped to meet Mr. Talbot at his apartment and get my book from him. That book had been sent in error to his address by the booksellers over eleven days ago and it had taken me many phone calls to establish its whereabouts. I needed it urgently for a lecture I was due to deliver the following day and I had been informed that no replacement book was available locally. Despite the fact that the war had ended over four years ago, obtaining scientific books from overseas was not always quick or easy. I was troubled as to why Mr. Talbot had not returned the book to the booksellers, seeing that he had not ordered it. Perhaps he had planned to keep it – a free book on the history of chemistry. Not everyone's taste in reading perhaps, but some people can be surprisingly inconsiderate.

Disappointed, I re-mounted my bicycle and rode the short distance to the post office, arriving over half an hour before mid-day. The day was overcast, the weather reflecting my mood. I stood and looked around. My attention was drawn to a wedding party exiting jubilantly from the church a short distance away. It was a large church, one I remembered from my childhood. Showers of confetti added to the colour of the scene. Photographers moved around trying to obtain the best pictures of the memorable day. Through the loud conversations and laughter, the final chords of Mendelssohn's Wedding March were just audible from the church organ. Slowly, the joyous crowd dispersed, their motorcade horns blaring incessantly. The organ had stopped playing. I still had some time to wait, assuming Mr. Talbot would arrive as the landlady had said. My impatience was mounting and I found myself planning what to say to him. I would tell him in no uncertain terms what I thought of his lack of consideration.

Glancing down at my bicycle, I noticed that my front tyre was soft. It was losing air rapidly. That was all I needed now. I would have to look for a bicycle shop. I had already cycled several miles and the possibility of having to undertake that long walk home only added to my annoyance. It was all Mr. Talbot's fault for causing me to take this trip across the city and I would tell him that.

Just then, the faint peals of the organ struck my ears once again. It was the dramatic opening notes of Bach's Toccata and Fugue, a popular but challenging composition for organists. I was instinctively drawn across the road towards that wonderful flow of chords. Having locked my bicycle to the railings, I mounted the confetti-strewn steps and entered the church. The pews were empty. It was one of the oldest churches in the city and I knew its magnificent pipe organ had been restored recently. Immediately, the powerful tones enveloped me as if demanding my attention. That king of instruments, as it has been termed, had sprung to life and was now living inside me. There was something unique about this performance that captivated me as the organist's superb mastery of his instrument became evident. Sitting in the back pew almost under the organ gallery, I felt the whole church had assumed the spirit of his music, as the intricacies of the composition unfolded in magnificent succession and rose to the apex of the high vaulted ceiling. The timbers resonated from the pedal bass notes as the climax approached. The organist was pouring his soul into that music and that soul was flowing from those pipes and was lifting me out of my narrow world, expressing the inexpressible, as if opening the door to divinity. For a few moments, I was transported to another existence through a sense of euphoria, transcending the human sphere. Then the music ceased, the sounds fading into space, until all was silent. I sat still for a moment, allowing the experience to linger in my being.

With the final chords still resounding in my head, I exited the church. My frustration returned, however, as thoughts of Mr. Talbot, my missing book and my flat tyre jolted me back to reality. In my mind, I couldn't help rehearsing once again what I was going to say to Mr. Talbot about his lack of consideration. To my surprise, as I was unlocking my bicycle, a couple slowly walked out from the church. I thought it strange that I hadn't noticed them there. His white overcoat fitted loosely over his tall thin frame. Surely this was him. An elderly woman was linking him. I approached the couple. The young man's sunken grey eyes seemed to be staring into nothingness.

'Mr. Talbot?' I asked. He confirmed that he was. As soon as I mentioned my book, the woman smiled and produced a neatly wrapped parcel from her large shoulder bag. It was addressed to the booksellers from which I had ordered my book. She explained that her son, Mr. Talbot, had opened the parcel in error and, when she visited him several days later, she saw it was not for him. 'I visit my son only once a week, you see,' she explained. They were on their way to the post office at that moment to post it. Profuse apologies for the inconvenience followed. 'The book was of no use to me,' Mr. Talbot said with a faint smile. 'I couldn't have read it anyway.' His mother handed him his folded white cane. They turned and moved away. The slow rhythmic tapping of that cane, receding into the city's grey background, penetrated me like a succession of tiny darts, bringing with them a torrent of guilt. A passer-by, a grey-haired man who had seen me speaking with the couple, smiled and commented: 'Do you know he's one of the best organists in the country?'.

In reflective mood, I slowly wheeled my bicycle home

with the tapping still sounding in my mind.

POEMS

Imagination is the only weapon in the war against reality.

LEWIS CARROLL

Inspiration

You know you need me for your task, to make your work unique,
You search for my constructive nudge, my special gift you seek.
You wonder where you'll find me when you want me as your guide,
I may be on those wave-licked sands or waiting by your side.
I'm in those things familiar that deserve a second look —
That suitcase in your attic or those pages in your book.

An empty house and garden wild where nettles multiply,
The distant sylvan silhouettes where hilltops meet the sky.
You find me in the moon beams casting shadows on the ground,
In ripples on a placid lake, in nature's whispered sound.
I'm on the flat horizon, in those ships from far off lands,
The sandy mollusc shell you got with love from tiny hands.

The yellow of one primrose in a crack between grey slabs,
The silver of the wriggling fish a hungry seagull grabs.
I'm in the scent of lilac blooms, the sounds from thrushes' throats,
The songs and melodies from yore, the haunting pipers' notes.
I'm in the tiny candle piercing darkness with its light,
The writing on a gravestone, or a fox's eyes at night.

I'm peering from those faces in that photo dulled with age,
Or from the lines of Shakespeare claiming 'All the world's a stage'.
I'm there in love most powerful that spans the deep divide
Between the human spirits and the selves that dwell inside.
You listen for my prompts in conversations overheard,
In voices rich in content, in thoughts and feelings shared.

The lonely foghorn moaning to the cloaking mists at sea,
The final russet leaf of autumn clinging to that tree,
Those feelings never spoken that your daydreams leave behind,
The transcendental footsteps in the hallway of your mind.
I am that sudden upsurge that unleashes thoughts anew,
Those miracles of genius, precious fragments rare and few.

I come at busy noontime when your intellect is bright,
Or when your mind is darkened by the silence of the night.
I'll startle you with lucid thought, a vivid flash of light,
A sparkling new idea, and creations that excite.
So, find me in those sights and sounds and words and thoughts and
*   things,*
That's when your own creative self, unfettered, will take wings.

I am Dublin

I am a mix of people's lives, of those from far and near,
I am a country's guiding voice, for those who wish to hear.
I am the seat of government, of legislators great,
I am the proud curator of the history of this state.
I am the source of cultured thought, of writers new and old,
I am the garner of the minds, of talents strong and bold.

I am the beating heart of trade, of failure and success,
I am the keen investment hub for those with more or less.
I am the home of commerce strong, on which this land is built,
I am the inspiration for elation, joy or guilt.
I am the desperation dire that plagues the destitute,
I am the voice of loneliness, the silent and the mute.

I am the bed of properties, of fortunes made and lost,
I am the home of homelessness and those who count the cost.
I am the strength of outward thrust, at never ending pace,
I am the bells, the chimes, the peals of sanctity and grace.
I am the face of welcomes warm as visitors arrive,
I am the opportunity for those who care to strive.

I am the beacon of delight for those from other lands,
I am the gentle feel of surf as waves caress the sands.
I am the flowing mass of people, liberated, free,
I am the tidal waterway conversing with the sea.
I am the font of liquid black for those who parch with thirst,
I am the largest in the land, the proudest and the first.

I am the cheers from stadia, the roars when net greets ball,
I am the strength of sportsmanship, as champions rise and fall.
I am the love for animals, of species wild and rare,
I am the doctors, nurses, those who give the sick their care.

I am the brunt of jokes and jibes and praise and voiced frustration,
I am the complex urban sprawl, the foremost in this nation.

I am the hopes of young and old, of aspirations strong,
I am the tastes of cuisines rare, where connoisseurs belong.
I am the sound of music live from café, pub and street,
I am the clubs and venues where good friends will plan to meet.
I am the cranes, the scaffolding in building works deployed,
I am the fields of promise and of greenery destroyed.

I am the cogent critic of the skyline's elevation,
I am the fountain, rich and rare, for poets' inspiration.
I am the whispers from the past, of liberators dead,
I am the ghosts of history stained with blood that martyrs shed.
I am the strength from conflicts gained, when brave men fought and
*   died,*
I am the thrust of heads held high, endowed with strength and pride.

I am the controversial blend of happiness and strife,
I am a country's spirit strong, its soul, its blood, its life.

I am Dublin.

Time

What is time? A paradox? Mysterious, unseen,
Defining past and future, and that moment in between.
The universe's rhythm, which nature's laws obey,
As Spring turns into Summer and as night turns into day.
The intervals at which it's right to wake, to work, to sleep,
To start, to stop, to do, to play, to help, to laugh, to weep.

Director of activities, their schedules and pace,
Reminder of impermanence for all the human race.
A vapour trail of nothingness behind us, as we swim
Through mists of life's uncertainties towards horizons dim.
Invisible dimension that encompasses our lives,
As all our worlds disintegrate, then only it survives.

That abstract lifeless entity on which all life depends,
Continuum of threads without beginnings, without ends.
Coordinate of spacetime that defines the adverb 'when',
A mystical obsession that controls us now and then.
Subjective ghost of abstractness, to challenge and defy
The scientists, philosophers and all of those who try
To ponder on its nature, its structure and its pace,
Modifying their perceptions as it warps in outer space.

For ages, an illusion captivating scribes and bards,
But its tantalising mysteries it resolutely guards.
We're carried like a landslide down a never-ending slope;
Behind us lie our memories; before us, only hope.

So, what is time? Again I ask. It's all of these and more,
Our temporal companion at the universe's core
That bars us from the future and the past, so let us vow
To live with zeal that precious blip – that moment we call NOW!

Roots & Wings

What would we do without our Roots, those anchors that impart
The formative beginnings that give our beings a start;
Our conduits of nourishment, from which we build our lives,
Of wisdom, love, stability on which a sound life thrives;
Our families and memories of those who've gone before,
They build our wings of fortune for whatever lies in store.

What would we do without our Wings to let us fly the nest
To catch our spirits' thermals as they lift us on our quest
To relish nature's treasures in the world through which we fly,
With vast ambitions to achieve and dreams to satisfy.
To view our earth through macro lens, then micro lens as well –
That miracle called life in which we're fortunate to dwell.

But if, like Icarus of old, who flew beside the sun,
We carelessly misuse our wings when good advice we shun,
We fall to earth and seek our roots to help us on our way,
But with that love and nourishment, we find some time to stay.

From birth to death we make our way, whatever fortune brings,
To help us on the paths of life, we all need Roots & Wings.

ACKNOWLEDGEMENTS

I would like to acknowledge the help and support of the following people, all of whom I sincerely thank:

My devoted wife Suzanne for listening patiently as I discussed my various pieces and for her thoughtful critiques of my initial drafts. She also generously ensured I was allowed time to concentrate on my writing. Without her loving assistance, this book would never have come to fruition.

Our children, Jeanne-Marie, Brenda, Sinéad, Lara and Gavin, for their interest and encouragement.

Our grandchildren for giving me inspiration, perhaps unwittingly, for some of my stories – Seán, Sophia, Karl, Adam, Cian, Max, Clara, Rory, Róisín, Hannah, Zoe and Robyn. I dedicate this book, with my love, to all of them.

My sister-in-law, Sonya, for her helpful appraisals.

My many colleagues and fellow writers in the Dalkey Creative Writing Groups, and in particular the excellent facilitators Ferdia Mac Anna and Christine Ryan, and our ever-active organiser, Anna Fox. Their guidance during my lengthy attempts to master the art of creative writing, together with their constructive criticisms during the preparation of many of these stories, were of invaluable assistance.

In addition, Ferdia has also been a most helpful editor and a great pleasure to work with, generously offering his vast creative experience to enhance my stories.

Helen Bovaird Ryan and my colleagues in her Creative Writing Classes for their help and guidance, and their valuable and detailed critiques on some of the stories included here.

Adrian White for his detailed work in bringing the book to market and with whom I enjoyed working.

My very good friend and talented fellow writer, Adrian Taheny, who was the first to encourage me to publish my stories and who offered constructive comments on many of my writings. Adrian also patiently guided me through the self-publishing procedure and suggested this wonderful title for the book.

Adrian's gifted brother, Tom, who produced this imaginative cover design.

My fellow writer Zoë Devlin, who had the patience to carefully read and offer many valuable suggestions on a number of these stories.

Again, thank you all!

Printed in Poland
by Amazon Fulfillment
Poland Sp. z o.o., Wrocław